Quantitative Portfolio Management

Quantitative Portfolio Management

The art and science of statistical arbitrage

Michael Isichenko

WILEY

Published by John Wiley & Sons, Inc., Hoboken, New Jersey.
Published simultaneously in Canada.

For general information on our other products and services or for technical support, please contact our Customer Care Department within the United States at (800) 762-2974, outside the United States at (317) 572-3993 or fax (317) 572-4002.

Wiley also publishes its books in a variety of electronic formats. Some content that appears in print may not be available in electronic formats. For more information about Wiley products, visit our web site at www.wiley.com.

Library of Congress Cataloging-in-Publication Data

Names: Isichenko, Michael, author.
Title: Quantitative portfolio management : the art and science of
    statistical arbitrage / Michael Isichenko.
Description: Hoboken, New Jersey : John Wiley & Sons, Inc., [2021] |
    Includes bibliographical references and index.
Identifiers: LCCN 2021013923 (print) | LCCN 2021013924 (ebook) | ISBN
    9781119821328 (cloth) | ISBN 9781119821229 (adobe pdf) | ISBN
    9781119821212 (epub)
Subjects: LCSH: Portfolio management—Mathematical models. | Arbitrage.
Classification: LCC HG4529.5 .I83 2021 (print) | LCC HG4529.5 (ebook) |
    DDC 332.6—dc23
LC record available at https://lccn.loc.gov/2021013923
LC ebook record available at https://lccn.loc.gov/2021013924

Cover Design: Wiley
Cover Image: © Michael Isichenko
SKY10077049_060724

Contents

.

List of Figures

Code Listings

Preface

This book describes the process used by quantitative traders, or *quants*, a community the author has belonged to for a number of years. Quants are not usually trained as quants, but often come from one of the "hard sciences" such as mathematics, statistics, physics, electrical engineering, economics, or computer science. The author, a physicist by training, feels guilty for (ab)using the word describing a fundamental concept of quantum physics in the context of quantitative trading, but this slang is too rooted in the industry to be avoided. Having quantitative finance professionals in mind, the intended audience is presumed interdisciplinary, fluent in mathematical notation, not foreign to algorithmic thinking, familiar with basic financial concepts such as market-neutral strategies, and not needing a definition of *pnl*. This book could be also interesting to those readers who are thinking of joining the quant workforce and wondering if it is worth it.

The quant trading business, especially its *alpha* part, tends to be fairly secretive, but the traffic of portfolio managers and analysts between quant shops has created a body of common knowledge, some of which has been published in the literature. The book is an attempt to cover parts of this knowledge, as well as to add a few ideas developed by the author in his own free time. I appreciate the concern of some of the more advanced colleagues of mine about letting the tricks of the trade "out in the wild." Those tricks, such as machine learning and optimization algorithms, are mostly in the public domain already but are spread over multiple fields. In addition to academic research, Wall Street can learn a lot from Silicon Valley, whose inhabitants have generated a tremendous and less secretive body of knowledge. Using an analogy with cryptography, *security through obscurity* is a popular approach in quantitative trading, but it gradually gives way to *security by design* ultimately rooted in the increasingly difficult forecasting of future asset prices, the holy skill and grail of quantitative portfolio management. The rest of the quant trading process, while not exactly trivial in scope, is within the reach of a reasonably trained scientist, this author included, who is willing and able to read Wikipedia[1] and learn better coding.

The choice of topics for this book is aligned with the author's personal interests in the field, although an honest attempt is made to cover, in depth or in passing, all relevant parts of *statistical arbitrage*, a quantitative approach to equity trading. Whether or not a particular formula or approach is expected to help make money (or avoid losses) is not disclosed or opined upon, in part because any application success is data- and implementation-dependent, and in part to keep the reader in suspense. The book is also an attempt to strike a balance between what the author could say and is comfortable saying. In the field of quantitative trading, the more interesting stuff doesn't usually get published. In this book, the reader will hopefully find a few things that might be interesting or at least entertaining.

Any resemblance of described quantitative practices to past or existing firms is coincidental and may not be statistically significant. As Kurt Vonnegut admitted in Slaughterhouse-Five, *All this happened, more or less.* This book is for quants and, occasionally, *about* quants.

A lot of the quantitative portfolio management process involves data and code. The exposition style adopted in this book does not include too many charts, tables, or code snippets, although there are some. Instead, the focus is on ideas, motivation for various approaches, and mathematical description seeking a terse and elegant exposition whenever possible.

---

[1] Accordingly, and for the reader's convenience, the electronic version of this book has multiple hyperlinks to Wikipedia and other URLs.

Mathematical formulas tend to be more compact and expressive than code written in any programming language. In addition, and quoting Eugene Wigner,[2] *the enormous usefulness of mathematics in the natural sciences is something bordering on the mysterious and ... there is no rational explanation for it.*

This book is an unlikely result of some 20 years of trial-and-error discovery. It is also a work in progress. The author will appreciate indication of any omission or error, as well as any feedback from the reader, whose comments are most welcome at `michael.isichenko@gmail.com`.

M.I.

New York-Montauk, June 2020–May 2021.

---

[2] E. Wigner, *The Unreasonable Effectiveness of Mathematics in the Natural Sciences*, Communications in Pure and Applied Mathematics, 13(I), February 1960.

About this Book

Quantitative trading of financial securities is a multi-billion dollar business employing thousands of portfolio managers and quantitative analysts ("quants") trained in mathematics, physics, or other "hard" sciences. The quants trade stocks and other securities creating liquidity for investors and competing, as best they can, at finding and exploiting any mispricings with their systematic data-driven trading algorithms. The result is highly efficient financial markets, which nonetheless are not immune to events of crowding, bubbling, occasional liquidation panic, and "cobra effects" including the high-frequency trading (HFT) arms race. This book attempts a systematic description of the quant trading process by covering all its major parts including sourcing financial data, "learning" future asset returns from historical data, generating and combining forecasts, diversification and its limitations, risk and leverage management, building optimal portfolios of stocks subject to risk preferences and trading costs, and executing trades. The book highlights the difficulties of financial forecasting due to quantitative competition, the curse of dimensionality, and the propensity to overfitting. Some of the topics included in the book have not been previously discussed in the literature. The exposition seeks a balance between financial insight, mathematical ideas of statistical and machine learning, practical computational aspects, actual stories and thoughts "from the trenches," as observed by a physicist turned a quant, and even tough or funny questions asked at countless quant interviews. The intended audience includes practicing quants, who will encounter things both familiar and novel (such as lesser-known ML algorithms, combining multiple alphas, or multi-period portfolio optimization), students and scientists thinking of joining the quant workforce (and wondering if it's worth it), financial regulators (mindful of the unintended cobra effects they may create), investors (trying to understand their risk-reward tradeoff), and the general public interested in quantitative and algorithmic trading from a broad scientific, social, and occasionally ironic standpoint.

Abstract

The book presents a systematic review of the quantitative equity trading process, aka statistical arbitrage, including market and other financial data, alpha generation, risk, trading costs, and portfolio construction. Financial forecasting involves statistical learning of future asset returns on features extracted from relevant current and past data, including price-volume, fundamental and analyst, holdings and flows, news, alternative, and other publicly available datasets. Both theoretical and algorithmic machine learning (ML) aspects of financial forecasting are reviewed with an emphasis on regularization methods, bias-variance and other tradeoffs, generalization error, the curse of dimensionality, and traps of overfitting. ML involves a wealth of parametric, nonparametric, deep, online, and latent structure algorithms, whose success is data-dependent according to the "No free lunch" theorem. Meta-learning methods include hyperparameter optimization, boosting, and other ensemble methods. An important context of financial ML is competition-based market efficiency imposing limits on the acceptable complexity and expected performance of predictive models. Some topics of active research such as "benign overfitting" in interpolating deep neural nets and other ML algorithms are also covered. Several approaches of combining multiple forecasts are discussed using secondary

ML, dimensionality reduction, and other methods, while highlighting correlation-based limits on alpha diversification. Multi-factor risk models and trading costs are reviewed including both theoretical and empirical aspects relevant to portfolio construction. Effects of price impact on stock market macro elasticity are also discussed. A unified framework of multi-period portfolio optimization is presented with several special closed-form solutions with impact and slippage costs and approximations for efficient algorithmic approaches. Optimal portfolio capacity and leverage are discussed, including a critical review of the Kelly criterion. The book also presents a brief review of intraday algorithmic execution and high-frequency trading (HFT) and raises fundamental questions of more efficient market design to benefit the general investing public.

Acknowledgments

This book wouldn't be possible without the author's interaction with many colleagues in academia and coworkers, competitors, and friends in the financial industry. The role of the early mentors, Vladimir Yankov (in physics) and Aaron Sosnick (in finance), was especially valuable in forming the author's ways of thinking about challenging problems and asking better questions.

Special thanks to all my superiors in the industry for prudently hiring or dismissing me, as appropriate for each occasion, and to all my peers and direct reports for the opportunity to learn from them.

I would like to thank Marco Avellaneda and Jean-Philippe Bouchaud for encouraging me to write up this material, as well as Aaron for discouraging it. A few fellow quants including, but not limited to, Colin Rust and Alexander Barzykin provided valuable comments and critique on various parts of the book draft. Their feedback is gratefully acknowledged.

Warm regards to those interviewers and interviewees who made the endless Q&A sessions more fun than they are supposed to be.

And thank you, Angela, for food, books, love, and understanding.

The time needed to write this book was an unexpected byproduct of the spread of the SARS-CoV-2 virus, which may have caused a temporary loss of smell, taste, or job, but hopefully not of sense of humor.

Introduction

Science is what we understand well enough to explain to a computer.
Art is everything else we do.

Donald Knuth

Financial investment is a way of increasing existing wealth by buying and selling assets of fluctuating value and bearing related risk. The value of a bona fide investment is expected to grow on average, or in expectation, albeit without a guarantee. The very fact that such activity, pure gambling aside, exists is rooted in the global accumulation of capital, or, loosely speaking, increase in commercial productivity through rational management and technological innovation. There are also demographic reasons for the stock market to grow— or occasionally crash.

Another important reason for investments is that people differ in their current need for money. Retirees have accumulated assets to spend while younger people need cash to pay for education or housing, entrepreneurs need capital to create new products and services, and so forth. The banking and financial industry serves as an intermediary between lenders and borrowers, facilitating loans, mortgages, and municipal and corporate bonds. In addition to debt, much of the investment is in equity. A major part of the US equity market is held by pension funds, including via mutual funds holdings.[1] Aside from occasional crisis periods, the equity market has outperformed the inflation rate. Stock prices are correlated with the gross domestic product (GDP) in all major economies.[2] Many index and mutual funds make simple diversified bets on national or global stock markets or industrial sectors, thus providing inexpensive investment vehicles to the public.

In addition to the traditional, long-only investments, many hedge funds utilize long-short and market-neutral strategies by betting on both asset appreciation and depreciation.[3] Such strategies require *alpha*, or the process of continuous generation of specific views of future returns of individual assets, asset groups, and their relative movements. Quantitative alpha-based portfolio management is conceptually the same for long-only, long-short, or market-neutral strategies, which differ only in exposure constraints and resulting risk profiles. For reasons of risk and leverage, however, most quantitative equity portfolios are exactly or approximately market-neutral. Market-neutral quantitative trading strategies are often collectively referred to as *statistical arbitrage* or *statarb*. One can think of the long-only market-wide investments as sails relying on a breeze subject to a relatively stable weather forecast and hopefully blowing in the right direction, and market-neutral strategies as feeding on turbulent eddies and waves that are zero-mean disturbances not transferring anything material—other than wealth changing hands. The understanding and utilization of all kinds of pricing waves, however, involves certain complexity and requires a nontrivial data processing, quantitative, and operational effort. In this sense, market-neutral quant strategies are at best a zero-sum game with a natural selection of the fittest. This does not necessarily mean that half of the quants are doomed to fail in the near term: successful quant funds probably feed more on imperfect decisions and execution by retail investors, pension, and mutual funds than on less advanced

---

[1] Organization for Economic Co-operation and Development (OECD) presents a detailed analysis of world equity ownership: A. De La Cruz, A. Medina, Y. Tang, *Owners of the World's Listed Companies*, OECD Capital Market Series, Paris, 2019.

[2] F. Jareño, A. Escribano, A. Cuenca, *Macroeconomic variables and stock markets: an international study*, Applied Econometrics and International Development, 19(1), 2019.

[3] A.W. Lo, *Hedge Funds: An Analytic Perspective - Updated Edition*, Princeton University Press, 2010.

quant traders. By doing so, quant traders generate needed liquidity for traditional, long-only investors. Trading profits of market-neutral hedge funds, which are ultimately losses (or reduced profits) of other market participants, can be seen as a cost of efficiency and liquidity of financial markets. Whether or not this cost is fair is hard to say.

Historically, statistical arbitrage started as trading pairs of similar stocks using mean-reversion-type alpha signals betting on the similarity.[4] The strategy appears to be first used for proprietary trading at Morgan Stanley in the 1980s. The names often mentioned among the statarb pioneers include Gerry Bamberger, Nunzio Tartaglia, David E. Shaw, Peter Muller, and Jim Simons. The early success of statistical arbitrage started in top secrecy. In a rare confession, Peter Muller, the head of the Process Driven Trading (PDT) group at Morgan Stanley in the 1990s, wrote: *Unfortunately, the mere knowledge that it is possible to beat the market consistently may increase competition and make our type of trading more difficult. So why did I write this article? Well, one of the editors is a friend of mine and asked nicely. Plus, chances are you won't believe everything I'm telling you.*[5] The pair trading approach soon developed into a more general portfolio trading using mean reversion, momentum, fundamentals, and any other types of forecast quants can possibly generate. The secrets proliferated, and multiple quantitative funds were started. Quantitative trading has been a growing and an increasingly competitive part of the financial landscape since early 1990s.

On many occasions within this book, it will be emphasized that it is difficult to build successful trading models and systems. Indeed, quants betting on their complex but often ephemeral models are not unlike behavioral speculators, albeit at a more technical level. John Maynard Keynes once offered an opinion of a British economist on American finance:[6] *Even outside the field of finance, Americans are apt to be unduly interested in discovering what average opinion believes average opinion to be; and this national weakness finds its nemesis in the stock market... It is usually agreed that casinos should, in the public interest, be inaccessible and expensive. And perhaps the same is true of stock exchanges.*

---

[4] M. Avellaneda, J.-H. Lee. *Statistical arbitrage in the US equities market*, Quantitative Finance, 10(7), pp. 761–782, 2010.

[5] P. Muller, *Proprietary trading: truth and fiction*, Quantitative Finance, 1(1), 2001.

[6] J.M. Kaynes, *The General Theory of Employment, Interest, and Money*, Macmillan, 1936.

This book touches upon several theoretical and applied disciplines including statistical forecasting, machine learning, and optimization, each being a vast body of knowledge covered by many dedicated in-depth books and reviews. Financial forecasting, a poor man's time machine giving a glimpse of future asset prices, is based on big data research, statistical models, and machine learning. This activity is not pure math and is not specific to finance. There has been a stream of statistical ideas across applied fields, including statements that *most research findings are false for most research designs and for most fields*.[7] Perhaps quants keep up the tradition when modeling financial markets. Portfolio optimization is a more mathematical subject logically decoupled from forecasting, which has to do with extracting maximum utility from whatever forecasts are available.

Our coverage is limited to topics more relevant to the quant research process and based on the author's experience and interests. Out of several asset classes available to quants, this book focuses primarily on equities, but the general mathematical approach makes some of the material applicable to futures, options, and other asset classes. Although being a part of the broader field of quantitative finance, the topics of this book do not include financial derivatives and their valuation, which may appear to be main theme of quantitative finance, at least when judged by academic literature.[8] Most of the academic approaches to finance are based on the premise of *efficient markets*[9] precluding profitable arbitrage. Acknowledging market efficiency as a pretty accurate, if pessimistic, zeroth-order approximation, our emphasis is on quantitative approaches to trading financial instruments for profit while controlling for risks. This activity constitutes statistical arbitrage.

When thinking about ways of profitable trading, the reader and the author would necessarily ask the more general question: what makes asset prices move, predictably or otherwise? Financial economics has long preached theories involving concepts such as fundamental information, noise and informed traders, supply and demand, adaptivity,[10] and,

---

[7] J.P.A. Ioannidis, *Why Most Published Research Findings Are False*, PLoS Med 2(8): e124, 2005.

[8] P. Wilmott, *Frequently Asked Questions in Quantitative Finance*, Wiley, 2009.

[9] P.A. Samuelson, *Proof That Properly Anticipated Prices Fluctuate Randomly*, Industrial Management Review, 6, pp. 41–49, 1965.

[10] A.W. Lo, *The Adaptive Markets Hypothesis: Market Efficiency from an Evolutionary Perspective*, Journal of Portfolio Management, 30(5), pp. 15–29, 2004.

more recently, inelasticity,[11] which is a form of market impact (Sec. 5.4). In contrast to somewhat axiomatic economists' method, physicists, who got interested in finance, have used their field's bottom-up approach involving market microstructure and ample market data.[12] It is definitely supply and demand forces, and the details of market organization, that determine the price dynamics. The dynamics are complicated, in part due to being affected by how market participants learn/understand these dynamics and keep adjusting their trading strategies. From the standpoint of a portfolio manager, price changes are made of two parts: the impact of his own portfolio and the impact of others. If the former can be treated as trading costs, which are partially under the PM's control, the latter is subject to statistical or dynamical modeling and forecasting.

Among other things, this book gives a fair amount of attention to the combination of multiple financial forecasts, an important question not well covered in the literature. Forecast combination is a more advanced version of the well-discussed theme of investment diversification. Just like it is difficult to make forecasts in efficient markets, it is also difficult, but not impossible, to optimally combine forecasts due to their correlation and what is known as the *curse of dimensionality*. To break the never ending cycle of quantitative trial and error, it is important to understand fundamental limitations on what can and what can't be done.

The book is structured as follows. Chapter 1 briefly reviews raw and derived market data used by quants. Alpha generation, the central part of the quant process, is discussed in Chapter 2. This chapter starts with additional financial data usable for forecasting future asset returns. Both theoretical and algorithmic aspects of machine learning (ML) are discussed with an emphasis on challenges specific to financial forecasting. Once multiple alphas have been generated, they need to be combined to form the best possible forecast for each asset. Good ways of combining alphas is an alpha in itself. ML approaches to forecast combining are discussed in Chapter 3. A formal view of risk management, as relevant to portfolio construction, is presented in Chapter 4. Trading costs, with an emphasis on their mathematical structure, are reviewed in Chapter 5.

---

[11] X. Gabaix, R.S.J. Koijen, *In Search of the Origins of Financial Fluctuations: The Inelastic Markets Hypothesis*, Swiss Finance Institute Research Paper No. 20-91, Available at SSRN: https://ssrn.com/abstract=3686935, 2021.

[12] J.-P. Bouchaud, J.D. Farmer, F. Lillo, *How markets slowly digest changes in supply and demand*, arXiv:0809.0822 [q-fin.TR], 2008.

There a case is made for a linear impact model that, while approximate, has a strong advantage of making several closed-form multi-period optimization solutions possible. Impact of a net flow of funds at a macro scale is also discussed with implications for stock market elasticity and bubbles. Chapter 6 describes the construction of a portfolio optimized for expected future profits subject to trading costs and risk preferences. This part tends to use the most math and includes previously unpublished results for multi-period portfolio optimization subject to impact and slippage costs. Related questions of portfolio capacity and optimal leverage, including the Kelly criterion, are also discussed. Chapter 7 concerns the purpose and implementation of a trading simulator and its role in quant research. A few auxiliary algorithmic and mathematical details are presented in appendices.

Computation is a primary tool in most parts of the quantitative trading process and in machine learning. Several aspects of computing, including coding style, efficiency, bugs, and environmental issues are discussed throughout the book. A few important machine learning concepts, such as bias-variance tradeoff (Secs. 2.3.5 and 2.4.12) and the curse of dimensionality (Sec. 2.4.10), are supported by small self-contained pieces of Python code generating meaningful plots. The reader is encouraged to experiment along these lines. It is often easier to do productive *experimental mathematics* than real math.

Some of the material covering statistics, machine learning, and optimization necessarily involves a fair amount of math and relies on academic and applied research in various, often disjoint, fields. Our exposition does not attempt to be mathematically rigorous and mostly settles for a "physicist's level of rigor" while trying to build a qualitative understanding of what's going on. Accordingly, the book is designed to be reasonably accessible and informative to a less technical reader who can skip over the more scary math and focus on the plain English around it. For example, the fairly technical method of boosting in ML (Sec. 2.4.14) is explained as follows: *The idea of boosting is twofold: learning on someone else's errors and voting by majority.*

The field of quantitative portfolio management is too broad for a single paper or book to cover. Important topics either omitted here or just mentioned in passing include market microstructure theory, algorithmic execution, big data management, and non-equity asset classes.

Several books cover these and related topics.[13,14,15,16,17] While citing multiple research papers in various fields, the author could not possibly do justice to all relevant or original multidisciplinary contributions. The footnote references include work that seemed useful, stimulating, or just fascinating when developing (or explaining) forecasting and optimization ideas for quantitative portfolio management. Among the many destinations where Google search brings us, the arXiv[18] is an impressive open source of reasonably high signal-to-noise ratio[19] publications.

A note about footnotes. Citing sources in footnotes seems more user-friendly than at the end of chapters. Footnotes are also used for various reflections or mini stories that could be either meaningful or entertaining but often tangential to the main material.

Finally, in the spirit of the quant problem-solving sportsmanship, and for the reader's entertainment, a number of actual interview questions asked at various quant job interviews are inserted in different sections of the book and indexed at the end, along with the main index, quotes, and the stories.

---

[13] R.C. Grinold, R.N. Kahn, *Active Portfolio Management: A Quantitative Approach for Producing Superior Returns and Controlling Risk.* McGraw-Hill, New York, 2000.

[14] R.K. Narang, *Inside the Black Box: A Simple Guide to Quantitative and High Frequency Trading, 2nd Edition,* Wiley, 2013.

[15] J.-P. Bouchaud, J. Bonart, J. Donier, M. Gould, *Trades, Quotes and Prices. Financial Markets Under the Microscope,* Cambridge University Press, 2018.

[16] Z. Kakushadze, J.A. Serur, *151 Trading Strategies,* Available at SSRN: https://ssrn .com/abstract=3247865, 2018.

[17] *Finding Alphas: A Quantitative Approach to Building Trading Strategies, 2nd Edition,* Edited by I. Tulchinsky, Wiley, New York, 2019.

[18] https://arxiv.org.

[19] A. Jackson, *From Preprints to E-prints: The Rise of Electronic Preprint Servers in Mathematics,* Notices of the AMS, 49, 2002.

Quantitative Portfolio Management

Chapter 1

Market Data

1.1 Tick and bar data

Perhaps the most useful predictor of future asset prices are past prices, trading volumes, and related exchange-originated data commonly referred to as *technical*, or *price-volume* data. Market data comes from quotes and trades. The most comprehensive view of the equity market includes exchange-specific limit order book by issue, which is built from limit orders forming buy and sell queues at different price depths, market orders, and their crossing (trades) per exchange rules such as price/time priority. In addition to the full depth of book tick stream, there are simplified datafeeds such as Level 2 (low-depth order book levels and trades), Level 1 (best bid and offer and trades), minute bars (cumulative quote and trade activity per discrete time intervals), and daily summary data (open, close, high, low, volume, etc).

Depth of book data is primarily used by high frequency trading (HFT) strategies and execution algos provided by brokers and other

1

firms, although one can argue that a suitable analysis of the order book could detect the presence of a big directional trader affecting a longer-term price movement. Most non-HFT quant traders utilize either daily or bar data—market data recorded with certain granularity such as every 5 minutes—for research and real-time data for production execution.[1]

Major financial information companies such as Thompson Reuters and Bloomberg offer market data at different levels of granularity, both historical and in real time. A quant strategy needs the history for research and simulation (Chapter 7) and real time for production trading. Historical simulation is never exactly the same as production trading but can, and must, be reasonably close to the modeled reality, lest research code have a lookahead bug, that is, violate the causality principle by using "future-in-the-past" data. As discussed in Chapter 2, highly competitive and efficient financial markets keep the predictability of future price movements at a very low level. As a result even a subtle lookahead (Sec. 2.1.1) in a quant trading simulator can be picked up by a sensitive machine learning (ML) algorithm to generate a spurious forecast looking great in simulation but never working in production.

1.2   Corporate actions and adjustment factor

Compute the products:

a. $\prod_{0<i<j<\infty}(i^{1/i} - j^{1/j})$

b. $\prod_{0<i<j<2020}(i^{1/i} - j^{1/j})$

From a quant interview

Equities as an asset class are subject to occasional corporate actions ("cax") including dividends, splits, spin-offs, mergers, capital restructuring, and multi-way cax. Maintaining an accurate historical cax database is a challenge in itself. Failure to do so to a good approximation results in wrong asset returns and real-time performance not matching simulation

---

[1] Sometimes even real-time trading is done on bar data. The author has observed peculiar periodic pnl fluctuations of his medium-frequency US equity portfolio. The regular 30-minute price spikes indicated a repetitive portfolio rebalancing by a significant market participant whose trades were correlated with the author's positions.

(Sec. 7.1). For alpha research purposes it is generally sufficient to approximate each cax with two numbers, dividend D and split S.[2] The dividend can be an actual dividend paid by the issue in the universe currency such as US dollar (USD) or the current total value of any foreign currency dividend or stock spin-off.

Security return for day d is defined as the relative change in the closing price C from previous day $d - 1$ to current day d:

$$R_d = \frac{C_d}{C_{d-1}} - 1. \tag{1.1}$$

To account for corporate actions, the prices are adjusted, that is, multiplied by an adjustment factor A_d so (1.1) give a correct return on investment after the adjustment. In general, a multi-day return from day d_1 to day d_2 equals

$$R(d_1, d_2) = \frac{A_{d_2} C_{d_2}}{A_{d_1} C_{d_1}} - 1. \tag{1.2}$$

The adjustment factor A_d is used only in a ratio across days and is therefore defined up to constant normalizing coefficient. There are two ways of price adjustment: backward and forward. The backward adjustment used, for example, in the *Bloomberg terminal* is normalized so today's adjustment factor equals one and changes by cax events going back in time. On a new day, all values A_d are recomputed.

Another way is forward adjustment, in which scheme A_d starts with one on the first day of the security pricing history and then changes as

$$A_d = \prod_{d' \leq d} \frac{S_{d'}}{1 - D_{d'}/C_{d'-1}}. \tag{1.3}$$

Cax events are understood as those with $S_d \neq 1$ or $D_d \neq 0$. The past history of the forward adjustment is not changed by new entries. Therefore, the forward adjustment factor can be recorded and incrementally maintained along with price-volume data. If backward adjustment factor is desired as of current date, it can be computed as

$$A_d^{(back)} = \frac{A_d}{A_{\text{today}}}. \tag{1.4}$$

---

[2] This is clearly not enough for updating an actual trading portfolio for newly spun off regular or when-issued stock. For this, portfolio managers usually rely on maintenance performed by the prime broker.

The rationale for Eq. (1.3) is as follows. Dividend and split for day d are always known in advance. One perfectly logical, if impractical, way to reinvest a dividend D_d (including a monetized spin-off) per share is to borrow cash to buy x additional shares of the same stock at the previous day close and then return the loan the morning after from the dividend proceeds. To stay fully invested, the total dividend amount $(1 + x)D_d$ must equal the loan amount $x C_{d-1}$, therefore

$$(1 + x)D_d = x C_{d-1} \implies x = \frac{D_d}{C_{d-1} - D_d}. \tag{1.5}$$

In terms of value at hand, this manipulation is equivalent to a $1 : (1 + x)$ stock split. If there is also a post-dividend split S_d, one-day adjustment factor equals

$$a_d = S_d(1 + x) = \frac{S_d}{1 - D_d/C_{d-1}}, \tag{1.6}$$

and formula (1.3) follows.[3]

Some quant shops have used a similar reinvestment logic of buying D_d/C_d shares of stock at the new closing price C_d resulting in a somewhat simpler day adjustment factor,

$$a_d' = S_d\left(1 + \frac{D_d}{C_d}\right). \tag{1.7}$$

This formula is fine as far as only daily data is concerned, but applying this adjustment to intraday prices results in a lookahead (Sec. 2.1.1) due to using a future, while intraday, closing price C_d. Intraday forecast features depending on such adjustment factor can generate a wonderful forecast for dividend-paying stocks in simulation, but production trading using such forecasts will likely be disappointing. Formula (1.6) differs from the "simple" Eq. (1.7) by a typically small amount $O(D^2/C^2)$ but is free from lookahead.

Dividend (including any spin-off) values D_d found in actual historical data can occasionally reach or exceed the previous close value C_{d-1} causing trouble in Eq. (1.3). Such conditions are rare and normally due

---

[3] Eqs. (1.3) and (1.6) apply to the convention that a dividend is paid on a pre-split (previous day) share. A post-split dividend convention is used by some data vendors and requires a straightforward modification of the adjustment factor. Simultaneous dividends and splits are infrequent.

to a datafeed error or a major capital reorganization warranting a termination of the security and starting a new one via a suitable entry in the security master (Sec. 2.1.2), even if the entity has continued under the same name.

Price adjustment is also used for non-equity asset classes. Instead of corporate actions, futures contracts have an expiration date and must be "rolled" to continue position exposure. The roll is done by closing an existing position shortly before its expiration and opening an equivalent dollar position for the next available expiration month. For futures on physical commodities, such as oil or metals, the price of a contract with a later expiration date is normally higher than a similar contract with an earlier expiration due to the cost of carry including storage and insurance. The monthly or quarterly rolling price difference can be thought of as a (possibly negative) dividend or a split and handled by a backward or forward adjustment factor using Eq. (1.3). Brokers provide services of trading "continuous futures," or automatically rolled futures positions.

1.3 Linear vs log returns

Given a list of consecutive daily portfolio pnls, compute, in linear time, its maximum drawdown.

From a quant interview

The linear return (1.1), also known as simple or accounting return, defines a daily portfolio pnl Q_d through dollar position $\mathbf{P}_d$:

$$Q_d = \mathbf{P}_{d-1} \cdot \mathbf{R}_d. \tag{1.8}$$

Here boldface notation is used for vectors in the space of portfolio securities. For pnl computation, the linear returns are *cross-sectionally* additive with position weights. Risk factor models (Sec. 4.2) add more prominence to the cross-sectional linear algebra of simple returns.

It is also convenient to use log returns

$$\tilde{R}_{ds} = \log(1 + R_{ds}) = \log \frac{A_{ds} C_{ds}}{A_{d-1,s} C_{d-1,s}}, \tag{1.9}$$

which, unlike the linear returns, are *serially* additive, for a fixed initial investment in one asset, across time periods. In quant research, both types of return are used interchangeably.

Over short-term horizons of order one day, stock returns are of order 1%, so the difference between the linear and the logarithmic return

$$\tilde{R} = \log(1 + R) = R - \frac{R^2}{2} + O(R^3) \qquad (1.10)$$

is of order 10^{-4}, or a basis point (bps), which is in the ballpark of the return predictability (Sec. 2.3.3). The expectation, or forecast, of the log return (1.10) is

$$E(\tilde{R}) \approx E(R) - \frac{\sigma^2}{2}, \qquad (1.11)$$

where σ is the volatility (standard deviation) of the return. Due to the negative sign of the correction in (1.11), its effect can be meaningful even for a slightly non-dollar-neutral or volatility-exposed portfolio. Volatility is one of commonly used risk factors (Sec. 4.3).

The difference between linear and log returns affects forecasting (Chapter 2), especially over longer horizons, because the operators of (linear) expectation and (concave) log do not commute. Even though statistical distribution of log returns may have better mathematical properties than those of linear returns, it is the linear return based pnl that is the target of portfolio optimization (Chapter 6). On the other hand, the log return plays a prominent role in the Kelly criterion (Sec. 6.9).

Chapter 2

Forecasting

It is very difficult to predict, especially the future.
Possibly Niels Bohr

For a non-gambler, investing money into moving things makes sense only when he or she is able to predict, more or less, where those things are moving. Predictability is actually not that bad in physics describing dynamics of matter by various ordinary or partial differential equations. The horizon of physical predictability is still limited by the *Lyapunov exponentiation* of nearby orbits. This exponential accumulation of uncertainty in a formally deterministic system is a signature of dynamical chaos, which almost invariably appears in dimensions greater than two.[1] For financial assets, it is also easier to predict returns over shorter horizons, mainly due to higher costs of faster trading

---

[1] A generic dynamical system $d\mathbf{x}(t)/dt = \mathbf{v}(\mathbf{x})$ in a d-dimensional state space free of special symmetries and associated conservation laws generates deterministic trajectories $\mathbf{x}(\mathbf{x}_0, t)$ typically filling allowed volume in a chaotic/fractal manner and exponentially sensitive to the initial condition $\mathbf{x}_0$, $\partial\mathbf{x}(\mathbf{x}_0, t)/\partial\mathbf{x}_0 \propto \exp(\lambda t)$, unless topology rules out chaotic trajectories.

(Chapter 5). The rules of the game and clear players' stimuli such as greed and fear provide a degree of dynamical description to the markets (Sec. 2.5), but those dynamics are very noisy due to many dimensions/ participants often making noisy decisions. In addition, actions of the more powerful and moneyed participants—informed traders—reduce the degree, and shorten the horizon, of price predictability. After all easy signals are *arbed out*, which they surely are, we are left with a pretty low predictability of future returns—on the order of ~ 1 bps[2] per day—vs $\sim 2\%$ stock volatility.

The predictability, or signal-to-noise ratio $\varepsilon \sim 10^{-2}$ is probably the most important *small parameter* of quantitative finance. In mathematics or theoretical physics, a small parameter such as the *fine structure constant*, makes it easier to work out useful analytics by perturbation theory or series expansion, but the low price predictability does not seem very helpful to quants, who also face non-trivial transaction costs. The zeroth order approximation in ε is of course the classical *efficient market hypothesis* preventing hedge funds from existence. The equivalent *no-arbitrage argument* is used in the Black-Scholes derivative pricing model.[3] Market efficiency does not necessarily imply the existence of a well-defined true asset value. As Fisher Black famously noted,[4] *We might define an efficient market as one in which price is within a factor of 2 of value.* In view of possibly inelastic dynamics of the aggregate stock market, the factor of 2 could easily turn 5 posing some difficulties for the market efficiency at the macro level (Sec. 5.4).

In the first order in ε, where quant traders operate, there exists a popular but flawed argument that small signal-to-noise ratio leaves viable only simple forecasts such as those based on low-dimensional ordinary least squares (OLS). While OLS regression (Sec. 2.4.3) remains one of the most frequently used forecasting tools, and for a good enough reason of low complexity if the number of predictors is low (Sec. 2.4.10), examples of sections 2.3 and 2.4 make the case for other methods as well.

---

[2] Here bps stands for *basis points*, or units of 10^{-4}, commonly used for measuring small returns.

[3] F. Black, M. Scholes, *The Pricing of Options and Corporate Liabilities*, Journal of Political Economy, 81(3), pp. 637–654, 1973.

[4] F. Black, *Noise*, The Journal of Finance, 41(3), pp. 529–554, 1986.

2.1 Data for forecasts

Given a CSV file with 11 columns $x_0, x_1, \ldots, x_9, y$ and 1000 rows, the last 10 rows with missing ys, fill in the blanks using this computer.

From a quant interview

Any future return prediction, or forecast (call it y), needs some *predictor* data (call it x), possibly multi-dimensional, so the forecast is a function of the predictor: $y = f(x)$. We will call this forecast function a *model*. The x data must be available at the time of forecasting; the y data is not yet directly observed and therefore modeled. To have predictive power, a predictor x must be relevant to the outcome y or, put simply, make sense for the context. Further, predictors are best cast in the form of *features*—formulaic or algorithmic combinations preferably expressing clear forecast ideas and maximizing predictive power. The terms *predictor* and *feature* are used interchangeably.

Forecasting financial time series involves both art and science. Feature engineering is mostly art based on financial intuition, educated *priors*, and a degree of understanding of market workings, although there are some general approaches as well.[5] Generating a forecast from features is mostly science, either using methods of classical statistics (Sec. 2.3) or those of the actively developing field of *machine learning* (Sec. 2.4).

In addition to the price-volume data mentioned in Sec. 1.1, below is an incomplete list of data sources commonly used for equity forecasting. Most types of data are available from more than one provider, which are not listed here.

2.1.1 Point-in-time and lookahead

What is the minimal vertical size of a wall mirror needed for a 6-foot-tall person to see himself from head to toe?

From a quant interview

---

[5] M. Kuhn, K. Johnson, *Feature Engineering and Selection: A Practical Approach for Predictive Models*, Chapman & Hall/CRC Data Science Series, 2019.

To be usable in quant research, financial data must be stored *point-in-time* (PIT), meaning a clear labeling of each record by the time when it had, or would, become available in the normal course of datafeed updates. An incorrect time labeling, either in data storage or upon data loading in RAM, can lead to *lookahead*, or a research bug of inadvertently using future data, whereas real-time production trading is clearly free of such "feature." If a researcher sees a too-good-to-be-true simulation (Sec. 7) performance,[6] the case for the lookahead is clear, but it is fair to assume that many quant strategies fail to perform due to never discovered subtle lookahead bugs.

Most financial data vendors provide both PIT history and a real-time feed. Some vendors have been noted for rewriting ("improving") history by better security mapping, error corrections, or worse. Unless the quant researcher has been collecting and timestamping vendor data in real time, it is hard to tell if the history is PIT.[7] Difficulty confirming that a third-party history is PIT is not uncommon. Predictive power of a dataset can also deteriorate due to market impact by trading strategies deployed soon after the dataset is made commercially available.

Survival bias discussed in Sec. 2.1.2 is a less obvious kind of lookahead that is more harmful for longer-term fundamental alphas.

There is another, more subtle, source of lookahead affecting a relatively large quant portfolio using the same forecasts over an extended period of time. Past trades done for this portfolio have affected prices by market impact (Sec. 5.2) making the forecast performance look better via a self-fulfilling prophecy. As with buggy lookaheads, self-impacted history can result in a too optimistic historical simulation deviating from production (Sec. 7.1). Ways to eliminate this effect are described in Sec. 2.6.

---

[6] The author once observed an "inexplicable" simulation performance improvement by shortening the forecast horizon. It turned out to be a one-day lookahead bug. When using the forecast over a long horizon, the first day lookahead was diluted by legitimate (poorly predicted) longer-term returns, and the simulation looked good within reason. When the forecast was applied to shorter and shorter horizons, the simulated pnl went miraculous.

[7] One of the first research projects assigned to this author was producing an equity forecast from insider trading data (Sec. 2.1.8) provided historically by a vendor. The real-time performance of this forecast turned out drastically worse than in historical simulation, and not due to a lookahead.

2.1.2 Security master and survival bias

An island is inhabited by 100 smart lions who are good at math.
A lion likes eating a human, but doing so would turn the lion into
a human. Assuming staying alive is the highest priority, if a human
arrives to the island, will he be eaten?

From a quant interview[8]

The simplest kind of company-specific historical data is company traits and attributes normally maintained in a security master, or *secmaster*. These fields include categorical data such as home and listing country, industrial attribution via Global Industry Classification Standard (GICS) or another grouping, membership in major equity indices, and so forth. Such data affect forecasting via grouping and decomposition (Sec. 4.4) and carries value as fundamental information independent of price.[9]

The primary purpose of the secmaster database is to map between multiple security symbols (IDs) to a common symbology used in the quant research and trading environment. Each major financial data vendor uses a vendor-specific symbology whose purpose is to provide unique string labels for individual securities. The maintenance of the labels across company name or ticker changes, mergers, spin-offs, and other corporate actions is a nontrival problem lacking a unique solution: it is a matter of judgment which of two similar-size companies, A or B, if any, should continue its identity as the merged $C = A + B$. Algorithmic approaches to resolving such inconsistencies are discussed in Sec. A1.

Another important function of the secmaster is the maintenance of securities listing and delisting dates. A correct lifespan information is important for avoiding *survival bias*, a fallacy of running quant research on assets alive today but ignoring those no longer active. Some web-based research portals catering to quant enthusiasts provide trading simulator APIs and financial data for currently active stocks, ETFs, and other instruments. While one wants to trade active instruments, it is also important to run alpha research historically, without the implicit

---

[8] This was a counter question offered by a would-be defector from Renaissance Technologies interviewing with the author long time ago. Counter-questioning, as well as asking *now give me* **your** *favorite question*, reflected a view of problem solving as a sport, or perhaps a form of science nostalgia, among some quant teams.

[9] Although running return correlations among companies with the same and other groups helps detecting occasional incorrect industry labels.

benefit of knowing which stocks would survive, say, by August 2020. The survival bias is another kind of buggy lookahead (Sec. 2.1.1).

2.1.3   Fundamental and accounting data

Data describing the details of company business are among the most important for long-term (weeks and months) forecasting. Quarterly and yearly company reports of earnings, sales, cash flows, R&D expenditure, and other financials are among the primary indicators of management quality, financial health, and competitiveness. These data are sparse (typically once per quarter) and fairly complex including hundreds of numeric and text fields per company. Forming relevant systematic features from company reports requires an accounting expertise. Cross-sectional application of accounting data would benefit from understanding differences between industries. For example, the capital structure of banks and manufacturers is not the same, so forming relative value predictors for a broad equity universe may be tricky.

To make fundamental analysis and forecasting more manageable, various accounting ratios are often used. These ratios include earnings to price, book value to price, debt to equity, dividend payout to income, assets to liabilities, profit to sales, and many others. Dimensionless ratios have long been employed by physicists in *dimensional analysis* to establish meaningful results such as the size of an atom estimated by Niels Bohr.[10] Financial ratios are less dimensionless than in physics, but they serve a similar purpose of dimensionality (the number of coordinates in the feature space) reduction (Sec. 2.4.10).

In addition to financial ratios, investors pay attention to broader themes such as *growth* and *value* operating with relevant subsets of the accounting ratios.[11] Due to being widely followed, and therefore subject to crowding (Sec. 4.7), these themes are also used as risk factors (Sec. 4.3).

---

[10] T. Hecksher, *Insights through dimensions*, Nature Physics, 13, p. 1026, 2017.
[11] B. Cornell, A. Damodaran, *Value Investing: Requiem, Rebirth or Reincarnation?*, NYU Stern School of Business. Available at SSRN: https://ssrn.com/abstract=3779481, 2021.

In addition to regular reports, companies occasionally issue earnings guidance statements or conference calls typically designed to manage investor expectations between the reports. Management guidance events often generate stock price shocks. Some providers collect and supply such data via the web or a direct feed service.

There is also a class of data providers supplying computer-friendly research-based *factor libraries*. The factor data can include a few or a few hundred fields per stock per day. They are derived from fundamental (sometimes called "quantamental"), analyst (Sec. 2.1.4), price-volume data, or even internal alpha research, and designed to be usable for apple-to-apple comparison of stocks. Such products can be used as risk factors (Sec. 4.2), raw alpha building blocks, or both.

2.1.4 Analyst estimates

> *There are two well informed stock analysts, one of whom always tells the truth and the other one always lies. You meet one of them but you don't know whether or not he is the liar. What question should you ask to find out if SPY is going up or down next week?*
>
> From a quant interview

Estimates and opinions on publicly traded companies published by sell-side analysts are used by quantitative and discretionary traders alike. The analysts follow a number of stocks or corporate bonds within their area of expertise and provide distilled/simplified views of the companies to clients and, via data vendors, to a broader investing community. Analyst reports are much simpler than original company reporting and contain estimates for a subset of accounting fields such as earnings or sales per share and opinions about stock price targets, upgrades/downgrades, bond credit ratings, and so forth. The structure of the analyst data is still complicated due to varying coverage by company, variation of estimates by analyst, and possible analysts' conflicts of interest.

Due to the attention investors pay to analyst reports, whatever their accuracy, analyst estimates and their revisions carry a predictive power for stock returns either directly or via statistics such as the variance of analysts' opinions.

2.1.5   Supply chain and competition

A sailor can pull with 100 lbs of force. With mooring cable wound one full round on a dock bollard, the sailor can hold a boat pulling with 10,000 lbs of force. How many cable rounds about the bollard are needed to hold a ship pulling with 1,000,000 lbs of force?

From a quant interview

Publicly traded companies form various explicit and implicit relationship graphs affecting their business, profitability, and stock price. This type of fundamental inter-company data includes clusters of firms competing in the same market or forming an interdependent supply chain. Depending on the type of relationship, stock prices within the chain can be positively or negatively correlated leading to a predictability of returns of some stock by returns of others. Supply chain fundamentals are available from several financial data vendors.

2.1.6   M&A and risk arbitrage

Among four stocks, Agilent, Barnes, Citigroup, and Dominion, six relative forecasts are available: $\phi_{ij} = f_i - f_j$, where $i,j = A, B, C, D$. Compute the individual forecasts f_i.

From a quant interview

Companies related by supply chain or competition are more likely to engage in mergers and acquisitions (M&A). Merger announcements are among the most important news affecting stock prices. After a merger announcement, the acquirer stock usually goes down and the target is sharply up due to an *acquisition premium* involved in a merger offer. The premium, usually in the ballpark of 20-30% of the target pre-merger stock price,[12] reflects the need of the acquirer to gain control and also perceived future benefits of synergy savings and reduced competition. The acquirer stock goes down due to the market perception of the acquisition premium often being overpriced and reflecting managerial hubris and self interest, in addition to the real economic synergy.

The target-acquirer price pattern can have a precursor if there is an information leak or just speculations of a possible deal. The price moves

---

[12] T. Laamanen, *On the role of acquisition premium in acquisition research*, Strategic Management Journal, 28(13), pp. 1359–1369, 2007.

revert if the deal doesn't go through or is in doubt. While identifying potential M&A targets and carrying out the transactions are investment banking functions, quants can build models estimating the probability of a merger initiation and/or its successful completion and trade affected stocks accordingly. This type of strategies is known as *risk arbitrage*.

2.1.7 Event-based predictors

This class of data is not distinct from the rest other than by a sparse and irregular time structure. Learning on such events is different as they tend to be infrequent but cause a stronger price response. One can use material company news, mergers and acquisitions, earning surprises, index rebalancing, or even dividends and splits: some market participants trade in predictable ways before or after dividend ex-date due to possible regulatory or tax implications. It is also possible that some portfolio managers miss or incorrectly book corporate actions or trade on false signals generated by a lookahead in the adjustment factor (Sec. 1.2).

Asset returns around such events are reasonably well understood and are usually learned by manual EDA methods (Sec. 2.4.6) rather than by the full power of machine learning (Sec. 2.4).

2.1.8 Holdings and flows

> *There are two non-intersecting trails between points A and B such that Alice and Bob can walk from A to B using different trails while always staying within one mile from each other. Is it possible for Alice to walk from A to B and for Bob to walk from B to A and to never get within a mile from each other?*
>
> From a quant interview

Large US funds are required to file quarterly reports of their long holdings, known as Form 13F. This data is made available by the U.S. Securities and Exchange Commission (SEC) and also through various data providers. Although not exactly timely, such holdings data have predictive value because the large funds, as possibly better informed traders, have their reasons to hold those securities and may need to liquidate them in the future. Hedge funds in aggregate hold around 10% of the US equity market while generating about a third of its total trading volume.[13]

Likewise, Financial Industry Regulatory Authority (FINRA) requires broker-dealers to periodically report aggregate *short interest* positions by issue (but not by institution), which are also made public.

Some brokers can route client order flow to market makers or HFT firms for a payment, before the orders hit public exchange. Aggregate routing information is reported per SEC Rule 606[14] on a quarterly basis. Real-time order flow not on exchange order books clearly carries alpha and can be available to select customers. This practice has sparked some controversy (Sec. 6.10.4). The SEC adopted additional order handing disclosure requirements in November 2018.[15]

In the US, officers and directors of publicly traded companies, as well as beneficial owners of $\geq$ 10% of company stock are treated as *corporate insiders* and are required to pre-announce and to report their trades in the company stock and derivatives on SEC Form 144 and Form 4, respectively. As other forms, these filings are made public by the SEC via its Electronic Data Gathering, Analysis, and Retrieval (EDGAR) system.[16]

Meaningful flow of funds occurs during major index rebalancing. This happens because index funds and index-tracking ETFs are required to have specific index exposures. Changes in index composition are published ahead of time and can be used to predict trading activity and related price changes.

Flows of funds affect both relative stock prices and absolute, or broad equity market fluctuations. The inelastic impact of net money flows is discussed in Sec. 5.4.

2.1.9   News and social media

Men don't care what's on TV. They only care what else is on TV.
Jerry Seinfeld

Publicly traded companies generate a stream of news releases and other messages appearing in major news wire services such as Thompson

---

[13] C. Cao, B. Liang, A.W. Lo, L. Petrasek, *Hedge Fund Holdings and Stock Market Efficiency*, The Review of Asset Pricing Studies, 8(1), pp. 77–116, 2018.

[14] https://www.sec.gov/tm/faq-rule-606-regulation-nms.

[15] https://www.sec.gov/rules/final/2018/34-84528.pdf.

[16] https://www.sec.gov/edgar.shtml.

Reuters, Associated Press, Dow Jones, and others. Company-specific news are usually tagged by company ticker or another ID for convenience of automated processing but are generally intended for a human reader.[17]

Several financial data providers entered the news data marketplace with better digitized and tagged news feeds including natural language processing, or NLP-based tags including relevance level and sentiment score. The data can be supplied in real time. Some quants have explored potential time advantage by automated translation of news feeds in other languages, before the English-based media catch the news. This extra layer can add noise and result in a signal lost in translation.[18]

In addition to official news wires, some of these providers also process social media postings such as stock-related tweets. Social-media-based sentiments often trail earlier news or price moves and can also be manipulative (Sec. 4.8).

2.1.10 Macroeconomic data

There are 10^{11} stars in the galaxy. That used to be a huge number. But it's only a hundred billion. It's less than the national deficit! We used to call them astronomical numbers. Now we should call them economical numbers.

Richard Feynman[19]

Governments, banks, and research institutions have traditionally published broad economic data such as inflation, interest rates, GDP,

---

[17] It appears that a fair amount of financial news articles are generated by robots. For example, it is not difficult to write a computer program generating a news about a company stock reaching a 52-week high or being among today's biggest movers.

[18] *Scene 1*. The author, an organizer of the Physics Department seminar at the University of California, San Diego, is talking with Prof. Terry Hwa, who is originally from Taiwan. Dr. Michael Longuet-Higgins, a distinguished British scientist and the invited speaker, is approaching us. Looking straight at Dr. Hwa the speaker says, "Hello, are you Dr. Isichenko?"

Scene 2. The author and his teenage daughter are picking up a takeout order at David Chen's Chinese restaurant in Armonk, NY, and talking in Russian. A friendly Asian waitress asks, "Are you guys from England?"

[19] Quoted by D.L. Goodstein, *Richard P. Feynman, Teacher*, Physics Today, 42(2), pp. 70-75, 1989.

unemployment, foreign exchange rates (FX), commodity prices, debt, consumer confidence survey, and so forth. An extensive macroeconomic dataset is maintained by the Federal Reserve.[20] Although not directly company related, such data can be useful for equity forecasting by identifying market regime changes (Sec. 2.4.17), residualization (Sec. 4.4), or conditioning (Sec. 2.9). For example, controlling for FX would make sense when forecasting stocks heavily relying on import/export operations.

2.1.11   Alternative data

Sometimes the road less traveled is less traveled for a reason.

Jerry Seinfeld

Traditional financial data has become a commodity and is freely or commercially available to all market participants. Quest for new alpha keeps bringing to life new, or "alternative," data sources. Examples include news and social media analytics already mentioned above, crowdsourcing (polls of professionals and *prediction markets*), retail credit card transactions, car registrations, employee benefit plans, goods shipments, job listings, internet search trends, web ad clicks, satellite images of crops, oil tankers or shopping mall parking lots, and so forth. Newborn datasets tend to generate meaningful trading profits for a period of time until the data, like the news sentiment, becomes a commodity.

Data accumulation rate is growing exponentially. Much of this stuff is poorly structured and is sitting there waiting for meaningful processing. No doubt there will be many more alternative data products available to quant researchers.

2.1.12   Alpha capture

A portfolio manager is hiring a quant analyst and is set to interview 100 candidates in a random order. The PM must make an offer during an interview; otherwise, the candidate will join a competitor and won't come back. What strategy would maximize the chance of hiring the best available quant?

From a quant interview

---

[20] https://www.federalreserve.gov/data.htm.

The field of systematic trading is highly competitive. The most successful hedge funds utilize vast amounts of data to generate multiple alpha signals. Many well-researched alphas are not strong enough to beat trading costs (Chapter 5) when used in isolation, but a combined forecast provides enough stability and strength to drive a high-capacity portfolio. Large quant funds employ sizable teams of quant researchers, sometimes outsourced to overseas locations with a higher talent/cost ratio. The quant teams generate alpha signals for a centralized alpha pool (Sec. 3.8) for subsequent combining (Chapter 3) and portfolio construction (Chapter 6). Other shops running a "silo" portfolio manager (PM) operation utilize internal alpha sharing for a fee. This *alpha capture* business is not limited to quant shops and can include trade ideas from discretionary traders, brokers, day traders,[21] and other sources. Some of the internally maintained alpha pools have $10^3 - 10^6$ items per stock per day and growing. Such alpha pools can be the largest and most valuable datasets whose optimal utilization poses unique challenges (Chapter 3).

2.2   Technical forecasts

Past security prices tend to be among the best predictors for future prices, at least in the short term (intraday to a few days). Without going into excessive detail, this section will try to explain the basic intuition behind technical forecasting commonly known as mean reversion and momentum. This discussion is specific to equities, which have both common traits and idiosyncratic properties. In addition, there are fairly many (hundreds to thousands) tradable stocks, which makes the law of large numbers (Sec. 2.3.4) work to the quant's advantage. The idea of common and idiosyncratic equity moves is not to be taken for granted. For better technical forecasts, one may need to work with separate groups of stocks, for example, by liquidity or sector (Sec. 2.8).

---

[21] This author once entertained a job offer from a firm providing data and execution services to day traders. The job description was to monitor trading success of the customers and build a book based on ideas of the best performers. When starting his quant career with three offers at hand, the author accepted the one with the lowest initial pay but seemingly the best team. (The day-trading shop offer was the highest.) Down the road, the choice turned out to be right. Other than track record, in the academia it is degree, and in hedge funds it is pedigree that seems to matter.

It is also best to avoid mixing stocks with exchange-traded funds (ETFs). ETFs are quoted and traded just like stocks, but their dynamics and forecasting are different from common stocks. There are thousands of ETFs. Most of them are tradable instruments tracking other securities, such as a group of stocks by industry (example: XBI for biotech), theme (ICLN for clean energy), geography (EWZ for Brazil), index (SPY for S&P500), or style (ESGV for environmental, social, and corporate governance).

2.2.1   Mean reversion

A lit candle is set on a table in a moving railroad car. Describe what will happen to the candle's flame when the train starts braking.

From a quant interview

Common trends among stocks can be already deduced from mainstream news soundbites discussing investors putting money into stocks, bonds, or fleeing to cash. At a basic level, this implies, and is supported by data, that most stock moves are correlated with, and can be "explained by," the *market*, or the mean return of a broad equity universe.

If we introduce a daily statistical weight w_{ds} for stock s on day d, the market return M_d is defined through stock returns R_{ds} as

$$M_d = \frac{\sum_s w_{ds} R_{ds}}{\sum_s w_{ds}}. \tag{2.1}$$

Each stock's return time series is correlated with, or partially explained by, the market. We can run a rolling-window or exponential moving average (EMA) linear regression $R_{ds} \sim M_d$ with the result (Sec. 2.4.3)[22]

$$R_{ds} = \beta_{ds} M_d + r_{ds},$$

$$\beta_{ds} = \frac{\sum_{d' \leq d} u_{d'} R_{d's} M_{d'}}{\sum_{d' \leq d} u_{d'} M_{d'}^2}, \tag{2.2}$$

where $u_{d'}$ is the time weight to cover the relevant trailing window, for example, $u_d = e^{\gamma d}$ for γ^{-1}-day EMA. Except for few special industries

---

[22] A standard market beta definition involves linear regression with an intercept. Alternatively, the time series of R_{ds} and M_d can be serially detrended before running the regression.

such as precious metals, the market betas β_{ds} are positive numbers of order one, usually smaller for staples and utilities and larger for technology and "glamour" stocks. The residual term r_{ds} in Eq. (2.2) is a stock-specific, or net-of-market, daily return. As seen from its definition, current residual return r_{ds} is a nonlinear function of $R_{d's'}$, the past and current returns of all stocks in the universe.

Quants, not unlike humans, want to know the reason, or "story," behind their forecasts. The story of mean reversion is herding. Although the meaning of Eq. (2.2) is purely statistical, one can think of it in loosely dynamical terms as if stocks were moving with the mean flow (market) and also experienced Brownian-like[23] chaotic residual motion in the frame of reference of that flow. It is therefore expected that residual deviations revert to keep stocks with the mean. This *mean reversion* behavior is indeed observed in the cross-sectional regression of future vs past residuals,

$$r_{d+1,s} = \beta^{(mr)} r_{ds} + \varepsilon_{ds},$$

$$\beta^{(mr)} = \frac{\sum_{d'<d,s} u_{d'} w_{d's} r_{d's} r_{d'+1,s}}{\sum_{d'<d,s} u_{d'} w_{d's} r_{d's}^2}, \tag{2.3}$$

with a small negative mean reversion coefficient $\beta^{(mr)}$. In this simplest closed form, however, the forecast is too weak to be practical. Further refinements include multi-factor (Sec. 4.2) residuals rather than just net of market, different horizons, multiple predictors including those sensitive to trading volume (Sec. 2.2.3), and so forth. Curiously, quite a few examples of mean-reversion-type forecast have been published.[24]

2.2.2   Momentum

> *A hockey player shoots a puck with initial velocity v without rotation. The puck stops after gliding a distance L. The player shoots the puck again with the same initial velocity but this time also with rotation. Will the puck go a distance smaller or larger than L?*
>
> From a quant interview

---

[23] The Ornstein-Uhlenbeck random process with attraction to the origin would probably be a better description of mean reversion than the Brownian motion.

[24] Z. Kakushadze, *101 Formulaic Alphas*, arXiv:1601.00991v3 [q-fin.PM], 2016.

Over longer horizons, stock returns tend to be positively autocorrelated. One can try to put a rationale behind this *momentum* phenomenon,
but it probably won't sound as convincing as mean reversion—assuming
the reader finds anything here convincing at all. Momentum has been
attributed to delayed information propagation and behavioral effects.[25]
It is more natural to expect momentum in group forecasts, such as for
industry or other factor returns,[26] where the oscillatory residual noise
tends to cancel out. Some reversion in factor returns may still exist as
indicated by the existence of *factor rotation* strategies. Momentum in equities and futures is associated with autocorrelation of price changes such
that the volatility "signature plot" shows a long-term volatility exceeding
daily volatility.[27]

2.2.3   Trading volume

There are two bottles: A with 1 liter of water and B with 1 liter of
ethanol. One pours a cup from bottle A into bottle B, shakes B, and
then pours the same amount back from B into A. Is there now more
water in ethanol or ethanol in water?

From a quant interview[28]

While past returns are of primary interest for future returns, technical
features routinely include trading volume. The effect of trading volume
on mean reversion and momentum has a story, too. One can argue that
if a stock has moved relative to others without a significant change in
volume, this is likely a temporary deviation which is expected to revert to
the mean. On the other hand, a price move accompanied by an abnormal
trading activity indicates there was a material company news behind the
price change, which could persist or even further increase as the market
digests the news—this is momentum.

---

[25] R.J. Bianchi, M.E. Drew, J.H. Fan, *Commodities momentum: A behavioral perspective*,
Journal of Banking & Finance, 72(11), pp. 133–150, 2016.

[26] R.D. Arnott, M. Clements, V. Kalesnik, J.T. Linnainmaa, *Factor Momentum*, 2019.
Available at SSRN: https://ssrn.com/abstract=3116974.

[27] T.-L. Dao, T.-T. Nguyen, C. Deremble, Y. Lempérière, J.-P. Bouchaud, M. Potters,
Tail protection for long investors: Trend convexity at work, arXiv:1607.02410 [q-fin.GN],
2016.

[28] Inspired by D.I. Mendeleev, *On the Combinations of Water with Alcohol*, Sc.D. thesis (in
Russian), Faculty of Physics and Mathematics, St. Petersburg University, 1865.

2.2.4 Statistical predictors

Alice's model predicts the USD to EUR exchange rate to increase 10% in one year. Bob's forecast indicates the same increase for the EUR to USD rate over the same period. Can Alice and Bob both be right?

From a quant interview

In addition to pointwise predictors such as past return from time $t - h$ to time t, various statistical means have some predictive power either directly or via conditioning (Sec. 2.9). For example, historical stock volatility used to be a reasonable predictor of future returns for a number of years (not anymore). More subtle statistics such as fractal dimension and Hurst exponent have been measured and applied to financial time series prediction.[29,30]

The Hurst exponent H is a fractal property of a time series $R(t)$ whose increments, after detrending, scale on average as

$$|R(t + \tau) - R(t)| \propto \tau^{H}. \tag{2.4}$$

A Wiener process describing an unpredictable Brownian motion has $H = 1/2$. Values of $H \neq 1/2$ correspond to a fractional Brownian motion and indicate persistence ($H > 1/2$) or antipersistence ($H < 1/2$) of the time series.[31] Such behavior is associated with a longer time series memory with implications for its predictability (Fig. 2.1). Persistence indicates momentum (Sec. 2.2.2), and antipersistence describes a mean reversion behavior of returns (Sec. 2.2.1).

In addition to the properties of a single time series, one can also utilize statistical relations between different time series (Sec. 2.10).

2.2.5 Data from other asset classes

This is my quant. He doesn't even speak English.

From the 2015 movie *The Big Short*

[29] L. Borland, J.-P. Bouchaud, J.-F. Muzy, G. Zumbach, *The Dynamics of Financial Markets—Mandelbrot's multifractal cascades, and beyond*, arXiv:cond-mat/0501292, 2005.

[30] S. Tzouras, C. Anagnostopoulos, E. McCoy, *Financial time series modeling using the Hurst exponent*, Physica A: Statistical Mechanics and its Applications, 425(1), pp. 50–68, 2015.

[31] M.B. Isichenko, *Percolation, statistical topography, and transport in random media*, Reviews of Modern Physics, 64, pp. 961–1043, 1992.

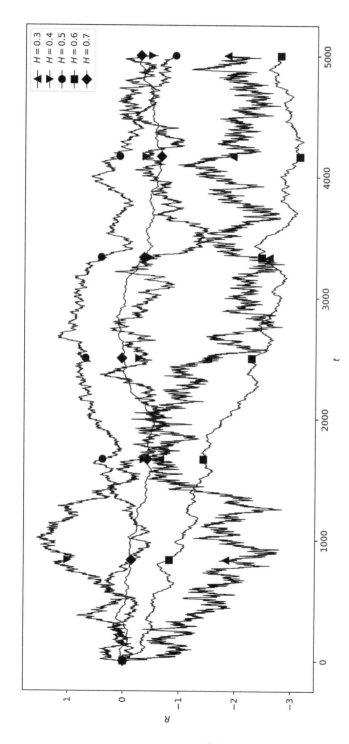

Figure 2.1 Examples of fractional Brownian paths for different Hurst exponents H generated as Gaussian processes $R(t)$ with zero mean and covariance $\mathrm{Cov}(R(t_1), R(t_2)) = (t_1^{2H} + t_2^{2H} - |t_1 - t_2|^{2H})T^{-2H}$ for $0 < t < T$. Larger H makes a smoother (more persistent) process.

24

There are a few non-equity asset classes associated with publicly traded companies. These include corporate bonds, stock and bond options, single stock futures, and credit default swaps. Price-volume data for these instruments are correlated with the company stock price and carry certain predictive power for future equity returns.

Stock options are sensitive to stock price and volatility. Option-implied volatility can predict future stock returns[32] and can be used as a risk factor (Sec. 4.3). Insider trading, both legal and illegal, tends to be active in stock options,[33] which are often used for compensation of corporate officers and provide a higher leverage for individuals trading on material information.

A credit default swap (CDS) is an over-the-counter credit derivative similar to an insurance on the underlying debt. The debt can be mortgage-based, municipal, sovereign, or corporate. A corporate CDS spread (cost of yearly insurance premium per $1 debt) reflects the market view on the firm's balance sheet and creditworthiness. A CDS differs from an insurance on corporate bonds in that the holder of a (naked) long CDS position does not have to own the actual debt and is set to benefit from the company's credit events such as a downgrade or a default, similarly to a short stock position. Data for CDS written on corporate bonds are available from several data providers and can be used for predicting stock returns.[34]

An unregulated counterparty risk involved in buying and selling CDSs contributed to the troubles of several large financial institutions including AIG, Bear Stearns, and Lehman Brothers in 2008. CDSs have been used to structure more complex synthetic securities such as collaterized debt obligations (CDO). The CDOs built on mortgage-based securities have been blamed for obscuring credit risk and contributing to the subprime mortgage bubble and crash and the global financial crisis of 2007-2008, events well depicted in the 2015 movie *The Big Short*.

---

[32] B.-J. An, A. Ang, T.G. Bali, N. Cakici, *The Joint Cross Section of Stocks and Options*, The Journal of Finance, 69(5), 2014.

[33] P. Augustin, M. Brenner, M.G. Subrahmanyam, *Informed Options Trading Prior to Takeover Announcements: Insider Trading?* Management Science, 65(12), pp. 5449–5956, 2019.

[34] *Credit Default Swap Pricing and Equity Returns*, IHS Markit white paper, November 2012. Available at https://cdn.ihs.com/www/pdf/Credit_Default_Swap_Pricing_and_Equity_Returns.pdf.

2.3 Basic concepts of statistical learning

An average potato weighs a quarter of a pound. What is the probability for a potato to weigh over half a pound?

From a quant interview

A quote from Stephen Smale would be a succinct statement of what this section is about: *The goal of learning theory (and a goal in some other contexts as well) is to find an approximation of a function $f : X \to Y$ known only through a set of pairs (x_i, y_i) drawn from an unknown probability measure.*[35] In this section we briefly review the concepts of classical statistical learning theory that are relevant for financial forecasting. There are many excellent books on the subject, both theoretical[36,37,38] and with an emphasis on software.[39] Statistical software tools are evolving quickly with a significant recent shift toward Python, `scikit-learn` being one of the most popular, yet not the only one, statistical/ML libraries. The laconic expressiveness of Python makes it possible to write short pieces of nontrivial code, including several examples used in this book and reproducible by the reader.

Statistical theory operates on mathematical concepts of probability and distribution. A continuous random multi-dimensional variable $\mathbf{z}$ is said to have a distribution function, or probability density, $F(\mathbf{z})$ if the probability for the variable to be found in an infinitesimal volume $d\mathbf{z}$ around point $\mathbf{z}$ is $F(\mathbf{z})d\mathbf{z}$. If one of the dimensions of $\mathbf{z} = (\mathbf{x}, y)$ is treated as dependent (aka response, target) variable y and the rest, $\mathbf{x}$, as independent (aka covariates, predictors, regressors, features) variables, their joint distribution $F(\mathbf{x}, y)$ provides information about the relation between $\mathbf{x}$ and y, which can be used for forecasting unknown y based on known $\mathbf{x}$.

---

[35] F. Cucker, S. Smale, *Best Choices for Regularization Parameters in Learning Theory: On the Bias-Variance Problem*, Foundations of Computational Mathematics, 2, pp. 413–428, 2002.

[36] V.N. Vapnik, *Statistical Learning Theory*, Wiley, 1998.

[37] S. Hochreiter, *Theoretical Concepts of Machine Learning*, Institute of Bioinformatics, Johannes Kepler University Linz, Lecture Notes, 2014

[38] B. Efron, T. Hastie, *Computer Age Statistical Inference: Algorithms, Evidence, and Data Science*, Institute of Mathematical Statistics Monographs. Cambridge University Press, 2016.

[39] G. James, D. Witten, T. Hastie, R. Tibshirani, *An Introduction to Statistical Learning with Applications in R*, Springer, 2017.

Given a predictor value $\mathbf{x}$, the target distribution conditional on $\mathbf{x}$ is given by Bayes' theorem:

$$F(y|\mathbf{x}) = \frac{F(\mathbf{x}, y)}{\int F(\mathbf{x}, y)dy}, \qquad (2.5)$$

where the denominator is the *marginal density* of the predictor.

In a practical setting, the joint distribution $F(\mathbf{x}, y)$ is unknown and exists, as a continuous entity, only in our mathematical imagination. Instead, we have a data sample in the form of historical observations $(\mathbf{x}_i, y_i)$. These are used to *learn*, one way or another, the hypothetical distribution $F(\mathbf{x}, y)$ with the goal to predict y using Eq. (2.5). In quant alpha research, the target y is typically the future return of a security over a specified time horizon, and the primary quantity of interest is its expected value, or the *forecast*

$$f(\mathbf{x}) = E(y|\mathbf{x}) = \int yF(y|\mathbf{x})dy. \qquad (2.6)$$

One can also define the forecast as a conditional median,

$$f_{med}(\mathbf{x}) = \text{Med}(y) = \Phi^{-1}(1/2), \qquad (2.7)$$

where Φ^{-1} is the inverse of

$$\Phi(y|\mathbf{x}) = \int_{-\infty}^{y} F(y|\mathbf{x})dy, \qquad (2.8)$$

the cumulative target distribution conditional on the features.

The distribution of y around the forecast is usually less interesting. It is typically a skewed, fat-tailed distribution with the width proportional to the security volatility σ, a quantity much larger than the forecast f. A smaller, and more informative than σ, quantity is the *model uncertainty*, or confidence band $\delta f(\mathbf{x})$, which depends on data learnability and the learning algorithm (Sec. 4.9). If the model is learned on a large amount of training data, the forecast uncertainty $\delta f(\mathbf{x})$ can be relatively small due to the law of large numbers (Sec. 2.3.4) or its variants (Sec. 2.4.3).

In practice, one rarely learns the joint distribution $F(\mathbf{x}, y)$ and learns the forecast, or the *model $y \sim f(\mathbf{x})$*, instead. Nevertheless, distribution-based statistical theory provides a useful framework for developing forecasting algorithms and analyzing their *generalization error* (Secs. 2.3.3, 2.3.6).

2.3.1   Mutual information and Shannon entropy

Three (x, y) datasets are represented by scatter plots uniformly filling the three shapes in Fig. 2.2. Rank the datasets by predictive power.

From a quant interview

If the joint distribution is factored into a product as[40]

$$F(\mathbf{x}, y) = F(\mathbf{x})F(y), \qquad (2.9)$$

then $\mathbf{x}$ and y are independent, so the predictor $\mathbf{x}$ has nothing specific to say about y. In the other extreme, y is a well-defined function of $\mathbf{x}$:

$$F(\mathbf{x}, y) = F(\mathbf{x})\delta(y - f(\mathbf{x})), \qquad (2.10)$$

where $\delta(\cdot)$ is the Dirac delta function. In a financial setting, the situation is somewhere in the middle, or perhaps much closer to the former case.

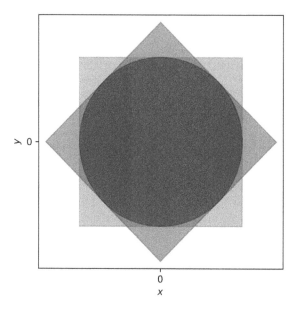

Figure 2.2   Three datasets.

---

[40] In this section a liberty is taken to denote different distributions with the same letter F, using a loosely C++–like convention that different argument types indicate totally different functions.

A measure of the dependence of two random variables $\mathbf{x}$ and y, or how much information about y is gained by knowing $\mathbf{x}$, is given by their *mutual information* function, aka *information gain*,

$$I(\mathbf{x}, y) = H(\mathbf{x}) - H(\mathbf{x}|y)$$
$$= H(y) - H(y|\mathbf{x}) \tag{2.11}$$
$$= H(\mathbf{x}) + H(y) - H(\mathbf{x}, y),$$

The mutual information is symmetric, $I(\mathbf{x}, y) = I(y, \mathbf{x})$, and expressible via individual, conditional, and joint *entropy*

$$H(\mathbf{x}) = -\int F(\mathbf{x}) \log F(\mathbf{x}) \, d\mathbf{x},$$
$$H(\mathbf{x}|y) = -\int F(\mathbf{x}, y) \log F(\mathbf{x}|y) \, d\mathbf{x} \, dy, \tag{2.12}$$
$$H(\mathbf{x}, y) = -\int F(\mathbf{x}, y) \log F(\mathbf{x}, y) \, d\mathbf{x} \, dy.$$

The information–theory entropy H was originally introduced for discrete random variables by Claude Shannon.[41] The (differential) entropy $H(x)$, a functional of a random distribution $F(x)$, is a measure of uncertainty in the value of a continuous random variable. The smaller the entropy $H(x)$, the more information about x is available. If only a limited prior is given about x, e.g., $x \in [a, b]$, a distribution $F(x)$ can be chosen to maximize $H(x)$. For a finite support $[a, b]$, the entropy is maximized by the least informative uniform distribution

$$F(x) = (b - a)^{-1} \quad \text{for} \quad x \in [a, b], \tag{2.13}$$

and zero otherwise. Conversely, the minimum entropy is reached for a definite value of $x = c \in (a, b)$:[42]

$$F(x) = \delta(x - c). \tag{2.14}$$

---

[41] C.E. Shannon, *A Mathematical Theory of Communication*, Bell System Technical Journal, 27(3), 1948.
[42] This minimum of $H(x)$ is formally a negative infinity due to some drawbacks of extending Shannon's theory to continuous distributions. For a discrete distribution with probabilities p_i, the entropy is defined as $-\sum_i p_i \log p_i$.

Quite remarkably, if only the mean μ and the variance σ^2 are known, the maximum-entropy distribution is normal:

$$F(x) = \mathcal{N}(\mu, \sigma^2) \equiv \frac{1}{\sigma\sqrt{2\pi}} \exp\left(-\frac{(x-\mu)^2}{2\sigma^2}\right). \qquad (2.15)$$

There is a connection[43] between Shannon entropy and the Central limit theorem (CLT) stating that a sum of n independent, generally non-normal, random variables tends toward a normal distribution as $n \to \infty$. There is also a link[44] between Shannon entropy and Kolmogorov complexity having to do with programmatic encoding of information. A family of lossless compression algorithms related to Kolmogorov complexity[45] is now in use in the Linux kernel, the workhorse of cloud computing (Sec. 2.4.19), and for data transmission and storage.

Regardless of the nature and the dimensionality of $\mathbf{x}$ and y, their mutual information $I(\mathbf{x}, y)$ is a nonnegative scalar; it equals zero if and only if $\mathbf{x}$ and y are statistically independent. Unlike the correlation coefficient and R-squared (Sec. 2.3.3), which express a degree of linear dependence of random variables, mutual information (2.11) is a criterion of a general nonlinear relationship. As such, mutual information is more useful than correlation for detecting nonlinear and nonparametric predictability (Sec. 2.4.6), although estimation of mutual information from data is generally more challenging.[46] In the simple example of a jointly normal distribution of two scalar random variables with means $\mu_{1,2}$ and variances $\sigma_{1,2}^2$,

$$F(x_1, x_2) = \mathcal{N}\left[\begin{pmatrix} \mu_1 \\ \mu_2 \end{pmatrix}, \begin{pmatrix} \sigma_1^2 & \rho\sigma_1\sigma_2 \\ \rho\sigma_1\sigma_2 & \sigma_2^2 \end{pmatrix}\right], \qquad (2.16)$$

their mutual information depends only on the correlation coefficient ρ and plays the role of a nonlinear R-squared:

$$I(x_1, x_2) = -\frac{1}{2}\log(1 - \rho^2). \qquad (2.17)$$

---

[43] O. Johnson, *Information Theory and the Central Limit Theorem*, World Scientific, 2004.

[44] P. Grunwald, P. Vitanyi, *Shannon Information and Kolmogorov Complexity*, arXiv:cs/0410002 [cs.IT], 2004.

[45] J. Ziv, A. Lempel, *A Universal Algorithm for Sequential Data Compression*, IEEE Transactions on information theory, IT-23(3), pp. 337–343, 1977.

[46] L. Paninski, *Estimation of Entropy and Mutual Information*, Neural Computation 15, pp. 1191–1253, 2003.

If the correlation is small, $|\rho| \ll 1$, (2.17) simplifies to

$$I(x_1, x_2) = \frac{1}{2}\rho^2, \tag{2.18}$$

which is one-half the OLS R-squared (Sec. 2.4.3). Unlike R-squared, mutual information can be larger than one and in fact goes to infinity for the perfect correlation $\rho = \pm1$. Adding an independent Gaussian noise ε to a Gaussian variable x reduces the mutual information as

$$I(x, x + \varepsilon) = \frac{1}{2}\log\frac{\sigma_x^2 + \sigma_\varepsilon^2}{\sigma_\varepsilon^2}, \tag{2.19}$$

where $\sigma_{x,\varepsilon}^2$ are the respective variances.

The general nonlinear nature of the mutual information

$$I(\mathbf{x}, y) = \int F(\mathbf{x}, y)\log\frac{F(\mathbf{x}, y)}{F(\mathbf{x})F(y)}\,d\mathbf{x}dy \tag{2.20}$$

is seen in the invariance of $I(\mathbf{x}, y)$ under a one-to-one change of variable $y \to h(y)$:

$$I(\mathbf{x}, h(y)) = I(\mathbf{x}, y), \tag{2.21}$$

as is easily verified from the definition (2.20). In general, a transformation of variables does not introduce any new mutual information and can only reduce it:

$$I(\mathbf{g}(\mathbf{x}), h(y)) \leq I(\mathbf{x}, y), \tag{2.22}$$

a statement known as *data-processing inequality*. This type of inequalities appears in quantum information theory and the *uncertainty principle*.[47]

It was reported that mutual information of pairs of stock return time series captures patterns different from those given by Pearson correlation.[48] Mutual information has been used for predictor selection and dimensionality reduction[49] (Sec. 3.5).

---

[47] M. Tomamichel, *Quantum Information Processing with Finite Resources – Mathematical Foundations*, arXiv:1504.00233 [quant-ph], 2020.

[48] P. Fiedor, *Mutual Information Rate-Based Networks in Financial Markets*, arXiv: 1401.2548 [q-fin.ST], 2014.

[49] L. Faivishevsky, J. Goldberger, *Mutual information based dimensionality reduction with application to non-linear regression*, IEEE International Workshop on Machine Learning for Signal Processing, pp. 1–6, Kittila, Finland, 2010. doi: 10.1109/MLSP.2010.5589176.

A related concept is *relative entropy*, or Kullback–Leibler (KL) divergence, of two distribution $F(\mathbf{x})$ and $G(\mathbf{x})$. This statistic is defined as

$$D_{KL}(F||G) = \int F(\mathbf{x}) \log \left(\frac{F(\mathbf{x})}{G(\mathbf{x})} \right) \, d\mathbf{x}. \qquad (2.23)$$

The scalar KL divergence expresses the difference between F and G for the same random variable $\mathbf{x}$. This difference is not a symmetric distance, because generally $D_{KL}(F||G) \neq D_{KL}(G||F)$. By Jensen's inequality, and due to the concavity of the logarithm, the Kullback–Leibler divergence is always nonnegative.

Cross-entropy of two distributions $F(\mathbf{x})$ and $G(\mathbf{x})$ (not to be confused with the joint entropy $H(\mathbf{x}, y)$ in (2.11)) is defined as the sum of the Shannon entropy of F and the Kullback–Leibler divergence:

$$H(F, G) = H(F) + D_{KL}(F||G) = -\int F(\mathbf{x}) \log G(\mathbf{x}) \, d\mathbf{x}. \qquad (2.24)$$

This statistic is mostly used for discrete distributions, e.g., as a loss function in logistic regression and multi-class classification (Sec. 2.4.1).

Entropy is a deep concept appearing in many branches of mathematics, computer science, and physics. In statistical physics, arguments of "most probable" or maximum-entropy states of macroscopic systems are the basis of the second law of thermodynamics and the Maxwell-Boltzmann distribution. Applying the ideas of statistical physics to other systems requires more than just a maximum of entropy. Statistical mechanics is based on the conservation of energy and also of phase volume known as Liouville's theorem, which, along with multi-dimensional dynamical chaos, results in a uniform (in suitable coordinates) mixing known as *ergodicity*. It is sometimes stated that the success of statistical mechanics is due to a *blessing of dimensionality*,[50] as opposed to the *curse of dimensionality* in machine learning (Sec. 2.4.10). Chaotic mixing of specific entropy (a known function of temperature and pressure) in atmospheric convection toward a uniform distribution results in a $10°/km$ temperature drop with altitude.[51] Similarly incompressible and chaotic phase space flows were investigated in other

---

[50] A.N. Gorban and I.Y. Tyukin, *Blessing of dimensionality: mathematical foundations of the statistical physics of data*, Philosophical Transactions of the Royal Society A 376(2118), 2018.

[51] E. Fermi, *Thermodynamics*, p. 26, Dover, New York, 1937.

complex systems including plasma turbulence,[52,53] but this description seems missing from agent-based dynamical models of markets (Secs. 2.5 and 2.6). The law of conservation of money was explored in econophysics literature.[54,55] This conservation law appears less than universal.[56] Any Liouvillean dynamics and ergodicity in finance yet remain to be discovered.

2.3.2 Likelihood and Bayesian inference

In a game, you are presented with two identical sealed envelopes known to contain \$x and \$10x, where x is a positive random number. You open one envelope and have the choice to either keep the money or exchange it for the other envelope. Is there a strategy whose expected return is higher than the one of always keeping the first envelope?

From a quant interview

A more general distribution-based learning uses *maximum likelihood* (MLE) or *maximum a posteriori* (MAP) estimates. These methods start with postulating a distribution $F(z, \theta)$ depending on parameters θ. Unless data has specific features such as multi-modality, the choice of distribution is often normal, in which case the parameters θ include the means and the covariance matrix of z.

The *likelihood function* is the probability of data conditioned on parameters:

$$L(\theta) = \text{Prob}(\{z_i\}|\theta) \propto \prod_{i=1}^{N} F(z_i, \theta). \tag{2.25}$$

[52] M.B. Isichenko, V.V. Yankov, *Turbulent equipartitions in two-dimensional drift convection*, Physics Reports, 283(1-4), pp. 161–175, 1997.

[53] V.V. Yankov, *From Solitons and Collapses to Hierarchy of Attractors*, Proceedings of Conference on Solitons, Collapses, and Turbulence (SCT-19), Yaroslavl, Russia, 2019.

[54] A. Drăgulescu, V.M. Yakovenko, *Statistical mechanics of money*, The European Physics Journal B, 17, pp. 723–729, 2000.

[55] V.M. Yakovenko, *Monetary economics from econophysics perspective*, arXiv:1608.04832 [q-fin.EC], 2016.

[56] At a court divorce hearing, a husband argued that his wife's claimed lifestyle expenses could not be true, for recorded time series of income, tax, and assets, due to the law of conservation of money. The wife's attorney countered this by: *Objection Your Honor, there is no concept of conservation of money in matrimonial law!* Objection sustained.

Given observations $\mathbf{z}_i$, $i = 1,\ldots, N$, it is possible to compute parameters $\boldsymbol{\theta}$ maximizing the likelihood. Depending on dimension and assumptions about covariances, MLE maximization can be a difficult (non-convex) problem.

Kullback-Leibler divergence (Sec. 2.3.1) can be used to analyze maximum likelihood estimates. Let $\boldsymbol{\theta}_0$ be the true value of the parameter vector. The KL divergence between the true distribution $F(\mathbf{z}, \boldsymbol{\theta}_0)$ and $F(\mathbf{z}, \boldsymbol{\theta})$ is zero at $\boldsymbol{\theta} = \boldsymbol{\theta}_0$ and nonnegative elsewhere, so the expansion of the KL divergence through quadratic terms is given by a positive semidefinite curvature matrix:

$$D_{KL}(F(\mathbf{z}, \boldsymbol{\theta}_0)||F(\mathbf{z}, \boldsymbol{\theta})) = \frac{1}{2} \sum_{ij} \mathcal{I}_{ij}(\boldsymbol{\theta}_0)(\theta_i - \theta_{0i})(\theta_j - \theta_{0j}). \quad (2.26)$$

The matrix is the expectation of the log-likelihood Hessian

$$\mathcal{I}_{ij}(\boldsymbol{\theta}) = E\left(\frac{\partial \log(F(\mathbf{z}, \boldsymbol{\theta}))}{\partial \theta_i} \frac{\partial \log(F(\mathbf{z}, \boldsymbol{\theta}))}{\partial \theta_j} \right) \quad (2.27)$$

and is called *Fisher information matrix*. Fisher information is a measure of sensitivity of a probability distribution function with respect to parameters providing a lower bound on the variance of their estimation. For a scalar θ,

$$\text{Var}(\theta) \geq \mathcal{I}^{-1}(\theta). \quad (2.28)$$

This inequality is known as Cramér-Rao bound. Fisher information is proportional to the number N of observations forming the likelihood (2.25). In the limit $N \to \infty$, the distribution of the estimated parameter θ is normal with the covariance given by the Fisher information $\mathcal{I}(\boldsymbol{\theta}_0)$.[57]

Maximum a posteriori (MAP) estimation is a generalization of MLE for the case when there is a pre-data *prior* in the form of a distribution $\Phi(\boldsymbol{\theta})$ of possible values of the parameters. For example, parameters $\boldsymbol{\theta}$ must meet certain constraints such as positive definiteness of the covariance matrix. An *a posteriori function*, or *posterior probability*, $A(\boldsymbol{\theta})$ is the probability of parameters conditioned on data. According to Bayes' theorem,

$$A(\boldsymbol{\theta}) = \text{Prob}(\boldsymbol{\theta}|\{\mathbf{z}_i\}) = \frac{\text{Prob}(\{\mathbf{z}_i\}|\boldsymbol{\theta}) \, \text{Prob}(\boldsymbol{\theta})}{\text{Prob}(\{\mathbf{z}_i\})} \propto L(\boldsymbol{\theta})\Phi(\boldsymbol{\theta}). \quad (2.29)$$

---

[57] L. Wasserman, *All of Nonparametric Statistics*, Springer, 2006.

If there is no prior on the parameters and each $\boldsymbol{\theta}$ is equiprobable, posterior probability equals likelihood, and both MLE and MAP result in the same parameter inference. A more consistent noninformative prior on the parameters is the Jeffreys prior,[58]

$$\Phi(\boldsymbol{\theta}) = \sqrt{\det \boldsymbol{I}(\boldsymbol{\theta})}, \qquad (2.30)$$

where $\boldsymbol{I}(\boldsymbol{\theta})$ is the Fisher information matrix (2.27).

A general Bayesian inference approach follows the same logic but does not stop at maximizing MLE or MAP, known as *point estimates*. Instead, unknown parameters are consistently treated as random with the posterior distribution (2.29), and any conclusions about data are made in expectation over a random $\boldsymbol{\theta}$. Bayesian methods were used to derive the *Akaike information criterion*[59] (AIC) and other statistics used to estimate out-of-sample model performance.

2.3.3   Mean square error and correlation

INTERVIEWER: You are applying for a job at 100 different hedge funds, with 1% probability of success at each. What is the probability of getting a job? Compute the answer without a calculator.

CANDIDATE: 100%.

INTERVIEWER: What if you are applying at 200 funds?

CANDIDATE: Oh..

From a quant interview[60]

Forecast learning is based on minimizing a loss function, typically in terms of the mean square error (MSE) over a sample of N observations:

$$\text{MSE} = \text{Mean}([y - f(\mathbf{x})]^2) = \frac{1}{N} \sum_{i=1}^{N} (y_i - f(\mathbf{x}_i))^2. \qquad (2.31)$$

When run on a *training sample*, or *in-sample*, (2.31) is used for model fitting by finding parameters of $f(\mathbf{x})$ minimizing the MSE. In statistical

---

[58] H. Jeffreys, *An invariant form for the prior probability in estimation problems*, Proceedings of the Royal Society A, 186(1007), 1946.

[59] H. Akaike, *A new look at the statistical model identification*, in IEEE Transactions on Automatic Control, 19(6), pp. 716–723, 1974.

[60] The answers to this question have ranged from 1% to 100%.

literature, the in-sample error is called *empirical risk*. Correspondingly, fitting a model to training data is called *empirical risk minimization* (ERM). Extended to a *test sample*, or *out-of-sample*, Eq. (2.31) quantifies the *generalization error*, *test risk*, *predictive risk*, or *true risk* of the fitted model. Inspection of the true risk can lead to reconsidering the choice of the model. This iterative process can be replaced by minimizing a regularized version of MSE as discussed in Sec. 2.4.11.

Financial forecast is often a poor approximation of the target: the expected future return is normally two orders of magnitude smaller than the return volatility: $|f| \ll |y|$. To remove a large unfittable target volatility, we can write $\text{MSE} = \text{const} - 2\text{Cov}(f, y) + \text{Var}(f)$. Introducing a scaling factor k in $f(\mathbf{x}) = k f_0(\mathbf{x})$ and minimizing over k, we have

$$\text{const} - \text{MSE} = \frac{\text{Cov}^2(f_0, y)}{\text{Var}(f_0)} \propto \text{Cor}^2(f, y). \tag{2.32}$$

So minimizing forecast mean square error is equivalent, up to scaling, to maximizing the absolute forecast-target correlation. For equities, one can hope to achieve a correlation of order 1%.[61]

In the context of OLS regression (Sec. 2.4.3), the square correlation coefficient (2.32) is also known as coefficient of determination, statistical significance, explained sum of squares (ESS) divided by total sum of squares (TSS), or just "R-squared." A correlation of 1% translates to $R^2 = 10^{-4}$.

It is often useful to define weighted MSE and correlation. The weights can reflect the importance of observations if there is a reason to pay more attention to some datapoints than to others. Changes to the algebra are straightforward, and most statistical software libraries support weighted data fitting.

Besides MSE, a few other loss functions are used including mean absolute error (MAE) and median absolute deviation (MAD). Fitting data to minimize these losses could introduce bias and requires somewhat more complicated algorithms. The main target of absolute-value- or median-based losses is enhanced robustness with respect to outliers and fat-tailed data.

---

[61] Shorter-horizon price movements are more predictable than longer horizons. This is in part due to higher trading costs and hence more difficult arbitrage for shorter horizons.

2.3.4 Weighted law of large numbers

The average temperature in Kathmandu is $+24°C$, whereas at the summit of Mount Everest it is $-27°C$. Why is it colder at a higher altitude?

From a quant interview

The weak predictability of financial returns makes it difficult, but not impossible, to generate consistent trading profits. The lack of strong forecasts is in part compensated by the large number of tradable securities, especially stocks, and the number of days (or perhaps seconds in the case of high frequency trading) during which a quantitative trading strategy is run. One can diversify a systematically traded portfolio both cross-sectionally (across securities) and serially (in time),[62] so noisy profits and losses tend to average out to a relatively stable, and hopefully positive, pnl.

The *law of large numbers* says that the variance of the average of N independent random variables x_i decreases as their number N increases. If the variance of each x_i equals σ^2, the variance of the sample mean is

$$\text{Var}(\overline{x}) = \text{Var}\left(\frac{\sum_{i=1}^N x_i}{N}\right) = \frac{1}{N^2}\sum_{ij}\text{Cov}(x_i, x_j) = \frac{\sigma^2}{N}, \qquad (2.33)$$

due to the assumed independence of x_i and x_j for $i \neq j$. Eq. (2.33) explains, among other things, why thermodynamic quantities like temperature and pressure are very accurately defined for the number of molecules $N \sim 10^{23}$.

It is straightforward to generalize the law of large numbers to a weighted mean of N independent observations with weights w_i. The result is

$$\text{Var}(\overline{x}) = \text{Var}\left(\frac{\sum_{i=1}^N w_i x_i}{\sum_{i=1}^N w_i}\right) = \frac{\sigma^2}{N_{\text{eff}}}, \qquad (2.34)$$

where

$$N_{\text{eff}} = \frac{\left(\sum_{i=1}^N w_i\right)^2}{\sum_{i=1}^N w_i^2} \qquad (2.35)$$

---

[62] Serial diversification is less effective than cross-sectional because investors are more sensitive to drawdowns—losses concentrated in time—than to patterns of cross-sectional pnl distribution.

is the *effective number of independent observations*. By Chebyshev's sum inequality, this number is always between 1 and N, the latter being the case only when all weights are equal. Eqs. (2.34)-(2.35) can be thought of as the *weighted law of large numbers*.

In a time-series context, an exponential moving average (EMA) is often used to maintain recent statistics, which is supposed to be more relevant (Sec. 2.7). If the index i runs over days, the EMA weights $w_i \sim e^{i/D}$ make the mean, the variance, and other statistics "forget" the contribution of past data by a factor of e^{-1} after D days. The online maintenance of EMA statistics can be done efficiently by adding new data and decaying sums on each time step (Sec. 2.4.13). If the history is much longer than the decay horizon D, the effective number of EMA observations is

$$N_{\textit{eff}} = \frac{1 + e^{-1/D}}{1 - e^{1/D}} \approx 2D \quad \text{for} \quad D \gg 1. \tag{2.36}$$

So the "large numbers" may end up not so large. If the observations are not independent, their effective number is further decreased (Sec. 3.1).

In addition to serial weights, financial statistical learning can use cross-sectional weights to emphasize some (e.g., more liquid) securities over others (Sec. 2.4.3). Due to the concentration of weights in more "important" securities, inhomogeneous cross-sectional weighting also decreases the effective number of independent observations. Formula (2.35) can be used for general weights to estimate the effective statistical coverage of learning algorithms.

2.3.5   Bias-variance tradeoff

> *An ant starts crawling on an expanding rubber band starting at its fixed end. The ant's speed relative to the rubber is u. The other end of the band is moving away from the fixed end at the speed v. Will the ant ever reach the moving end of the band?*
>
> From a quant interview

Mean out-of-sample square error (2.31), as a measure of forecast production performance, can be split in three logical parts:

$$\text{MSE} = \text{Bias}^2(f) + \text{Var}(f) + \text{Var}(\tilde{y}). \tag{2.37}$$

The bias part is in-sample difference between the model and the target, which can, in principle, be made arbitrarily small by using a more and more complex model $f(\mathbf{x})$. Doing so, however, will drive up the model variance $\mathrm{Var}(f)$, or generalization error, when switching from training to previously unseen test data. The last, but not least, term in (2.37) is noise error due to a target component $\tilde{y}$ not predictable by $\mathbf{x}$ however hard we try.

An important characteristic of a model is *complexity*, or ability to adjust to fit training data. In the case of linear regression (Sec. 2.4.3), the complexity is the number of predictors (degrees of freedom). For splines (Sec. 2.4.11), the complexity is the number of wiggles, for a regression tree (Sec. 2.4.6) it is the tree depth, and so forth. As a function of complexity, the bias is decreasing and the variance is increasing, so the model error (2.37) is minimized at some optimal complexity level that is data- and model-dependent. VC dimension (Sec. 2.3.6) is one way to define complexity formally. Another approach is to use regularization (Sec. 2.4.11) and compute both bias and variance as a function of the regularizing parameter such as λ in (2.83). This can be done analytically for a class of Tikhonov-regularized kernel regression problems (Sec. 2.4.11.6).[63]

Consider a synthetic example of N observations with correlated K-dimensional $\mathbf{x}$ data and y generated as a linear combination of $\mathbf{x}$ plus noise. All $\mathbf{x}$ variables are relevant and contribute to the OLS R-squared statistic for the training sample. The number of used predictors k is the OLS model complexity. The test sample R^2 is decreasing for $k > k^*$, so it is best to forego some of the less relevant variables for best out-of-sample performance. This is demonstrated in Fig. 2.3 generated with Python code in Listing 2.1.[64] The synthetic data are

---

[63] T. Poggio, S. Smale, *The Mathematics of Learning: Dealing with Data*, Notices of the American Mathematical Society (AMS), 50(5), pp. 537–544, 2003.

[64] Generation of correlated multivariate data with covariance C using numpy.random .multivariate_normal is slow in high dimensions $K \gg 1$. A faster approach would use $\mathbf{x} = A\xi$, where ξ is sampled from an uncorrelated normal distribution $\mathcal{N}(0, 1)$ (numpy.random.normal), and A is a $K \times K$ matrix such that $AA' = C$. The matrix A can be precomputed efficiently by a Cholesky decomposition of C (numpy.linalg .cholesky). The Python code in Listing 2.1 uses repeated batch learning via sklearn .linear_model.LinearRegression. Using an online covariance (Sec. 2.4.13) and its submatrices would result in a faster code.

drawn from a well-behaved normal distribution. Real financial data are less stationary and can produce a larger generalization error. More examples of bias-variance tradeoff for linear smoothers are presented in Sec. 2.4.11.

In financial forecasting, there are similar learning tradeoffs related to nonstationarity (Sec. 2.7) and asset grouping (Sec. 2.8). Section 2.4.12 describes a seeming violation of the bias-variance tradeoff principle and a "benign overfitting" traceable to less obvious kinds of regularization.

Listing 2.1 Bias-variance tradeoff for 100 OLS features. The output is in Fig. 2.3.

```python
import numpy as np
import sklearn.linear_model as lm
import matplotlib.pyplot as plt


np.random.seed(1)
N = 1000000        # total size
T = int(0.5*N)     # training size
K = 100            # max number of features
kk = range(1, K + 1) # feature subset sizes
signal2noise = 0.003
coefs = np.random.normal(size=K)
coefs = coefs[np.argsort(-np.abs(coefs))] # by descending abs value
fig = plt.figure()
for xcor in [0.75, 0.85, 0.95]: # x-x correlations
    # generate correlated features with this covariance:
    cov = (1 - xcor)*np.diag(np.ones([K])) + xcor*np.ones([K,K])
    X = np.random.multivariate_normal(np.zeros(K), cov, size=(N))
    # noisy response:
    y = signal2noise*np.dot(X, coefs) + np.random.normal(size=N)
    is_r2 = np.zeros(K + 1)
    os_r2 = np.zeros(K + 1)
    for k in kk:
        Xtrain, Xtest = X[0:T, 0:k], X[T:N, 0:k]
        ytrain, ytest = y[0:T], y[T:N]
        reg = lm.LinearRegression(fit_intercept=False).fit(Xtrain, ytrain)
        is_r2[k] = reg.score(Xtrain, ytrain) # training R**2
        os_r2[k] = reg.score(Xtest, ytest) # testing R**2
    is_label = f'IS xcor={xcor}'
    os_label = f'OS xcor={xcor}: $k^*$={np.argmax(os_r2)}'
    plt.plot(kk, is_r2[1:K + 1], '-', label=is_label)
    plt.plot(kk, os_r2[1:K + 1], '--', label=os_label)
plt.xlabel('$k$')
plt.ylabel('$R^2$')
plt.legend()
plt.show()
```

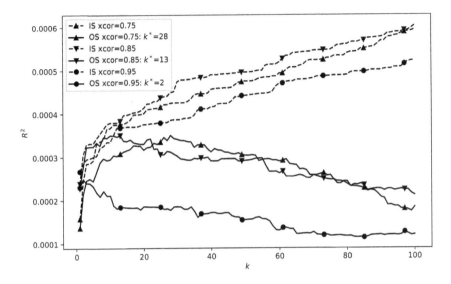

Figure 2.3   Bias-variance tradeoff in OLS demonstrated by in-sample (IS) and out-of-sample (OS) regression performance vs model complexity k (subset size of 100 correlated features). The regressions are run for three different correlation levels. Larger IS R^2 means decreasing bias. Smaller OS R^2 means increasing variance. k^* is the number of features maximizing OS R^2. The chart is generated by code in Listing 2.1.

2.3.6   PAC learnability, VC dimension, and generalization error bounds

Given a continuous function $a(t)$ defined on $[0, 1]$, find $\min_{x(t)}$ $[\max_t(x(t)) + \max_t(x(t) + a(t))]$ among all continuous $x(t)$ zero-mean on $[0, 1]$.

From a quant interview[65]

---

[65] This more difficult question originated in optics and was used for testing math aptitude of some quant analyst candidates. One candidate, a Harvard postdoc originally from China, was given this as a homework to think about. Soon, another candidate who had interviewed earlier, alerted this author about a post at a Mandarin-language web forum asking for a solution of exactly this problem, in English, which looked familiar to him. The crowdsourcing didn't seem effective: the Harvard candidate never sent in his answer.

It would be wrong to assume that statistical learning is a purely empirical science with a growing laundry list of recipes to try "until it works." There is a body of theoretical foundation for machine learning, which is both mathematically rigorous and addressing important practical questions such as bounds on generalization error and computability of learning in reasonable time. The *Probably Approximately Correct* (PAC) learning framework introduced by Valiant[66,67] studies a Boolean classification problem for $y \in \{0, 1\}$ with a set of Boolean predictors $\mathbf{x} \in \{0, 1\}^d$.[68] The main assumption of the PAC framework is the existence of an underlying joint probability distribution $F(\mathbf{x}, y)$. In simplified terms, a (Boolean) model $y = f(\mathbf{x})$ is called PAC-learnable if, given an unlimited number of learning examples available to draw from the distribution, the model's generalization (misclassification) error can be made smaller than any small bound $\varepsilon > 0$ by feeding the learning algorithm with sufficiently many training examples. If the number of such examples, $N(\varepsilon)$, is polynomial, as opposed to exponential, in ε, the learning model is considered *learnable*. To be more precise, the PAC learnability requires the generalization error to be smaller than ε with probability larger than $1 - \delta$, and the sufficient training sample size $N(\varepsilon, \delta)$ be polynomial in both small parameters. The minimum sample size $N(\varepsilon, \delta)$ needed to learn the model to a given accuracy is called the *sample complexity*. In the somewhat cryptic PAC nomenclature, the probability δ is the "probable" part and the accuracy ε is the "approximate" part. PAC-learnable, that is, converging to a true prediction in probability, models are also known as *consistent*.

The question of what kind of models provide a consistent learning was addressed starting with the concept of Vapnik-Chervonenkis (VC) dimension.[69] The VC dimension is a measure of complexity of

[66] L.G. Valiant, *A theory of the learnable*, Communications of the ACM, 27(11), pp. 1134–1142, 1984.

[67] M.J. Kearns, U. Vazirani, *An Introduction to Computational Learning Theory*, MIT Press, 1994.

[68] Like in the case of AdaBoost (Sec. 2.4.14), Boolean classification appear more conducive to theoretical analysis. Qualitative results of classification are applicable to regression learning after mild adjustments.

[69] V.N. Vapnik, A.Ya. Chervonenkis, *On the uniform convergence of relative frequencies of events to their probabilities*, Theory of Probability and Its Applications, 16(2), pp. 264–280, 1971.

the model $y = f(\mathbf{x}, \boldsymbol{\theta})$ roughly determined by the number of fittable parameters $\boldsymbol{\theta}$. The formal definition of the VC dimension is the maximum number of arbitrarily chosen test points $(\mathbf{x}_i, y_i)$, $i = 1, \ldots, n$, that the model can fit exactly, or "shatter," under a suitable choice of $\boldsymbol{\theta}$. For example, a binary hyperplane classification model

$$f(\mathbf{x}, \boldsymbol{\theta}) = \text{Sign}(\boldsymbol{\theta} \cdot \mathbf{x} + \tau) \tag{2.38}$$

in a d-dimensional predictor space, a building block of a support vector machine (SVM), has the VC dimension $d + 1$. This is because it is always possible to separate by color, say, 3 black or white points in a 2D plane by a straight line, but it can't be done for 4 or more points.

The VC dimension provides useful information about the model generalization error in terms of inequalities due to Vapnik.[70] Again, leaving out exact probabilistic details involving ε and δ, one can say that the out-of-sample error E_{OS} of a model exceeds its in-sample error E_{IS} by a margin that depends of the training sample size N and the model's VC dimension D:

$$E_{OS} = E_{IS} + O\left(\sqrt{\frac{\log(N/D)}{(N/D)}}\right). \tag{2.39}$$

It is therefore important to keep the ratio N/D large by using a large training sample and/or low-VC model. For a fixed training size N, e.g., due to timeliness constraints (Sec. 2.7), a lower VC dimension D (a simpler model) would likely elevate the training error E_{IS}, so (2.39) expresses the familiar bias-variance tradeoff (Sec. 2.3.5).

Rademacher complexity[71] is an alternative model complexity measure providing similar bounds on generalization error. Bounds like (2.39) do not necessarily require the PAC limit of almost perfect "oracle" ($\varepsilon \to 0$) and can be applied to moderately sized samples with $N/D \gtrsim 20$.

Another approach to theoretical error bounds uses stability of learning. One definition of stability is based on a *leave-one-out* (LOO) setup similar to cross-validation (Sec. 2.4.8). If the change of the loss

---

[70] V.N. Vapnik, *Statistical Learning Theory*, Wiley, 1998.
[71] S. Shalev-Shwartz, S. Ben-David, *Understanding Machine Learning: From Theory to Algorithms*, Cambridge University Press, 2014.

function at point z_i, upon the removal of z_i from training, is $O(1/N)$, the generalization error is also $O(N^{-1/2})$.[72,73]

The probabilistic bounds on generalization error for models trained on samples drawn from a fixed distribution are ultimately based on the law of large numbers (Sec. 2.3.4) and related concentration inequalities stating that empirical distribution measured on a large enough sample converges to the true distribution. The Kolmogorov-Smirnov test as well as Chebyshev's and Hoeffding's inequalities, among others, provide bounds on the rate of this convergence.[74]

PAC learnability, finite VC dimension, or uniform LOO stability are formal criteria of statistical modeling consistency in terms of the ability to deliver very accurate out-of-sample classification or forecast given a sufficiently large training sample. In practical terms, this situation applies to low-noise problems such as speech[75] or face[76] recognition, whose algorithms have been recently perfected to the point of being usable on smartphones in real time (Sec. 2.4.4). In financial forecasting, the situation is different in at least two respects. First, a stable underlying probability distribution is only a poor approximation. Indeed, it would be difficult to establish meaningful bounds on generalization error when the training and testing samples are drawn from different distributions. Second, and not unrelated to the first, the generalization error cannot be made arbitrarily small. Instead, due to trading competition arbing out market inefficiencies, it is rather the generalization accuracy which has a small upper bound. This asymptotic is conspicuously missing from the mathematical machine learning theory.

[72] O. Bousquet, A. Elisseeff, *Stability and Generalization*, Journal of Machine Learning Research, 2, pp. 499–526, 2002.

[73] T. Poggio, R. Rifkin, S. Mukherjee, P. Niyogi. *General conditions for predictivity in learning theory*, Nature, 428(6981), pp. 419–422, 2004.

[74] F. Cucker, S. Smale, *On the mathematical foundations of learning*, Bulletin of the American Mathematical Society, 39(1), pp. 1–49, 2001.

[75] S. Latif, R. Rana, S. Khalifa, R. Jurdak, J. Qadir, B.W. Schuller, *Deep Representation Learning in Speech Processing: Challenges, Recent Advances, and Future Trends*, arXiv: 2001.00378 [cs.SD], 2020.

[76] P. Grother, M. Ngan, K, Hanaoka, *Ongoing Face Recognition Vendor Test (FRVT)*, NIST Interagency Report (NISTIR) 8238, 2018.

Intuitively, the RHS of Eq. (2.39) needs another term involving a ratio of the level of unlearnable noise to the sample size N. Allowing for a non-stationarity of the underlying distribution $F(\mathbf{z})$, e.g., in terms of the rate of Kullback-Leibler divergence (Sec. 2.3.1), would also add to the generalization error.[77]

Proofs of learning consistency and theoretical bounds on generalization error serve as valuable foundations of ML and are based on somewhat strong assumptions. In a financial forecasting setting, the theory provides at best qualitative guidelines such as controlling an urge to overfit. Quant ML largely remains a growing laundry list of recipes to try "until it works"—or overfits (Sec. 2.4.2).

2.4   Machine learning

A smart machine will first consider which is more worth its while: to perform the given task or, instead, to figure some way out of it.
Stanisław Lem, The Futurological Congress

Since the beginning of this millennium, or perhaps since the internet era, machine learning (ML) has become a major industry and even a pop culture icon replacing the earlier buzzwords of cybernetics and artificial intelligence. Data science helps, and occasionally supplants, fundamental science by *learning*, rather than discovering, the laws of nature. A Princeton physicist recently suggested that planetary motion in the Solar system can be accurately predicted by an ML algorithm fed with past astronomical observations, rather than relying on Newton's laws.[78] Interesting as this approach might sound philosophically, the paper still operates in terms of *symplectic coordinates* preserving phase volume—an important feature of Newton-Hamilton-Liouville mechanics.

Machine learning and data science are a lot more helpful in automating things, extracting structure from big noisy data, and detecting fraud

---

[77] V. Kuznetsov, M. Mohri, *Generalization bounds for non-stationary mixing processes*, Machine Learning, 106, pp. 93–117, 2017.
[78] H. Qin, *Machine learning and serving of discrete field theories*, Sci. Rep., 10, 19329, 2020.

in credit card transaction or national elections.[79] ML is a vast field with both mature and developing methods having many applications in and outside finance. Any comprehensive review of the field would be a major undertaking likely to be outdated in a few years. *Dive into Deep Learning*[80] is an innovative live online book project by Amazon data scientists incorporating theory, applications, code, and contributions from the machine learning community.

In this section we discuss machine learning both generally and specifically for financial forecasting characterized by a low signal-to-noise ratio. We continue the theme of statistical learning (Sec. 2.3) with more focus on algorithms and other practicalities. While simple predictable patterns such as momentum or mean reversion have understandable reasons to exist, many ML-generated forecasts may have no simple "story" behind them due to the complexity of multi-dimensional inputs already impacted by trades generated by other ML signals, which, in turn, are learned on the impacted prices, and so on. ML forecasts are sophisticated and delicate black boxes that need to be handled with care.

Some systematic trading strategies are based on rigid rules for entering and exiting positions under specified conditions (Sec. 6.2). If you have a good rule-based strategy, chances are it can be improved by rewriting it in terms of an ML forecast with features based on the trade rules.

Identifying good features is the most important part of the ML process. Feature engineering should be based on the domain knowledge and understanding of the relevance of potential predictors for the target. This understanding can be characterized as an *inductive bias*.[81] Inductive biases can also include the shape or smoothness properties of the model $y = f(\mathbf{x})$ thus affecting the choice of a learning algorithm and its hyperparameters (Sec. 2.4.7). Inductive bias is a good thing not to be confused with the training error in the context of the bias-variance tradeoff (Sec. 2.3.5).

---

[79] D. Kobak, S. Shpilkin, M.S. Pshenichnikov, *Putin's peaks: Russian election data revisited*, Royal Statistical Society: Significance, (8), June 2018. https://doi.org/10.1111/j.1740-9713.2018.01141.x.

[80] A. Zhang, Z.C. Lipton, M. Li, A.J. Smola, *Dive into Deep Learning*, Online: http://d2l.ai.

[81] T.M. Mitchell, *The need for biases in learning generalizations*, CBM-TR 5-110, New Brunswick, New Jersey, USA: Rutgers University, 1980.

There are many learning algorithms to choose from. It is certainly possible to identify a few bad ones, such as *head and shoulders* or other charts used by the "chartered market technicians" (CMT), but there is no way to tell which one is the best before running on actual data (Sec. 2.4.18). A basic understanding of weak and strong sides of various ML algorithms is helpful in deciding which ones to try for each occasion.

2.4.1 Types of machine learning

Machine learning algorithms are broadly classified into the following categories:

1. **Unsupervised learning** is used to summarize data in terms of a low-dimensional, smooth, or otherwise simplified representation. Among the examples of unsupervised learning are principal components (Sec. 3.5.1), clustering (Sec. 3.5.2), latent structure (Secs. 3.7 and 2.4.17), autoencoders (Sec. 2.4.5), and *density estimation*—one of the most fundamental statistical learning problems.[82]

2. **Supervised learning** computes a mapping from features $\mathbf{x}$ to target y based on examples with given targets. The distinction between supervised and unsupervised learning is not set in stone. Unsupervised estimation of the probability density $F(\mathbf{x}, y)$ or data smoothing (Sec. 2.4.6) implicitly provides the mapping $y = f(\mathbf{x})$.

3. **Reinforcement learning** has to do with a choice of optimal actions in a time series environment under a stochastic or delayed feedback and can be considered as a branch of optimization theory similar to optimal control (Sec. 6.7). Elements of reinforcement learning are used in online optimization[83] of hyperparameters (Sec. 2.4.7).

Another way to characterize ML functionality is to split ML algorithms into **discriminative** and **generative**. Discriminative models include regression, classification, and clustering of data. Generative models create new data such as density estimation, recovery of latent variables in collaborative filtering (Sec. 3.7) or in hidden Markov models (HMM) (Sec. 2.4.17), optimal policy in reinforcement learning, or new samples mimicking existing data (Sec. 2.4.4).

---

[82] L. Wasserman, *All of Nonparametric Statistics*, Springer, 2006.
[83] E. Hazan, *Introduction to Online Convex Optimization*, arXiv:1909.05207 [cs.LG], 2019.

Many financial applications deal with supervised regression. We are given a number of observations $(\mathbf{x}_i, y_i)$, or tuples of (features, response), and need to *learn* a functional dependence $y = f(\mathbf{x})$ usable for predicting y for a new previously unseen $\mathbf{x}$. Algorithms implementing such learning are called *learners*. The model function $f(\mathbf{x})$ can be specified explicitly in a formulaic form, with a set of parameters to fit to the data, or constructed by the algorithm implicitly. The former class of learners is called **parametric** (Secs. 2.4.3, 2.4.4) and the latter **nonparametric** (Sec. 2.4.6).

Features $\mathbf{x}$ can be of multiple types including numerical, categorical, or more complex such as sequences of signals (sound), characters (text), pixels (image), and so forth. The target y is usually either numerical or categorical. The case of numerical targets, such as future asset returns hunted for in statistical arbitrage, is called **regression**.[84] Learning categorical targets is known as **classification** and has its own methods powerful enough for some quants willing to switch to classification by coarse-graining asset returns into just "ups" and "downs."

Both regression and classification can be **single-target** or **multi-target**, the latter jointly predicting multiple outcomes $\mathbf{y}$. Examples include stock return predictions for multiple horizons (Sec. 2.4.13), joint returns of equity risk factors (Sec. 4.4) or major world currencies, or computing bounding boxes for faces recognized in a photograph. A generalization of multi-target learning is structured learning used, for example, in natural language processing (NLP) with data structure targets encoding tree-like representations of text syntax and semantics.

Learning algorithm are usually **deterministic** even when running on random-looking data. However, there is a class of **randomized** learners using explicitly generated random numbers (Sec. 2.4.16).

Implementation-wise, ML algorithms can be set up as either **batch** or **online**. Batch learning runs on a full-size training sample. The batch setting is conceptually simpler, used in most theoretical studies establishing generalization error bounds (Sec. 2.3.6), and is well suited for various methods of cross-validation (Sec. 2.4.8). Online learning (Sec. 2.4.13) allows for inexpensive updates of the learned "knowledge" by additional

---

[84] Not to be confused with ordinary least squares (OLS) regression often meant by "regression."

examples as they become available. Learners capable of online updates provide a more efficient ML framework in a time series setting such as historical trading simulation (Chapter 7).

2.4.2   Overfitting

> *The first principle is that you must not fool yourself—and you are the easiest person to fool.*
>
> Richard Feynman[85]

The central issues in financial ML include feature selection and control of overfitting. Alpha carrying features are the holy grail of quant trading, and the reader should not expect to find many (useful) features in textbooks. Overfitting is a problem of a frustrating out-of-sample performance of a model fit in-sample, also known as high *generalization error*. A more colloquial definition of overfitting is foolishly thinking we found structure when searching through noise.

To minimize the generalization error, one wants to learn on data *patterns* rather than on datapoints or, idiomatically speaking, to see the forest for the trees. A suitably identified bigger picture, agnostic to noisy details, requires a certain level of coarse-graining to have a better chance of generalizability for previously unseen data. This is a wish, not an algorithm. Methods of avoiding overfitting include selection of more meaningful features and regularization (Sec. 2.4.11) enforcing lower model complexity. The choice of right features has its own data-dependent traps dangerous to even disciplined statisticians.[86]

In general, the danger of overfitting is higher for lower signal-to-noise ratio in the data, a typical situation in financial ML. In a batch setting, the bias-variance tradeoff (Sec. 2.3.5) is found almost universally and tuned by cross-validation (Sec. 2.4.8). In a financial time-series setting, the search for middle ground between under- and overfitting is complicated by additional overfitting traps. It is fair to say that overfitting of quant models is a widespread issue resulting from

---

[85] R.P. Feynman, *Cargo cult science*, A commencement address at the California Institute of Technology, 1974.
[86] A. Gelman, E. Loken, *The Statistical Crisis in Science*, American Scientist, 102(6), 460, 2014.

quants not doing their homework (notably, reading ML textbooks) and getting into the common pitfall of polishing their backtests to the extent of ultimately moving all available data to the training sample and running out of the test sample. In statistical learning, this fallacy is known under the nomenclature of data snooping, data dredging, or *p*-hacking.[87]

How much should a quant care about overfitting? Too much is almost enough. Benign overfitting (Sec. 2.4.12) is not normally the case. Repeated and excessive backtest optimization leads to *information leakage* from the test to the train sample, which is a fairly explicit lookahead (Sec. 2.1.1). It is not clear how to quantify the information leakage due to each round of "learning by backtest."[88] It is difficult to identify an overfit limit on the number of attempted backtests, ML data passes, or similar research cycles in general. Use statistical theory, where applicable, and your judgment.

2.4.3   Ordinary and generalized least squares

Alice drew a square on a board and marked 4 points on its different sides. Then came Bob and erased the square, but he couldn't erase the marked points. Help Alice restore the original square.

From a quant interview

The simplest ML approach uses the classical statistical inference by parameter fitting, often in terms of a linear model[89] $y = f(\mathbf{x}) = \boldsymbol{\beta} \cdot \mathbf{x}$.

---

[87] J.P. Simmons, L.D. Nelson, U. Simonsohn, *False-Positive Psychology: Undisclosed Flexibility in Data Collection and Analysis Allows Presenting Anything as Significant*, Psychological Science, 22(11), 2011.

[88] A mathematically advanced quantitative analyst insisted on running quantamental forecast research using multiple historical simulations, the argument being that it would be highly improbable to get a good-looking multi-year simulation by massaging the forecast model were it based on pure noise. Estimating this low probability, or the *p*-value of thus researched forecasts, did not seem feasible, though, and the overall out-of-sample results were mixed.

[89] It is common to demean $\mathbf{x}$ and y data or, equivalently, add a constant of one to the list of predictors.

One would generally introduce observation weights w_i and fit the model by minimizing a square loss function, yielding a closed-form result for the coefficients of the ordinary least squares (OLS) regression:

$$\beta = \text{argmin} \sum_i w_i \left(y_i - \sum_k \beta_k x_{ik} \right)^2 = (X'WX)^{-1}X'WY. \quad (2.40)$$

Here X is the $N \times K$ matrix of N observations for K predictors referred to as a *design matrix*, W is the $N \times N$ diagonal matrix of weights, and Y is the N-vector observation of the dependent variable. If some of the predictors are not independent (collinear) or $N < K$, the $K \times K$ covariance matrix $X'WX$ is not full rank and cannot be inverted. In this case the OLS problem is called underdetermined or overparameterized and has multiple sets of β coefficients giving the same minimum of the mean square error. This situation is usually handled by choosing minimum-norm regression coefficients β. For both full rank or underdetermined OLS regression, the coefficients are compactly written using the notation of weighted pseudo inverse (2.120):

$$\beta = X_W^+ Y. \quad (2.41)$$

In an overparameterized ($K > N$) regression, the minimum-norm solution provides a useful regularization with a benign kind of overfitting (Sec. 2.4.12).

The goodness of an in-sample OLS fit is measured by a single number called *coefficient of determination* or R-squared. This number is the ratio of the "explained" variance of the dependent variable y and its total variance:

$$R^2 = \frac{\sum_i w_i \left(\sum_k \beta_k x_{ik} \right)^2}{\sum_i w_i y_i^2}. \quad (2.42)$$

In matrix notation and for full-rank X features, R-squared involves the covariances of the features and the target:

$$R^2 = \frac{Y'WX(X'WX)^{-1}X'WY}{Y'WY}. \quad (2.43)$$

For univariate OLS, R-squared equals the square correlation coefficient of x and y. In any dimension, R^2 is always between 0 and 1 and can be thought of as a degree of predictability or signal-to-noise ratio. In high-noise financial forecasting, the R-squared is often of order 10^{-4}.

The weights matrix W in the RHS of Eq. (2.40) need not be diagonal. A generalized version of the least squares (GLS) regression does not assume the residuals $\epsilon = \mathbf{y} - X\boldsymbol{\beta}$ independent of each other and, instead of the weighted residual square error, minimizes the total residual variance. The result is the same expression for the regression coefficients, but now the weights matrix $W = C^{-1}$ is the inverse of the covariance of the residuals $C_{ij} = \text{Cov}(\varepsilon_i, \varepsilon_j)$.

Weighted OLS can be seen as a special case of GLS with the weights $w_i = \sigma_i^{-2}$ equal to the reciprocal residual variances. More generally though, financial least-squares weights can express one or more of the following: historical relevance (recent history is more relevant due to non-stationary statistics), conviction level for a noisy observation, importance of an observation (illiquid securities have lower investment capacity and therefore are less interesting to learn on), and dynamic universe definition (a zero weight means the security is currently not in the universe).

Classical statistics addresses the question of generalization error in OLS and GLS regression by estimating the in-sample variance of the result (2.40). This usually involves additional assumptions such as the observations $(\mathbf{x}_i, y_i)$ being drawn from a joint normal distribution. Assuming full-rank predictors, the logic goes as if $\mathbf{x}$ were non-random and y random, thus rendering the fitted coefficients (2.40) random with expectation (2.40) and, by *propagation of error*, the covariance

$$\text{Cov}(\boldsymbol{\beta}, \boldsymbol{\beta}) = DX'W\text{Cov}(Y, Y)WXD, \quad D \equiv (X'WX)^{-1}. \quad (2.44)$$

If the y observations are independent,[90]

$$\text{Cov}(Y, Y) = \Sigma^2 = \text{Diag}(\sigma_i^2), \quad (2.45)$$

the variance of the estimated regression coefficients is given by the symmetric $K \times K$ matrix

$$\text{Cov}(\boldsymbol{\beta}, \boldsymbol{\beta}) = DX'W\Sigma^2WXD. \quad (2.46)$$

---

[90] This assumption can break badly for daily observations of multi-day returns. If this overlap is not corrected for, the uncertainty in the OLS regression coefficients will be underestimated.

In the special case of Gauss-Markov reciprocal-variance weights $w_i = \sigma_i^{-2}$, the variance of the coefficients simplifies to

$$\text{Cov}(\boldsymbol{\beta}, \boldsymbol{\beta}) = D = (X'WX)^{-1}, \qquad (2.47)$$

an expression which is inversely proportional to the number of *independent* observations N thrown into the regression. The OLS version of the law of large numbers says that the uncertainty of the regression coefficients is proportional to $N^{-1/2}$, which is similar to other statistics (Sec. 2.3.4).

As a reference, for one-dimensional demeaned features x_i, independent demeaned targets y_i, and observation weights w_i, the OLS regression coefficient, R-squared, and the variance of the coefficient are given by the following expressions:

$$\beta = \frac{\text{Cov}(x, y)}{\text{Var}(x)} = \frac{\sum_i w_i x_i y_i}{\sum_i w_i x_i^2},$$

$$R^2 = \text{Cor}^2(x, y) = \frac{\left(\sum_i w_i x_i y_i\right)^2}{\left(\sum_i w_i x_i^2\right)\left(\sum_i w_i y_i^2\right)}, \qquad (2.48)$$

$$\text{Var}(\beta) = \sigma_y^2 \frac{\sum_i w_i^2 x_i^2}{\left(\sum_i w_i x_i^2\right)^2}.$$

The latter can be written as

$$\text{Var}(\beta) = \frac{\sigma_y^2}{\sigma_x^2 N_{eff}^{(x)}}, \qquad N_{eff}^{(x)} = \frac{\left(\sum_i w_i\right)\left(\sum_i w_i x_i^2\right)}{\sum_i w_i^2 x_i^2}. \qquad (2.49)$$

Here $N_{eff}^{(x)}$ is the effective number of weighted x observations, a regression counterpart of formula (2.35).

The variance of the regression coefficients (2.44) can be used for estimating the t-statistic

$$t_k = \frac{\beta_k}{\sqrt{\text{Cov}(\beta_k, \beta_k)}} \qquad (2.50)$$

expressing the statistical significance of the kth predictor. If the absolute t-value (2.50) is sufficiently large, the null hypothesis of $\beta_k = 0$ (irrelevance of the predictor) can be rejected as unlikely. A small t-value of a predictor would indicate that the predictor is irrelevant to the target or that there is not enough data to make a conclusion. OLS t-values are proportional to the square root of the number of effectively independent observations.

Assuming reasonably stationary statistics, the estimate of the uncertainty of an OLS forecast by propagation of error is a valid proxy of generalization error. However, quants do not often incorporate the variance estimate (2.44) in their forecast process or duly account for non-independent (overlapping) observations. Outside linear OLS, there are few closed-form estimates for generalization error. Most ML methods handle these issues computationally (Sec. 2.4.8). Forecast uncertainty measured in terms of parameter variance or mean generalization error is an important characteristic of a forecast rooted in the quality and quantity of available data. This information can help in portfolio construction (Sec. 6.8).

2.4.4 Deep learning

With four parameters I can fit an elephant, and with five I can make him wiggle his trunk.

John von Neumann[91]

If ordinary least squares (Sec. 2.4.3) is one of the simplest learners, then the class of artificial neural networks (ANN) is perhaps the most complicated. ANNs are parametric learners fitting complex nonlinear models $y = f(\mathbf{x})$ represented by layers of composition of a simpler *activation function* $\phi(\xi)$. An important example is the weighted vote function

$$\xi_i^{(1)} = \phi\left(\sum_i w_{ij}^{(0)} x_j\right), \tag{2.51}$$

where the increasing $\phi(\xi)$ can be a positive indicator (1 for $\xi > 0$ and zero otherwise), a smooth *sigmoid* function $\phi(\xi) = (1 + e^{-\xi})^{-1}$, or a *rectified linear unit* (ReLU) $\phi(\xi) = \max(\xi, 0)$. Applying another transformation like (2.51) to $\xi_i^{(1)}$ with new weights $w_{ij}^{(1)}$ gives the next layer of transformed variables $\xi_i^{(2)}$, and so on until the last layer representing the target y. The last (output) layer can have either one (regression or binary classification) or multiple nodes (multi-target regression or multi-label classification).

---

[91] Quoted by F. Dyson, *A meeting with Enrico Fermi*, Nature 427(22), p. 297, 2004.

The node weights $w_{ij}^{(l)}$ form a *tensor*—a 3D matrix in this case. The elements of the weight tensor are the learner's fitting parameters that are learned by minimizing training classification or regression error. The weights are modeling synaptic connections between neurons in the brain (Sec. 2.4.5). The size and the graph-like topology of the network, the activation function ϕ, any structural constraints on the weights, and various learning heuristics are the hyperparameters of the ANN.

If a linear activation function $\phi(\xi) = \xi$ is used, the neural network model reduces to a matrix factorization $y = \mathbf{UVx}$ similar to collaborative filtering (Sec. 3.7). Hidden layers of the network correspond to the latent structure, and their sizes determine the rank. Linearly activated networks are mostly used in theoretical analyses. Virtually all practical neural networks are nonlinear. The ReLU activation function is the most common, perhaps due to its scale invariance, which can provide more stability when learning from a randomized initial state (Sec. 2.4.16).

Multi-layer neural networks are called *deep neural networks* (DNN). Suitably designed DNNs are effective for learning low-noise complex-structure models,[92] but they are computationally expensive (Sec. 2.4.19). Variants of DNN are ubiquitous in classification of high-dimensional structured data such as gene sequences, sound, images, or text (Sec. 2.4.5). The success of DNNs is primarily driven by intuition-based software experimentation. Theoretical analysis of complex DNNs poses substantial difficulties and lags empirical findings (Sec. 2.4.12). The use of neural nets in statarb, a high-noise data environment, is not unheard of.

Empirical risk minimization of neural nets is usually non-convex and therefore often approximate. The number of parameters $w_{ij}^{(l)}$ can be very large, so neural networks can be prone to overfitting when used for noisy data. The large number of model parameters make them extremely flexible and similar to nonparametric learners such as Gaussian processes[93] (Sec. 2.4.11.5).

The power of DNNs is based, in part, on the representation of an arbitrary continuous function $f(\mathbf{x})$ via a composition of functions of one variable. The question of representation goes back to Hilbert's 13th problem. This problem was solved by Kolmogorov and Arnold, who showed that any continuous function of many variables can be written in

---

[92] Y. LeCun, Y. Bengio, G. Hinton, *Deep learning*, Nature, 521, pp. 436–444, 2015.

[93] J. Lee, Y. Bahri, R. Novak, S.S. Schoenholz, J. Pennington, J. Sohl-Dickstein, *Deep Neural Networks as Gaussian Processes*, arXiv:1711.00165 [stat.ML], 2017.

terms of sums and compositions of continuous univariate functions.[94,95] Further generalizations to multilayer topology[96,97,98] (recursive function composition) constitute the *universal representation theorem* stating that a chain of superpositions (2.51) can approximate, under a suitable choice of weights and for a broad class of scalar activation functions, any continuous model $y = f(\mathbf{x})$. An important question of neural network expressivity is how well an arbitrary function $f(\mathbf{x})$ can be approximated, under optimal choice of weights, for a fixed activation function $\phi(\xi)$. The result depends on the network size and, more importantly, its topology. Poggio et al.[99] show that a deep network, i.e., one with multiple layers of composition (2.51), has exponentially (in a large network size) better approximation properties than a wide shallow network of the same total size. Conversely, the same expressivity can be achieved by a smaller network of deep topology than for a shallow network.

One can think about DNN as a machine learning two things simultaneously: a nonlinear feature representation (in hidden layers) and a regression function for those features (in the output layer).

There are several open-source software libraries for design and training of neural networks. TensorFlow[100] by Google and PyTorch[101] by Facebook are among the best maintained and most popular packages. Hypertuning of DNNs is a difficult task due to a high dimension and topological nature of the hyperparameter space. Google Vizier[102] is a

[94] A. Kolmogorov, *On the representation of continuous functions of several variables by superpositions of continuous functions of a smaller number of variables*, Proceedings of the USSR Academy of Sciences, 108, pp. 179–182, 1956.

[95] V.I. Arnold, *On functions of three variables*, Proceedings of the USSR Academy of Sciences, 114, pp. 679–681, 1957.

[96] G. Cybenko, *Approximations by superpositions of sigmoidal functions*, Mathematics of Control, Signals, and Systems, 2(4), pp. 303–314, 1989.

[97] K. Hornik, *Approximation capabilities of multilayer feedforward networks*, Neural Networks, 4(2), pp. 251–257, 1991.

[98] P.K. Kidger, T.L. Tlyons, *Universal Approximation with Deep Narrow Networks*, arXiv:1905.08539 [cs.LG], 2020.

[99] T. Poggio, H. Mhaskar, L. Rosasco, B. Miranda, Q. Liao, *Why and When Can Deep—but Not Shallow—Networks Avoid the Curse of Dimensionality: a Review*, arXiv: 1611.00740 [cs.LG], 2016.

[100] https://www.tensorflow.org.

[101] https://pytorch.org.

[102] D. Golovin, B. Solnik, S. Moitra, G. Kochanski, J. Karro, D. Sculley, *Google Vizier: A Service for Black-Box Optimization*, ACM, 2017.

closed-source software for complex black-box optimization available as a cloud service. There are some open-source clones.[103,104]

2.4.5 Types of neural networks

HUMAN: Give a one-word definition of the internet.

AI MACHINE: Cats.

Internet folklore

Deep neural networks are inspired by the human brain, which has proven efficient in recognizing images and spoken word, not to mention various creative endeavors. The brain has about 10^{11} interconnected neurons.[105] The reader's cerebellum forms a pretty deep hierarchical network connecting each neuron to some 10^4 other neurons via synapses in a way more complex than a straight feedforward layer architecture. The biological neural network runs a massively parallel analog (electrochemical) computation when regulating motor functions or enjoying this book. Although the brain structure is very different from the *von Neumann architecture*,[106] it can be thought of as an analog computer processing potentially billions of threads in parallel, albeit at the clock frequency of order 30 Hz. Unlike artificial neural networks, the organization of the biological brain supports multiple mixed learning tasks.[107] The brain organization appears to share, in a distributed multi-dimensional manner, the same neurons and synapses among multiple task-specific logical networks. The redundant brain

---

[103] https://github.com/tobegit3hub/advisor.

[104] https://github.com/LGE-ARC-AdvancedAI/auptimizer.

[105] R. Lent, F.A.C. Azevedo, C.H. Andrade-Moraes, A.V.O. Pinto, *How many neurons do you have? Some dogmas of quantitative neuroscience under revision*, European Journal of Neuroscience, 35, pp. 1–9, 2012.

[106] J. von Neumann, *First Draft of a Report on the EDVAC*, Contract No. W-670-ORD-4926 Between the United States Army Ordinance Department and the University of Pennsylvania, June 30, 1945. Reprinted by M.D. Godfrey in IEEE Annals of the History of Computing, 15(4), p. 27, 1993.

[107] M. Rigotti, O. Barak, M.R. Warden, X.-J. Wang, N.D. Daw, E.K. Miller, S. Fusi, *The importance of mixed selectivity in complex cognitive tasks*, Nature, 497, pp. 585–590, 2013. https://doi.org/10.1038/nature12160.

structure provides certain learning benefits[108] as well as a necessary fault tolerance—like a hologram still capable of generating a satisfactory image after a large portion of its diffraction fringes is compromised.

For comparison, the brain of a fly contains about 10^5 neurons. A recent electron microscopy study[109] indicates several types of neurons with a complicated connectivity structure. Everyone who tried to catch a fly would appreciate the quality of this natural design. Learning future stock prices may be easier than learning to evade a fly swatter.

Practicalities of digital computers, which are faster but not as parallelized as biological brains, dictated simplified network architectures with nodes organized in layers and fewer connections between the nodes. In addition, digital sequential algorithms, unlike analog systems, often hit the wall of *NP-hardness* meaning an exponential complexity in the problem size. This is what happened to the early general models of associative memory and computation, such as Hopfield network[110] and the thermodynamics-inspired Boltzmann machine.[111] At the time of this writing, digital neural networks remain smaller and simpler than biological ones, but the evolution rates of the two differ by about 4 orders of magnitude.[112]

There are many practical designs and topologies of artificial neural networks. Their choice depends on the learning task. Below are listed some of the more common architectures.

1. **Feedforward network**, or multilayer perceptron (MLP), is a basic architecture organized as a direct acyclic graph, i.e., a graph that doesn't form closed loops. In a feedforward network, a layer is connected only to its nearest neighbor layers.

---

[108] N. Hiratani and T. Fukai, *Redundancy in synaptic connections enables neurons to learn optimally*, Proceedings of the National Academy of Sciences, 115(29), pp. E6871-E6879, 2018.

[109] Z. Zheng, J.S. Lauritzen, E. Perlman, S. Saalfeld, R.D. Fetter, D.D. Bock, *A Complete Electron Microscopy Volume of the Brain of Adult Drosophila melanogaster*, Cell, 174(3), pp. 730–743, E22, 2018.

[110] J.J. Hopfield, *Neural networks and physical systems with emergent collective computational abilities*, Proceedings of the National Academy of Sciences, 79(8), pp. 2554–2558, 1982.

[111] G.E. Hinton, T.J. Sejnowski, *Learning and Relearning in Boltzmann Machines*, in D.E. Rumelhart, J.L. McClelland (eds.), *Parallel Distributed Processing: Explorations in the Microstructure of Cognition. Volume 1: Foundations*, pp. 282–317, 1986.

[112] S. Neubauer, J.-J. Hublin, P. Gunz, *The evolution of modern human brain shape*, Science Advances, 4(1), 2018. DOI: 10.1126/sciadv.aao5961.

2. **Convolutional neural network** (CNN) is a feedforward network with fewer connections or, equivalently, with many of the weights $w_{ij}^{(l)}$ set to zero and/or subject to other constraints. This is a version or regularization that helps prevent overfitting. In addition, a convolution-type structure is imposed on the weights tensor further limiting degrees of freedom and expressing a translational invariance desirable for certain image- or time series-related tasks. CNNs bear some resemblance to the visual cortex of animals. AlexNet, a CNN designed by Alex Krizhevsky,[113] achieved a breakthrough improvement in image classification due to the depth of the network having millions of parameters, which were trained using GPU hardware.

3. **Recurrent neural network** (RNN) allows cyclic dependencies on the network graph. This results in a memory-like behavior useful for learning sequences of patterns. Training an RNN is more difficult due to convergence issues and requires special handling such as in long short-term memory (LSTM) networks used for natural language processing (NLP) and translation.

4. **Residual network** (ResNet) is a CNN or an RNN where connections skip some layers. ResNets have useful theoretical properties of local minima of the training loss.[114]

5. **Randomized neural network** is a feedforward or recurrent network with most nodes assigned fixed randomized weights. Relatively few nodes, typically only in the output layer, are subject to supervised learning. Such networks can be learned much faster due to far fewer degrees of freedom solvable by essentially an OLS procedure. The predictive performance of suitably randomized networks can be only marginally below that of a comparable fully trainable network. Nomenclature for randomized neural networks has stirred an academic controversy. Introduction of the sexy term "Extreme learning machine" (ELM)[115] was criticized[116] as an act of plagiarism without a proper reference to earlier similar or identical designs with

[113] A. Krizhevsky, I. Sutskever, G.E. Hinton, *ImageNet classification with deep convolutional neural networks*, Communications of the ACM, 2017.

[114] O. Shamir, *Are ResNets Provably Better than Linear Predictors?*, arXiv:1804.06739 [cs.LG], 2018.

[115] G.-B. Huang, Q.-Y. Zhu, C.-K. Sieq *Extreme learning machine: a new learning scheme of feedforward neural networks.* IEEE International Joint Conference on Neural Networks, pp. 985–990, 2004.

[116] https://elmorigin.wixsite.com/originofelm.

comparable or better performance. The earlier approaches include Random Vector Functional Link (RVFL),[117] random-feature kernel ridge regression (KRR)[118] (Sec. 2.4.11.6), and RBF networks.[119] Randomization of hidden layers creates a complex nonlinear mix of inputs, which appears useful for the network generalization properties. Perhaps the reason is that the fixed random layers mimic the random nature of DNN parameters learned by the stochastic gradient descent (SGD) algorithm.[120]

6. **Autoencoder** is a feedforward network with one or more hidden layers and an output layer of the same size K as the input layer. The hidden layers are either smaller than K or have constraints such as requiring that at most $H \ll K$ weights be nonzero, in which case it is a *sparse autoencoder*.[121] The parameters of the network are learned to minimize, for a training set, the difference between the input and the output, e.g., in terms of their KL divergence (Sec. 2.3.2). The hidden layers then represent a training-set-specific compressed data representation (encoder) usable for dimensionality reduction[122] (Sec. 3.5) or automatic feature selection. The path from the hidden to the output layer represents a decoder. Note that this is a unsupervised type of learning (Sec. 2.4.1).

7. **Restricted Boltzmann machine** (RBM) is a version of the Boltzmann machine with a partition of all nodes into two subsets, visible and hidden, so that there is no internal communication within each subset. This restriction enables fast learning algorithms.[123] RBM is a generative network that can be used for learning a probability

[117] Y.-H. Pao, Y. Takefuji, *Functional-link net computing: theory, system architecture, and functionalities*, Computer, 25(5), pp. 76–79, 1992.

[118] A. Rahimi and B. Recht, *Random Features for Large-Scale Kernel Machines*, Proceedings of the 20th Int. Conf. on Neural Information Processing, pp. 1177–1184, 2007.

[119] D. Lowe, D. Broomhead, *Multivariable functional interpolation and adaptive networks*, Complex Systems, 2(3), pp. 321–355, 1988

[120] A. Steland, B.E. Pieters, *Cross-Validation and Uncertainty Determination for Randomized Neural Networks with Applications to Mobile Sensors*, arXiv:2101.01990 [stat.ML], January 2021.

[121] A. Ng, *Sparse autoencoder*, https://web.stanford.edu/class/cs294a/sparseAutoencoder_2011new.pdf, Lecture notes, Stanford University, 2011.

[122] G.E. Hinton, R.R. Salakhutdinov, *Reducing the Dimensionality of Data with Neural Networks*, Science, 313(5786), pp. 504–507, 2006.

[123] G. Hinton, *A Practical Guide to Training Restricted Boltzmann Machines*, http://www.cs.toronto.edu/~hinton/absps/guideTR.pdf, Lecture notes, University of Toronto, 2010.

distribution of training data and generating new data matching the distribution.

8. **Deep belief network** (DBN) is a generative DNN built by stacking multiple simpler RBM or autoencoder units. The separability of such units admits an efficient stagewise ("greedy") learning including unsupervised feature selection and supervised classification of data.[124] A DBN is capable of unsupervised learning high-level features such as people and animals in images. A Wikipedia article on ML timeline lists Google's success of recognizing cats in YouTube videos[125] among major ML achievements.

9. **Attention**, or **Transformer network**[126] is a neural net, normally embedded in a larger DNN stack, designed to learn the relative importance of components in sequence (text or image) data. The data is encoded in a way so the more important features be given more weight for downstream learning, not unlike in other weighted learning models (Sec. 2.4.3).[127] Transformers are replacing previously state-of-the-art RNNs for natural language processing.[128]

10. **Generative adversarial network** (GAN) is a combination of two coupled neural nets, a generator and a discriminator, competing in a zero-sum game.[129] Both networks learn a distribution of objects such as images. The generator network generates new "fake" samples

---

[124] G.E. Hinton, S. Osindero, Y.-W. Teh, *A fast learning algorithm for deep belief nets*, Neural computation, 2006. https://doi.org/10.1162/neco.2006.18.7.1527.

[125] Q.V. Le, M.A. Ranzato, R. Monga, M. Devin, K. Chen, G.S. Corrado, J. Dean, A.Y. Ng, *Building High-level Features Using Large Scale Unsupervised Learning*, arXiv:1112.6209 [cs.LG], 2011.

[126] A. Vaswani, N. Shazeer, N. Parmar, J. Uszkoreit, L. Jones, A.N. Gomez, L. Kaiser, I. Polosukhin, *Attention Is All You Need*, arXiv:1706.03762 [cs.CL], 2017.

[127] If you take a phone picture of the fascinating Moon craters on a clear full Moon night, the result will be far less interesting than seen by the naked eye. The reason is that the phone camera has a uniform resolution over the whole picture, whereas your eye's *macula* is densely packed with cone photoreceptors responsible for sharp central vision. Packing a few million cones in a tiny central area of the eye's retina is the *attention mechanism* missing from the same number of pixels spread over the iPhone retina display.

[128] T. Wolf, L. Debut, V. Sanh, J. Chaumond, C. Delangue, A. Moi, P. Cistac, T. Rault, R. Louf, M. Funtowicz, J. Davison, S. Shleifer, P. von Platen, C. Ma, Y. Jernite, J. Plu, C. Xu, T. Le Scao, S. Gugger, M. Drame, Q. Lhoest, A.M. Rush, *HuggingFace's Transformers: State-of-the-art Natural Language Processing*, arXiv:1910.03771 [cs.CL], 2019.

[129] I.J. Goodfellow, J. Pouget-Abadie, M. Mirza, B. Xu, D. Warde-Farley, S. Ozair, A. Courville, Y. Bengio, *Generative Adversarial Networks*, arXiv:1406.2661 [stat.ML], 2014.

mimicking the "real" training distribution, and the discriminator network attempts to tell fake from real. The generator learns to minimize the alarms sounded by the discriminator. The discriminator learns on fakes with which the generator has successfully fooled the discriminator. Variational autoencoder[130] is an alternative design with similar generative features. GANs have been used to generate real-looking abstract art,[131] portraits of inexistent people,[132] and also "deepfake" manipulation of images and videos.[133] Fast improving AI tools for manipulating news and social media have raised public concerns.[134] Generative networks are perhaps the first candidates for what can be called *artificial creativity*—to disambiguate from the overhyped and beaten term of *artificial intelligence* (AI). The meaning of AI has evolved from describing optical character recognition to chess playing[135] to algorithmic trading[136] to the discounted "AI effect" formulated by Larry Tesler: *AI is whatever hasn't been done yet.*

2.4.6   Nonparametric methods

$$\text{Solve the equation } \sqrt{a - \sqrt{a + x}} = x.$$

From a quant interview

Minimization of mean square error is a convenient way of fitting a known model $y = f(\mathbf{x}, \boldsymbol{\theta})$ with a few unknown parameters $\boldsymbol{\theta}$. If very little predictive power is expected, as is the case in financial forecasting,

---

[130] D.P. Kingma, M. Welling, *An Introduction to Variational Autoencoders*, arXiv: 1906.02691 [cs.LG], 2019.

[131] A. Elgammal, B. Liu, M. Elhoseiny, M. Mazzonem, *CAN: Creative Adversarial Networks, Generating "Art" by Learning About Styles and Deviating from Style Norms*, arXiv:1706.07068 [cs.AI], 2017.

[132] https://www.thispersondoesnotexist.com.

[133] T.T. Nguyen, C.M. Nguyen, D.T. Nguyen, D.T. Nguyen, S. Nahavandi, *Deep Learning for Deepfakes Creation and Detection: A Survey*, arXiv:1909.11573 [cs.CV], 2019.

[134] S. Parkin, *The rise of the deepfake and the threat to democracy*, The Guardian, June 22, 2019.

[135] B. Pandolfini, *Kasparov and Deep Blue: The Historic Chess Match Between Man and Machine*, Fireside Chess Library, 1997. ISBN 9780684848525.

[136] The title tag of http://www.foracapital.com, a statarb fund where this author has invested, is "FORA Capital | The AI Fund".

one should stick to very simple functions in low dimensions, such as a linear $f(\mathbf{x})$ discussed in Sec. 2.4.3. However, there are reasons for nonlinear dependencies as well.

For example, if x is an obscure accounting ratio such as *operating cash flow to enterprise value*, only extreme values of the factor may have an effect on future stock performance, so one would expect a flattish $f(x)$ with some structure on the left and/or right tails.

Technical forecasts (Sec. 2.2) can also have reasons for nonlinearity. A small residual deviation would indicate a temporary impact from some random trade; the price is expected to revert to the mean. But a larger deviation, especially if accompanied by an abnormal volume (Sec. 2.2.3), could be a collective reaction to a material news leading to a momentum pattern.

Parameterizing nonlinear functions is possible with polynomials or other basis functions within the OLS framework, but this practice is ripe with instabilities and is best avoided by switching to *nonparametric learners*. The general idea behind a nonparametric model is the same as for the (continuous) parametric $y = f(\mathbf{x}, \boldsymbol{\theta})$, except there is no f and no $\boldsymbol{\theta}$. Instead, a principle of continuity is used stating that similar $\mathbf{x}$ (as cause) are expected to lead to similar y (as effect). Some examples:

1. **Smoothing and denoising** (Sec. 2.4.11). Any smoothing representation of a set of datapoints $(\mathbf{x}_i, y_i)$ can be used for prediction of y corresponding to a new $\mathbf{x}$. The level of smoothing is a hyperparameter determining the model complexity and is subject to the usual bias-variance tradeoff. Over- (under-) smoothing means under- (over-) fitting. There are many ways to draw a smooth line or surface through a set of datapoints, such as splines, total variation denoising, kernel smoothing, or Gaussian process. One can think of almost any ML regression as a kind of smoothing. Indeed, a forecast (2.6) is defined by the underlying joint probability density $F(\mathbf{z})$ for $\mathbf{z} = (\mathbf{x}, y)$, which is implicitly estimated by learning on training data. A process of density estimation from discrete observations $\mathbf{z}_{1:N}$ is essentially a smoothing of the highly singular empirical probability density

$$\tilde{F}(\mathbf{z}) = \frac{1}{N} \sum_{i=1}^{N} \delta(\mathbf{z} - \mathbf{z}_i). \tag{2.52}$$

2. **K-nearest neighbor** (KNN) predictor specifies y for a new $\mathbf{x}$ as the mean of ys for training observations with $\mathbf{x}_i$ in the vicinity of $\mathbf{x}$. No particular structure of $f(\mathbf{x})$ is prescribed. To avoid the lookup of nearest neighbor over all datapoints, a more efficient approach of locality-sensitive hashing (LSH) has been proposed.[137]

3. **Regressogram**[138] is a version of a histogram for simple smoothing. It is most effective for one-dimensional x. Recall that a histogram counts the numbers N_j of datapoints x_i contained in bins B_j—suitably chosen intervals of x. A histogram is usually represented as a graph of the function $N_j(\text{center of } B_j)$. A regressogram also uses x bins, but computes the means of $\{y_i : x_i \in B_j\}$ instead of the datapoint counts. A regressogram is a nonparametric learner implementing a simple approximation of the model (2.6) from data. It is also a tool of exploratory data analysis (EDA) to detect any $y(x)$ dependency structure, including nonlinearity.[139] A scatter plot of (x_i, y_i) serves the same EDA purpose, but its utility in a high-noise setting is low. A regressogram is a special, and by no means the best, case of the kernel regression.

4. **Isotonic regression** is used for a scalar predictor. This algorithm finds a monotonically increasing or decreasing $f(x)$ minimizing a training error,

$$\sum_i w_i(f(x_i) - y_i)^2 \quad \text{or} \quad \sum_i w_i|f(x_i) - y_i|. \qquad (2.53)$$

The algorithm complexity is linear or $O(N \log(N))$ in the training set size.[140] Whether or not the function must be increasing is dictated by a prior such as expecting the predictor to be bullish or bearish. The monotonicity constraint is a powerful regularizer.

---

[137] A. Andoni, P. Indyk, *Near-optimal hashing algorithms for near neighbor problem in high dimensions*, Communications of the ACM, 51(1), pp. 117–122, 2008.

[138] E.G. Portugués, *Notes for Nonparametric Statistics*, https://bookdown.org/egarpor/NP-UC3M, 2020.

[139] A simple yet effective command-line tool for data visualization including 2D plots, histograms, and regressograms is available at https://github.com/michael-isichenko/plot.

[140] P. Mair, K. Hornik, J. de Leeuw, *Isotone Optimization in R: Pool-Adjacent-Violators Algorithm (PAVA) and Active Set Methods*, Journal of Statistical Software, 32(5), pp. 1–24, 2009.

5. **Additive models**[141,142] seek to soften the curse of dimensionality by imposing an additive structure because smoothing in the full K-dimensional space of predictors requires a sample growing exponentially with K. Additive nonparametric learning seeks K one-dimensional smoothers $f_k(x)$ minimizing the square error

$$\sum_i w_i \left(y_i - \sum_k f_k(x_{ik}) \right)^2. \tag{2.54}$$

It might seem that the additive model is a generalization of the OLS linear regression (Sec. 2.4.3) and is even more prone to overfitting. This is in fact not true due to the backfitting algorithm sidestepping the curse of dimensionality. The minimization of (2.54) alternates between 1D smoothing of $(x_{ik}, y_i^{(res)})$ for the residuals $y_i^{(res)}$ of the other smoothers combined and updating the residuals in a way similar to boosting (Sec. 2.4.14). A version of an additive model for linear combinations of $\mathbf{x}_i$ is called projection pursuit regression (PPR). The linear combinations, normally much fewer than K, are computed on each iteration to maximize their (smoothed) explanatory power for current residuals in a way resembling CCA (Sec. 3.5.1).

6. **Classification and regression trees** are piecewise-constant functions with splits along the axes in the feature space. An example of a regression decision tree (using a C-like syntax):

$$y = x[0] < a\ ?\ b : x[2] > c\ ?\ d : x[1] < e\ ?\ f : g. \tag{2.55}$$

Here the split points a, c, e, the order of the conditionals, and the leaf values b, d, f, g are the model parameters. Trees are among the most flexible ML algorithms with many recent improvements based on randomized ensembles. These approaches include *random forest*[143]

---

[141] J.H. Friedman, W. Stuetzle, *Projection Pursuit Regression*, Journal of the American Statistical Association, 76(376), pp. 817–823, 1981.

[142] A. Buja, T. Hastie, R. Tibshirani, *Linear smoothers and additive models (with discussion)*. The Annals of Statistics, 17, pp. 453–555, 1989.

[143] T.K. Ho, *The random subspace method for constructing decision forests*, in IEEE Transactions on Pattern Analysis and Machine Intelligence, 20(8), pp. 832–844, 1998.

and extremely randomized trees[144] ("ExtraTrees") performing random, rather than utility-based, splits. Tree learners are also used for boosting (Sec. 2.4.14), where they are called "boosted trees."

Model variance is a by-product of many nonparametric learners. For example, smoothers such as KNN and regressogram provide both the mean (predicted) y and its variance. Most other methods rely on cross-validation (Sec. 2.4.8).

2.4.7 Hyperparameters

Nonparametric learners, ironically, do need parameters such as smoothing scale, number of nearest neighbors, bin size, decision tree depth, and so forth, but these characterize the learning algorithm rather than the model $f(\mathbf{x})$ and are therefore called *hyperparameters*. If the parameters of a parametric learner or the internal state of a nonparametric ML are learned by fitting to the training data, hyperparameters are not learned from the data directly and must be chosen by the researcher before fitting the model to the data. The choice should be based on an inductive bias but can also be optimized for by simulation, cross-validation (Sec. 2.4.8), and other methods.[145,146] To distinguish from model *fitting* to the training data, the process of hyperparameters selection is sometimes call *tuning*.

Adding the ML level of hypertuning requires multiple training runs and carries a potential for overfitting, and care should be taken to avoid information leakage (Sec. 2.4.2). Isotonic regression (Sec. 2.4.6) has just one Boolean hyperparameter—whether or not the model $f(x)$ is increasing. Convex regression (Sec. 2.4.9) has no tunable hyperparameters.

In a more general ML decision framework such as AutoML (Sec. 2.4.18), discrete choices among alternative models are also part of hypertuning. In the process of financial forecasting, aka alpha research,

---

[144] P. Geurts, D. Ernst, L. Wehenkel, *Extremely randomized trees*, Machine Learning, 63, pp. 3–42, 2006.
[145] M. Feurer, F. Hutter, *Hyperparameter Optimization*, In: F. Hutter, L. Kotthoff, J. Vanschoren (eds), *Automated Machine Learning. The Springer Series on Challenges in Machine Learning*. Springer, 2019.
[146] T. Yu, H. Zhu, *Hyper-Parameter Optimization: A Review of Algorithms and Applications*, arXiv:2003.05689 [cs.LG], 2020.

there is one recurring Boolean hyperparameter: whether or not the model in question is worth it or if it is better to drop it and try something else.

2.4.8   Cross-validation

Write a C conditional efficiently testing whether an integer is a power of two.

From a quant interview

Cross-validation (CV) is a machine learning idiom for estimating the model generalization error. Statistical learning theory provides estimates for the generalization error, e.g., in terms of OLS coefficient variance (Sec. 2.4.3) or the model's VC dimension (Sec. 2.3.6), but those estimates are based on assumptions of a stable underlying distribution and are often more conceptual than explicit. In a computational setting, one can estimate the generalization error by splitting the data into two non-overlapping subsets: a training set and a holdout, or testing, set. To have a reasonably good estimate of the test (out-of-sample) error, the test data should be (a) never used for training the model, (b) large enough, and (c) drawn from the underlying distribution without a bias. Downsides of cross-validation include additional computational costs and withholding some data from training.

A popular learning approach is splitting data into three subsets: training, validation, and testing. The model is fitted on the training set and hypertuned on the validation set. It is allowed to iterate between training and validation, but the final testing verdict is supposed to be rendered only once. Partitioning of data is subject to tradition and rule of thumb rather than quantitative rationale. Typical train:validate:test ratios are 70:15:15 and 80:10:10.

There are several CV recipes:

1. **Fixed holdout** under a single train/test pass. An effort should be made to have the holdout unbiased to fairly represent future unseen data. The size of the holdout is subject to tradeoff between training vs testing statistical significance. In a financial time-oriented context, it is common to withhold data for the last year or so. This procedure would exclude the most recent market predictability structure (Sec. 2.7) from training and is sometimes replaced by withholding a historical period in the past.

2. **Leave-one-out** (LOO) cross-validation for a set of observations $\mathbf{z}_i = (\mathbf{x}_i, y_i)$, $i = 1, \ldots, N$, employs N rounds of training on each subset with a single observation $\mathbf{z}_j$ held out, with the model loss L_j computed on $\mathbf{z}_j$. The overall LOO CV loss is computed as the mean of all L_j, $j = 1, \ldots, N$. This approach is especially useful for learners whose predictions are linear in the dependent variable y_i:

$$f(\mathbf{x}) = \sum_i S_i(\mathbf{x}) y_i. \tag{2.56}$$

Examples include ordinary least squares (Sec. 2.4.3) and linear smoothers (Sec. 2.4.11).[147] For these learners, the LOO CV error can be computed in a closed form by "unlearning" one observation at a time after a single training on all N observations. This gives the "shortcut formula"[148]

$$L = \left(\sum_i w_i \right)^{-1} \sum_i w_i \left(\frac{y_i - f(\mathbf{x}_i)}{1 - S_i(\mathbf{x}_i)} \right)^2. \tag{2.57}$$

3. **k-fold** cross-validation splits the sample into k parts of about equal size and computes the loss on each part after training on the rest $k - 1$ parts combined. The splits can be done in many different, often randomized, ways. LOO CV is a special case of k-fold CV for k equal to the total sample size N.

In a financial time-series forecasting environment, LOO and k-fold CV are not directly applicable due to the overlap of features and targets: predictors of future returns often include past returns (Sec. 2.2). Excluding such overlaps leads to a "purged" version of k-fold,[149] but then some data are lost for training. In addition to a fixed holdout approach and purged k-fold, one can cross-validate on each newly observed target y before using it for training. This rolling cross-validation is occasionally termed *leave-future-out*[150] (LFO) CV, a method especially suited for

---

[147] Note that, for OLS regression (2.40), $S_i(\mathbf{x})$ is linear in $\mathbf{x}$ (but not in the training $\mathbf{x}_i$), and nonlinear in $\mathbf{x}$ for non-parametric smoothers. For the leave-one-out CV score (2.57) only linearity in y_i is important.

[148] L. Wasserman, *All of Nonparametric Statistics*, Springer, 2006.

[149] M. López de Prado, *Advances in Financial Machine Learning*, Wiley, 2018.

[150] P.-C. Bürkner, J. Gabry, A. Vehtari, *Approximate leave-future-out cross-validation for Bayesian time series models*, arXiv:1902.06281 [stat.ME], 2019.

online learning (Sec. 2.4.13). There are also efficient approximations for k-fold CV in an online setting.[151]

The purpose of cross-validation can be defeated by repeated model tuning based on CV results on the same test sample leading to over-fitting via information leakage (Sec. 2.4.2). This is often the case to some degree because an important function of cross-validation is feature and model selection in the first place. A disciplined approach would not allow iterations of model refitting as a result of the CV feedback. Information leakage via cross-validation can be prevented by training the model with a nested[152] CV-based hyperparameter tuning, a single-pass version of AutoML (Sec. 2.4.18), or online hyperparameter optimization.[153] Dwork et al.[154] proposed an interesting idea of reusable holdout set subject to some obfuscation by noise designed to limit the information leakage while still providing generalization error estimates.

2.4.9   Convex regression

> *Given a line and two points, construct a circle tangent to the line and passing through the two points.*
>
> From a quant interview

Convex regression seeks a best fit of training data $(\mathbf{x}_i, y_i)$, $i = 1, \ldots, N$, with a *convex function*. A convex function $f(\mathbf{x})$ is defined by the property that, for any two points $\mathbf{x}_{1,2}$ and for any $\alpha \in [0, 1]$,

$$f(\alpha \mathbf{x}_1 + (1 - \alpha)\mathbf{x}_2) \le \alpha f(\mathbf{x}_1) + (1 - \alpha) f(\mathbf{x}_2). \tag{2.58}$$

In one dimension, convexity means a monotonically increasing derivative $f'(x)$. Just like in isotonic regression, convexity is a regularizing constraint requiring a U-like shape of the graph of $y = f(\mathbf{x})$ and preventing its unnecessary wiggling.

---

[151] P. Joulani, A. György, C. Szepesvári, *Fast Cross-Validation for Incremental Learning,* arXiv:1507.00066 [stat.ML], 2015.

[152] S. Varma, R. Simon, *Bias in error estimation when using cross-validation for model selection,* BMC Bioinformatics, 7, Article number: 91, 2006.

[153] E. Hazan, *Introduction to Online Convex Optimization,* arXiv:1909.05207 [cs.LG], 2019.

[154] C. Dwork, V. Feldman, M. Hardt, T. Pitassi, O. Reingold, A. Roth, *Generalization in Adaptive Data Analysis and Holdout Reuse,* arXiv:1506.02629 [cs.LG], 2015; *The reusable holdout: Preserving validity in adaptive data analysis,* Science, 349(6248), pp. 636–638, 2015.

Convex and isotonic regressions are examples of *shape-constrained models*. Such models utilize a prior knowledge of, or express a preference for, the shape of $f(\mathbf{x})$. A useful property of a convex function is that it does not have local minima; any minimum of $f(\mathbf{x})$ is global. This makes convex regression suitable for tuning of ML hyperparameters (Sec. 2.4.11.7). Hypertuning involves a search of hyperparameters, often in a multi-dimensional space, minimizing ML testing or cross-validation error. Learning the noisy error function in convex terms kills two birds with one stone by regularizing the hyperlearning and by finding a unique minimum of the testing error. In addition, convex regression does not involve any tuning parameters.[155] A log-concavity assumption makes density estimation by shape-constrained methods free of tuning and more precise than by kernel methods.[156]

Convex regression, a nonparametric learning problem, is usually solved in terms of a piecewise-linear parametric regression:

$$f(\mathbf{x}) = \max_{1 \le k \le K} (\mathbf{a}_k \cdot \mathbf{x} + b_k), \qquad (2.59)$$

where the slopes (aka subgradients) $\mathbf{a}_i$ and the intercepts b_i define the convex polyhedron of the function graph (Fig. 2.4). Using Eq. (2.59) for fitting data directly results in a non-convex optimization problem

$$\{\mathbf{a}_i, b_i\} = \operatorname{argmin} \sum_{i=1}^{N} w_i \left[y_i - \max_{1 \le k \le K} (\mathbf{a}_k \cdot \mathbf{x}_i + b_k) \right]^2, \qquad (2.60)$$

with a combinatorial (exponential in K) complexity. Fortunately, convex data fitting can be made more computer-friendly by reformulating it as an inequality-constrained quadratic programming (QP) problem:[157]

$$\{\mathbf{a}_i, \hat{y}_i\} = \operatorname{argmin} \sum_{i=1}^{N} w_i \, (y_i - \hat{y}_i)^2,$$

$$\text{subject to: } \hat{y}_j - \hat{y}_i \ge \mathbf{a}_i \cdot (\mathbf{x}_j - \mathbf{x}_i), \quad 1 \le i,j \le N. \qquad (2.61)$$

---

[155] Although, for a small training sample, it appears useful to introduce a regularization hyperparameter penalizing for too large subgradients $|\mathbf{a}_i|$ in Eq. (2.61).

[156] M. Cule, R. Samworth, M. Stewart, *Maximum likelihood estimation of a multidimensional log-concave density*, arXiv:0804.3989 [stat.ME], 2008.

[157] S. Boyd, L. Vandenberghe, *Convex Optimization*, Cambridge University Press, 2004.

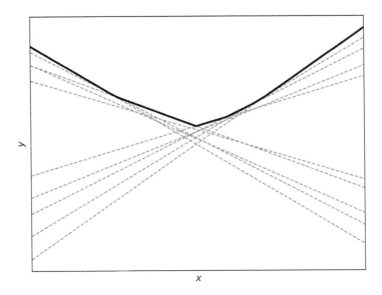

Figure 2.4 Building a piecewise-linear convex function as a maximum of linear functions per Eq. (2.59).

Solution of the QP problem (2.61) gives the fitted function values $\hat{y}_i$ at the training points $\mathbf{x}_i$. Outside this set, the prediction can be constructed as a non-smooth polyhedron-like linear interpolation (Fig. 2.4):

$$f_L(\mathbf{x}) = \max_{1 \leq i \leq N} \left[\hat{y}_i + \mathbf{a}_i \cdot (\mathbf{x} - \mathbf{x}_i) \right].$$ (2.62)

If a smoother prediction is desired, it can be obtained by interpolating the vertices of (2.62) with a *Moreau envelope*, aka *proximal operator*,

$$f_P(\mathbf{x}) = \min_{\xi} \left(f_L(\xi) + \frac{\lambda}{2}(\mathbf{x} - \xi)^2 \right),$$ (2.63)

where λ is a smoothing parameter.[158] The proximal interpolation can be solved as another, lighter QP problem.

Since the number of inequalities in (2.61) is $O(N^2)$, the complexity of the convex regression problem can be as high as $O(N^3 D^3)$, where $D = \dim(\mathbf{x})$, or $O(N^6)$ depending on the QP solver. Exploiting the special structure of (2.61) allows to reduce the cost of the convex fit

---

[158] N. Parikh, S. Boyd, *Proximal Algorithms*, Foundations and Trends in Optimization, 1(3), pp. 123–231, 2013.

computation. Mazumder et al.[159] and Lin et al.[160] present variants of the augmented Lagrangian method using $O(N^2)$ FLOPs per iteration, including options with guaranteed convergence.

Since there are typically few "active" constraints in the solution of (2.61), Bertsimas and Mundru[161] propose an algorithm starting with few, e.g., randomly chosen, constraints, and then adding, one at a time, constraints violated during the previous iteration and resolving. The iteration runs until all convexity constraints are met either by enforcement or by luck. The complexity of this approach scales as $O(N^{1.25})$.

There are also heuristic algorithms based on adaptive partitioning of the training data into K subsets and running linear OLS regressions $y \sim \mathbf{a}_k \cdot \mathbf{x} + b_k$ for each subset (cluster) meant to be used in the final model (2.59).[162,163] These algorithms need a choice of tuning parameters and benefit from cross-validation (Sec. 2.4.8). The complexity of convex adaptive partitioning can be $O(N \log(N) D^3)$. In addition to relative ease of implementation, partitioning-based algorithms can be used to simplify potentially complex, and overfitting, convex models, especially in higher dimensions. Limiting the number of clusters K can be used as a way dimensionality reduction aimed at mitigating the curse of dimensionality (Sec. 2.4.10). An example of convex regression is shown in Fig. 2.5.

2.4.10   Curse of dimensionality, eigenvalue cleaning, and shrinkage

In what dimension is the volume of a sphere with radius 1 the largest?

From a quant interview

Assume our dataset contains 100 relevant and correlated x predictors for the target y. Consider two options for learning a forecast. We can

---

[159] R. Mazumder, A, Choudhury, G. Iyengar, B. Sen. *A Computational Framework for Multivariate Convex Regression and its Variants*, arXiv:1509.08165 [stat.CO], 2015.

[160] M. Lin, D. Sun, K.-C. Toh, *Efficient algorithms for multivariate shape-constrained convex regression problems*, arXiv:2002.11410 [math.OC], 2020.

[161] D. Bertsimas, N. Mundru, *Sparse Convex Regression*, INFORMS Journal on Computing, 33(1), 2020.

[162] A. Magnani, S.P. Boyd, *Convex piecewise-linear fitting*, Optimization and Engineering, 10, pp. 1–17, 2009.

[163] L.A. Hannah, D.B. Dunson, *Multivariate convex regression with adaptive partitioning*, arXiv:1105.1924 [stat.ME], 2011.

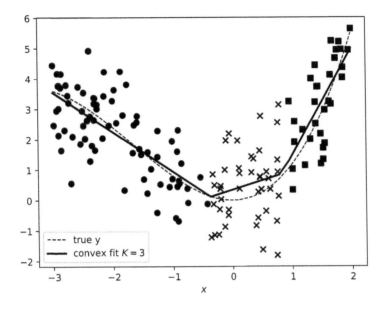

Figure 2.5 Piecewise-linear convex regression fit of noisy data. The data is the same as in Figs. 2.9 and 2.10. The algorithm is based on iterative OLS partitioning of Magnani and Boyd (2009). Different types of markers show the data partitioning. Each segment of the convex regression line is an OLS fit of the respective cluster.

run a single multivariate OLS regression with all the predictors thrown in.[164] Since the features interact (are correlated) with each other, the simultaneous regression looks like the right thing to do. Or we can try something more naive by running 100 univariate regressions of y on each x_i and build 100 separate, but clearly correlated, forecasts. Both ways are easy to experiment with, e.g., using synthetic data generated by the Python code in Listing 2.1. Now, something strange is happening. A combination such as the mean[165] of the 100 univariate forecasts can easily outperform, *out-of-sample*, the single multivariate regression, as demonstrated in Fig. 2.6. Why is that?

Running OLS, or any other ML for that matter, in a multi-dimensional space of predictors suffers from what is known as the *curse of dimensionality*, first noted by Bellman.[166] In high dimensions, the concepts of distance and angle, which are relevant to variance and

---

[164] One quant shop is rumored to use a linear regression forecast with 50 features.
[165] Which is hardly optimal—see Chapter 3 for discussion of other options.
[166] R.E. Bellman, *Adaptive Control Processes*, Princeton University Press, 1961.

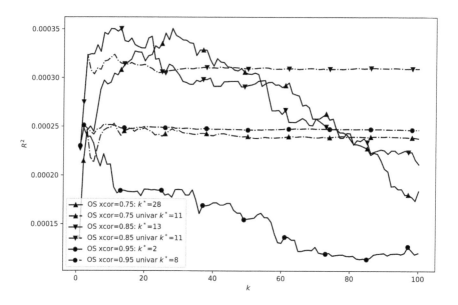

Figure 2.6   Comparison of out-of-sample performance of k-variate OLS regression forecasts (solid lines, identical to those in Fig. 2.3) and the mean of k univariate forecasts (dash-dotted lines) for the synthetic dataset of Fig. 2.3. For a large enough number of features k, a naive combination of the k univariate regressions beats, out-of-sample, the monolithic k-variate OLS forecast.

correlation, lose their discriminating power. For example, the nearest neighbor method suffers from poor space coverage by available training sample: to surround[167] a datapoint by neighbors on all sides, one would need an observation per vertex of a 100-dimensional cube—a sample of size 2^{100}. In general, it takes an exponentially large, in the dimensionality of the predictor, training sample to achieve a small testing error. Obversely, the ugly head of the curse of dimensionality is that no reasonable sample size is enough to learn a multi-dimensional distribution well. In the financial forecasting context, this generally means one must use an explicit or implicit dimensionality reduction (Sec. 3.5) to hope for any profitable forecast-driven portfolio. Last, but not least, it is even hard to think in multiple dimensions.

---

[167] Because interpolation is more reliable than extrapolation.

From an OLS learning perspective, a full 100×100 covariance matrix contains 5050 independent entries accumulated over whatever number of observations we have in the sample. Regression coefficients (2.40) depend on the inverse covariance matrix of the predictors,

$$D = (X'WX)^{-1}, \qquad (2.64)$$

which also appears in formula (2.44) for the (co)variance of the coefficients. If the training sample size is smaller than 100, the covariance is rank-deficient, which invalidates Eq. (2.40), but we still can use (2.41) delivering minimum-norm regression coefficients. The more serious problem is that a large covariance sampled over not a much larger dataset is *noisy*, or subject to random changes as we go out-of-sample, and its (pseudo) inverse can get even noisier. While finite-sampling noise is a general phenomenon, it is further amplified in financial forecasting by the low signal-to-noise ratio and a lack of a stationary distribution.

Matrices are fascinating things combining the apparent simplicity of a rectangular data table with deep and often unintuitive mathematics. Matrices are very important in quantum mechanics and quant trading alike. Among the most useful "personal" traits of a matrix are its eigenvalues and eigenvectors. To a large extent, the real nonnegative eigenvalues of a symmetric covariance matrix C give a compressed idea of what the matrix *is like*, just as one can imagine a drum by hearing its sound.[168] Matrix inversion accuracy and its sensitivity to noise are determined by the eigenvalue spectrum. The matrix condition number quantifies amplification of data error during matrix inversion or solving a linear system. The condition number of C is the ratio of its maximum to minimum non-zero[169] eigenvalues. To estimate the effects of noise on a covariance matrix one can use the theory of random matrices.

---

[168] M. Kac, *Can One Hear the Shape of a Drum?* The American Mathematical Monthly, 73(4), pp. 1–23, 1966.

[169] The presence of zero eigenvalues in a rank-deficient matrix is not really a problem if one is looking for a minimum-norm solution of a linear system or, equivalently, the Moore-Penrose matrix inverse C^+ (Sec. 2.11).

This theory, initially motivated by nuclear physics,[170,171] was put to use in finance.[172,173] Many insightful financial applications of the random matrix theory were published by the CFM team.

To demonstrate the idea of random matrices, consider the simplest case of uncorrelated K-dimensional features $\mathbf{x}$ drawn from a multivariate normal distribution $\mathcal{N}(0, C_{ij})$ with the diagonal (Kronecker) true covariance $C_{ij} = \delta_{ij}$. All eigenvalues of this covariance are equal to one. Now let's see what happens when the covariance is built empirically from data by drawing N samples of $\mathbf{x}$ from the underlying distribution. It takes a few seconds to run the code in Listing 2.2, and the reader is encouraged to experiment with it. The result in Fig. 2.7 shows that the eigenvalues of the empirical covariance generally have a broad distribution and are reasonably close to 1 only when the sample size N is a very large multiple of the dimension K. When the data coverage by observations is not that great—a typical situation in finance—the empirical covariance matrix is full of unintended eigenvalues resulting in a large condition number and prediction errors. Possible remedies include eigenvalue cleaning and shrinkage.

When both K and N are large, it is possible to compute the asymptotic distribution of the eigenvalues. The Marchenko-Pastur distribution gives the density of the eigenvalues λ_i:

$$F(\lambda) = \frac{\sqrt{(\lambda_+ - \lambda)(\lambda - \lambda_-)}}{2\pi\gamma\lambda},$$

$$\lambda_\pm = (1 \pm \sqrt{\gamma})^2, \quad \gamma = \frac{K}{N}. \tag{2.65}$$

Formula (2.65) can be seen as the baseline eigenvalue noise due to finite-size sample with $\gamma > 0$. The Marchenko-Pastur distribution

[170] E.P. Wigner, *Characteristic Vectors of Bordered Matrices With Infinite Dimensions*, Annals of Mathematics Second Series, 62(3), pp. 548–564, 1955.

[171] V.A. Marchenko and L.A. Pastur, *Distribution of eigenvalues for some sets of random matrices*. Matematicheskii Sbornik (N.S.) (in Russian), 72(114:4), pp. 507–536, 1967.

[172] J.-P. Bouchaud, M. Potters, *Financial Applications of Random Matrix Theory: a short review*, in The Oxford Handbook of Random Matrix Theory, edited by G. Akemann, J. Baik, and P. Di Francesco, 2015.

[173] M. López de Prado, *Machine Learning for Asset Managers (Elements in Quantitative Finance)*. Cambridge: Cambridge University Press, 2020.

slowly converges to the ground truth density $F(\lambda) = \delta(\lambda - 1)$ in the limit $\gamma \to 0$. The finite-sample distribution (2.65) can be generalized to features X with a general non-diagonal true covariance. The inverse problem of estimating the true covariance from the empirical covariance

Listing 2.2 Generation of empirical and Marchenko-Pastur distributions of the eigenvalues of a pure-noise covariance matrix. The result is in Fig. 2.7.

```python
import numpy as np
import matplotlib.pyplot as plt


K = 1000
fig = plt.figure()
ax1 = fig.add_subplot(121)
shrink = 0.5
gammas = [ 2.0, 1.0, 0.5, 0.01]
labels = [f'$N/K={1/gamma}$' for gamma in gammas]
slab = labels[0] + ' shrunk'
evalues = [None for gamma in gammas]
for idx, gamma in enumerate(gammas):
    N = int(K/gamma)
    X = np.random.normal(size=(N, K))
    C = X.T@X/N # (K, K)
    evalues[idx], _ = np.linalg.eigh(C)
    ax1.plot(range(K), np.flip(evalues[idx]), label=labels[idx])
    if idx == 0 and shrink:
        shrunk, _ = np.linalg.eigh(shrink*C + (1-shrink)*np.identity(K))
        ax1.plot(range(K), np.flip(shrunk), '-.', color='m', label=slab)
ax1.plot(range(K), np.ones(K), '--', color='grey')
ax2 = fig.add_subplot(122)
plt.yscale('log')
for idx, gamma in enumerate(gammas):
    # Marchenko-Pastur theory:
    a, b = (1 - np.sqrt(gamma))**2, (1 + np.sqrt(gamma))**2
    xx = np.linspace(a, b, 100)
    mp = np.sqrt((b - xx)*(xx - a))/(2*np.pi*gamma*xx)*max(gamma, 1)
    ax2.plot(xx, mp, label=labels[idx] + " (MP)")
for idx, gamma in enumerate(gammas):
    # histograms of eigenvalues:
    evals = evalues[idx]
    evals = evals[evals > 1e-3].reshape((-1, 1))
    ax2.hist(evals, bins=50, histtype='step', density=True,
             fill=True, alpha=0.1 + idx*0.05)
    if idx == 0 and shrink:
        # discard repeated lowest eigenvalues:
        shrunk = shrunk[shrunk > 1 - shrink + 1e-3]
        ax2.hist(shrunk, bins=40, histtype='step',
                 density=True, color='m', label=slab)
ax1.set_xlabel(r'$k$')
ax1.set_ylabel(r'$\lambda$')
ax1.legend();
ax2.set_xlabel(r'$\lambda$')
ax2.legend()
plt.subplots_adjust(wspace=0)
plt.show()
```

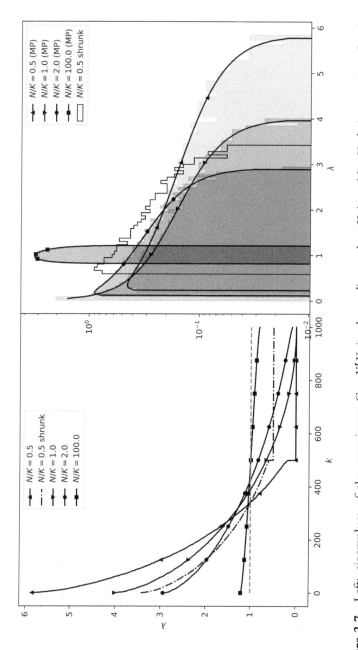

Figure 2.7 Left: eigenvalues of the covariance $C = X'X$ in descending order. X is a $N \times K$ design matrix of independent normal random features with $K = 1000$. Right: histograms of the non-zero eigenvalues of C (steps) and corresponding theoretical Marchenko-Pastur distributions (smooth lines) from Eq. (2.65). The chart is generated with the code in Listing 2.2.

is more difficult. Laloux et al.[174] describe a way of cleaning the covariance of stock returns by fitting its spectrum to the pure-noise Marchenko-Pastur distribution (2.65). In its simplest "clipping" form, the procedure involves classification of the empirical eigenvalues into the "bulk," i.e., falling within the matching Marchenko-Pastur bandwidth, and the "outliers." The bulk is likely due to sampling noise and can be replaced by a single repeated eigenvalue. The outliers express likely significant cross-feature correlations and can be trusted. Bun et al.[175] give an extensive review of various eigenvalue-cleaning covariance estimators including those with desirable invariant properties. These techniques are also applicable to features used in large OLS regression models.

It is worth noting that, while the sample covariance matrix C is the best unbiased estimate of the unobserved true covariance $\hat{C}$, this is not true of nonlinear functions of $\hat{C}$ such as its eigenvalues and inverse, which can be improved by the eigenvalue cleaning or by a simpler method of *linear shrinkage*.[176] Shrinkage of a covariance matrix is an artificial simplification such as suppression of its off-diagonal elements by transforming the empirical covariance matrix C in the direction of the identity matrix I:

$$C \to \alpha C + (1 - \alpha)I, \quad 0 < \alpha < 1. \tag{2.66}$$

The optimal shrinkage ratio α is data-dependent and can be be computed theoretically under certain assumptions.[177,178] The eigenvalues are transformed by the shrinkage as

$$\lambda_i \to \alpha\lambda_i + 1 - \alpha. \tag{2.67}$$

Fig. 2.7 includes the eigenvalues of a "shrunk" undersampled covariance with $N/K = 1/2$ and $\alpha = 1/2$. The regularizing effects of shrinkage

---

[174] L. Laloux, P. Cizeau, M. Potters, and J.-P. Bouchaud, *Random Matrix Theory And Financial Correlations*, International Journal of Theoretical and Applied Finance, 3(3), pp. 391–397, 2000.

[175] J. Bun, J.-P. Bouchaud, M. Potters, *Cleaning large correlation matrices: tools from random matrix theory*, arXiv:1610.08104 [cond-mat.stat-mech], 2016.

[176] W. James, C. Stein, *Estimation with Quadratic Loss*. Proceedings of the Fourth Berkeley Symposium on Mathematical Statistics and Probability, Volume 1: Contributions to the Theory of Statistics, pp. 361–379, University of California Press, Berkeley, 1961.

[177] A.B. Tsybakov. *Introduction to nonparametric estimation. Springer Series in Statistics*, Springer, New York, 2009.

[178] O. Ledoit, M. Wolf, *Nonlinear shrinkage estimation of large-dimensional covariance matrices*. The Annals of Statistics, 40(2), pp. 1024–1060, 2012.

are moving the eigenvalues away from zero and narrowing down their distribution.

Qualitatively, shrinkage implies that we trust the diagonal elements of the empirical covariance matrix, expressing the variance of individual features, more than the off-diagonal covariances across the features. After all, it is the noise in the off-diagonal elements that results in small eigenvalues, bad conditioning, and learning instability. Another way to express this sentiment is to keep the diagonal of C as is and to reduce the effective dimensionality of the rest, $\tilde{C} = C - \texttt{Diag}(C)$. This can be done by using the eigendecomposition

$$\tilde{C} = E\Lambda E', \quad \Lambda = \texttt{Diag}(\tilde{\lambda}_i), \tag{2.68}$$

where the columns of the matrix E are the eigenvectors of $\tilde{C}$ and $\tilde{\lambda}_i$ are the eigenvalues. Replacing in Λ smaller eigenvalues with zeros and leaving only a few largest ones will result in fewer degrees of freedom, including due to using only a few columns of matrix E, and better conditioning. This operation of "eigenectomy" is equivalent to the PCA dimensionality reduction (Sec. 4.5), which is a good thing to do when dealing with the curse of dimensionality. In the context of portfolio risk, this procedure corresponds to a multi-factor model with PCA risk factors (Sec. 4.2). Eigenectomy of predictor covariance and risk factor models are just another kind of shrinkage.

The ideas of regularization and shrinkage in multi-dimensional learning are often based on subtle mathematics including nonlinear statistical estimation and random matrix theory. It is relieving to know that computer simulation endows us with the convenience of being more superficial and engaging in productive *experimental mathematics*—once the general ideas of fighting the curse of dimensionality are understood.

In addition to the issues related to generalization error, handling multi-dimensional predictors poses computational difficulties and may require the use of online learning algorithms (Sec. 2.4.13).

2.4.11   Smoothing and regularization

Prove that $\sin(10°) > 1/6$.

From a quant interview

Correcting the covariance matrix is not the only way to improve out-of-sample forecast performance. One can also improve the learning process by redefining the loss function such as MSE (2.40) in ordinary least squares. A general theme in ML as a discipline is regularization.[179] Regularization controls the model complexity either explicitly or by penalizing a training loss function. Definitions of complexity and regularization are model- and even researcher-dependent.

Consider a few examples starting with nonparametric learners (Sec. 2.4.6).

2.4.11.1 Smoothing spline. A spline $f(x)$ minimizes the loss functional

$$L(f(x); \lambda) = \sum_i w_i \left[y_i - f(x_i) \right]^2 + \lambda \int \left[f''(x) \right]^2 dx. \qquad (2.69)$$

The loss includes a regularization term with the curvature penalty λ. The function $f(x)$ minimizing Eq. (2.69) can be worked out by calculus of variations. The result is a set of adjacent cubic splines with knots at the datapoints.[180] In the limit $\lambda \to 0$ it reduces to piecewise-linear interpolation between the training points (x_i, y_i) and to a straight OLS regression line for $\lambda \to \infty$.

2.4.11.2 Total variation denoising. Total variation denoising (TVD) is a smoothing algorithm allowing discontinuities of the function derivative. Instead of (2.69), TVD minimizes

$$L(f(x); \lambda) = \sum_i w_i [y_i - f(x_i)]^2 + \lambda \int |f'(x)| dx. \qquad (2.70)$$

The TVD penalty is proportional to the function's total variation, or the sum of all its absolute ups and downs. In the limit $\lambda \to \infty$, $f(x)$ approaches a constant equal to the weighted mean of ys.

The properties of a TVD smoother are easier to analyze in the continuous model,

$$f(x) = \operatorname{argmin} \int \left(w(x)[y(x) - f(x)]^2 + \lambda |f'(x)| \right) dx, \qquad (2.71)$$

[179] T. Hastie, R. Tibshirani, and J. Friedman, *The Elements of Statistical Learning*, Springer, 2009.
[180] G. Wahba, *Spline Models for Observational Data*, SIAM, 1990.

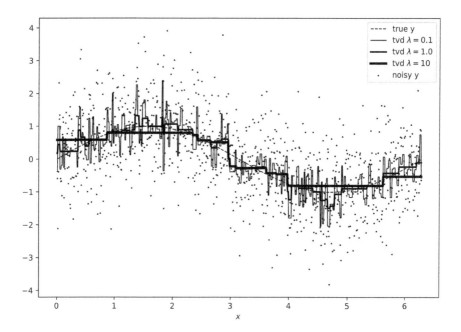

Figure 2.8   Total variation denoising of a noisy signal for different levels of the TVD penalty.

with a smooth input $y(x)$. A variational analysis of (2.71) shows that $f(x)$ is also continuous but generally has a discontinuous derivative: $f(x)$ consists of intervals where it either equals $y(x)$ or is constant, thereby avoiding the roundtrips associated with too sharp maxima or minima of $y(x)$ (Fig. 2.8). This behavior is similar to the "comfort range" pattern of optimal trading in the presence of slippage costs that are proportional to the total position variation (Sec. 6.4.5).

Among many other applications, total variation denoising is used for image reconstruction. The non-smooth result of TVD, while smoothing out speckles, can still capture sharp edges.[181] There is an efficient 1D TVD algorithm linear in the problem size.[182]

---

[181] P. Rodriguez, *Total Variation Regularization Algorithms for Images Corrupted with Different Noise Models: A Review*, Journal of Electrical and Computer Engineering, 1-4, pp. 1-16, 2013.

[182] L. Condat, *A Direct Algorithm for 1-D Total Variation Denoising*, IEEE Signal Processing Letters, 20(11), pp. 1054–1057, 2013.

2.4.11.3 Nadaraya-Watson kernel smoother.

A kernel smoother is defined as a weighted mean of the target values,

$$f(x) = \sum_i S_i(x) y_i, \quad S_i(x) = \frac{b_i(x)}{\sum_i b_i(x)}, \quad (2.72)$$

with location-specific weights:

$$b_i(x) = w_i K\left(\frac{x - x_i}{h}\right). \quad (2.73)$$

Here $K(\xi)$ is a nonnegative kernel function and h is the bandwidth. Eq. (2.72) is an x-local mean of training y_i similar to the regressogram. In the limit $h \to \infty$, the prediction for y is the global mean of y_i. The limit of $h \to 0$ gives a set of sharp peaks and zero elsewhere.

Listing 2.3 Local Linear Regression (LLR) solver based on Eqs. (2.74)-(2.75). The code is used for Fig. 2.9.

```
def EpanechnikovKernel(x):
""" A reasonable default kernel, numpy-vectorized
"""
    return 0.75*np.where(np.abs(x) < 1, 1 - x**2, 0)

def LLR(x, xx, yy, h, K=EpanechnikovKernel, weights=None):
    """ Compute Local Linear Regression for (xx, yy) data,
        kernel K, and bandwidth h at point x.
        Return: smoothing weights S, so the model is f(x) = np.dot(S, yy)
    """
    kk = K((xx - x)/h) if weights is None else weights*K((xx - x)/h)
    M1 = np.dot(kk, xx - x)
    M2 = np.dot(kk, (xx - x)**2)
    S = kk*M2 - kk*(xx - x)*M1
    denom = np.sum(S)
    return S/denom if denom > 0 else S
```

2.4.11.4 Local linear regression.

Local linear regression (LLR) is a simple refinement of kernel smoothing (2.72)-(2.73). LLR fits both the mean and the slope of the model with kernel-based local weights. Just like the Nadaraya-Watson smoother, the LLR prediction is linear in the training targets y_i, but nonlinear in x_i and the new location x:

$$f(x) = \sum_i S_i(x) y_i, \quad S_i(x) = \frac{b_i(x)}{\sum_i b_i(x)}, \quad (2.74)$$

where

$$b_i(x) = w_i K \left(\frac{x_i - x}{h} \right) (M_2(x) - (x_i - x)M_1(x)),$$

$$M_p(x) = \sum_i w_i K \left(\frac{x_i - x}{h} \right) (x_i - x)^p. \tag{2.75}$$

Adding the local fit of slope does not increase the number of degrees of freedom, or the potential for overfitting, relative to the local mean fit. LLR is just a smoother smoothing at the same computational complexity. An example of LLR is given in Fig. 2.9.

2.4.11.5   Gaussian process. A Gaussian process (GP) is a way of looking at $\{\mathbf{x}_i, y_i\}$ datapoints as realizations of a random function $y(\mathbf{x})$ from an underlying Gaussian distribution. A random process, including a Gaussian one, is a joint distribution of multiple random variables $y(\mathbf{x})$ "indexed" by an independent variable, which can be a scalar time or a multi-dimensional $\mathbf{x}$. A unique property of a multivariate Gaussian, or

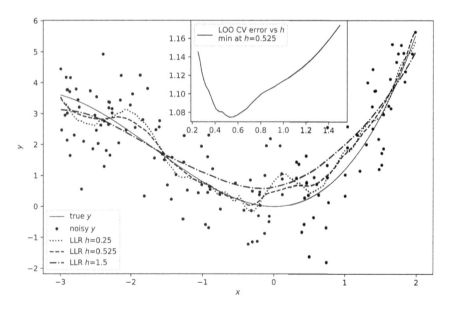

Figure 2.9   Local weighted linear regression smoothing of the (true) function $y = x^2 + x^3/5$ sampled, with noise, at 150 random points. LLR lines show smoothing for 3 different bandwidths: overfit $h = 0.25$, best fit $h = 0.525$, and underfit $h = 1.5$. LLR smoothers use the code in Listing 2.3. Inset: LOO cross-validation error (2.57) vs bandwidth h shows a familiar bias-variance tradeoff. An alternative (GP) smoothing of this data is shown in Fig. 2.10.

normal, distribution $\mathcal{N}(\mu, \kappa)$ is that it is completely defined by its mean $\mu(\mathbf{x})$ and its covariance

$$\kappa(\mathbf{x}, \mathbf{x}') = \text{Cov}(y(\mathbf{x}), y(\mathbf{x}')), \qquad (2.76)$$

also called a *kernel function*. The kernel function describes a degree of correlation between the values of y at two nearby (or remote) points $\mathbf{x}$ and $\mathbf{x}'$. Unless there is a compelling reason for anisotropy, the kernel is usually a radial basis function (RBF) depending only on the Euclidean distance between the points. A squared exponential RBF is a popular choice:

$$\kappa(\mathbf{x}_i, \mathbf{x}_j) = \sigma_f^2 \exp\left(-\frac{(\mathbf{x}_i - \mathbf{x}_j)^2}{2h^2}\right). \qquad (2.77)$$

Here σ_f^2 is the function variance and h is a correlation length playing the role of the smoothing bandwidth. These hyperparameters are based on data knowledge and can be tuned by cross-validation (Sec. 2.4.8). The RBF kernel is just one of many available options. Other kernels are used to express varying levels of smoothness of a typical realization of $y(\mathbf{x})$. Periodic or oscillatory kernels are used for time-based GP with a seasonality feature.

The flexibility contained in the kernel function is high enough, so it is common to assume a zero mean: $\mu(\mathbf{x}) = 0$. The idea behind GP smoothing is to choose a kernel function κ based on available inductive bias and to form a posterior distribution conditional on the training observations. This is a Bayesian inference approach (Sec. 2.3.2) applied directly to functions rather than parameters.[183]

The mathematics of Gaussian processes makes it possible to work out a closed-form Bayesian posterior conditional on observed data. Given N training points $(\mathbf{x}_i, y_i)$, $i = 1, \ldots, N$, the posterior distribution of $y(\mathbf{x})$ at a new point $\mathbf{x}$ is normal with the following mean and variance:

$$f(\mathbf{x}) = \sum_{ij} \kappa(\mathbf{x}_i, \mathbf{x}) K_{ij}^{-1} y_j,$$

$$\sigma^2(\mathbf{x}) = \kappa(\mathbf{x}, \mathbf{x}) - \sum_{ij} K_{ij}^{-1} \kappa(\mathbf{x}_i, \mathbf{x}) \kappa(\mathbf{x}_j, \mathbf{x}). \qquad (2.78)$$

Here

$$K_{ij} = \kappa(\mathbf{x}_i, \mathbf{x}_j) + \sigma_n^2 \delta_{ij} \qquad (2.79)$$

[183] C.E. Rasmussen, C.K.I. Williams, *Gaussian Processes for Machine Learning*, MIT Press, 2006. Available online: http://gaussianprocess.org/gpml.

is a symmetric $N \times N$ matrix, whose inverse appears in Eq. (2.78), and σ_n^2 is the optional y-observation noise variance. Just like in the Nadaraya-Watson or LLR kernel smoothers, the GP prediction for $f(\mathbf{x})$ is a weighted sum of the training values y_i. The smoothing weights

$$S_i(\mathbf{x}) = \sum_j K_{ij}^{-1} \kappa(\mathbf{x}_j, \mathbf{x}) \qquad (2.80)$$

tend to be larger—and the prediction variance $\sigma^2(\mathbf{x})$ smaller—for $\mathbf{x}$ closer to the training points $\mathbf{x}_j$. An example of GP fit of noisy data is given in Listing 2.4 and Fig. 2.10.

Listing 2.4 GP regression over noisy data. The result is in Fig. 2.10.

```
import numpy as np
import matplotlib.pyplot as plt
import sklearn.gaussian_process as gp

def TrueF(x):
    return x**2 + 0.2*x**3

N = 150
noise = 1.0
np.random.seed(1)
xx = np.random.uniform(low=-3, high=2, size=N)
xp = np.linspace(np.min(xx), np.max(xx), 200)
yy = TrueF(xx) + noise*np.random.normal(size=N)
fig = plt.figure()
rbf = gp.kernels.RBF(length_scale=2, length_scale_bounds=(0.1, 5))
white = gp.kernels.WhiteKernel()
gp = gp.GaussianProcessRegressor(kernel=rbf + white, alpha=noise)
fit = gp.fit(xx.reshape(-1, 1), yy)
yp, sigma = fit.predict(xp.reshape(-1, 1), return_std=True)
plt.plot(xp, TrueF(xp), '--', linewidth=1.5, label='true')
plt.plot(xx, yy, '.', label='noisy')
plt.plot(xp, yp, 'b-', label=f'GP prediction')
plt.fill(np.concatenate([xp, xp[::-1]]),
        np.concatenate([yp - 2*sigma, (yp + 2*sigma)[::-1]]),
        alpha=.1, fc='b', ec='None', label='95% confidence interval')
plt.legend()
plt.show()
```

An attractive feature of a GP smoother is that it provides a consistent estimate of the prediction f, its variance σ^2 (forecast uncertainty), and the full (Gaussian) distribution function

$$F(y|\mathbf{x}) = \mathcal{N}(f(\mathbf{x}), \sigma^2(\mathbf{x})). \qquad (2.81)$$

In addition to the single-point prediction, a Gaussian process also provides a multi-point joint distribution of ys at two or more $\mathbf{x}$ points if needed. These nice features come at a higher computation cost and the

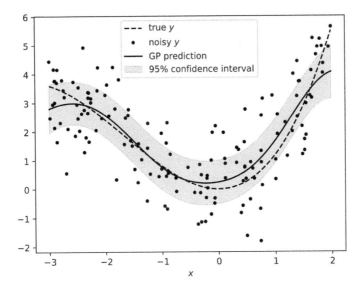

Figure 2.10 GP smoothing of noisy data of Figs. 2.5 and 2.9. The 95% confidence area is shaded. Note the difference between LLR and GP regression at the ends of the x interval. The chart is generated with the code in Listing 2.4.

need to choose and to tune the kernel function κ. As a natural model of a noisy function such as a CV loss vs hyperparameters, a Gaussian process is a useful tool for ML hypertuning.[184] However, a GP-based hypertuner has its own hyperparameters, which may need tuning too.

2.4.11.6 Ridge and kernel ridge regression.

For a parametric linear regression model,

$$f(\mathbf{x}) = \boldsymbol{\beta} \cdot \mathbf{x}, \tag{2.82}$$

a popular regularized loss function is the norm-penalized mean square error[185]

$$L(\boldsymbol{\beta}) = \frac{\sum_i w_i (y_i - \boldsymbol{\beta} \cdot \mathbf{x}_i)^2}{\sum_i w_i} + \lambda \sum_j |\beta_j|^p, \quad \lambda > 0. \tag{2.83}$$

---

[184] J. Snoek, H. Larochelle, R.P. Adams, *Practical Bayesian Optimization of Machine Learning Algorithms*, arXiv:1206.2944 [stat.ML], 2012.

[185] When using penalty based on a norm of coefficients, the predictors are best put on equal footing by serially prescaling each feature x to unit variance.

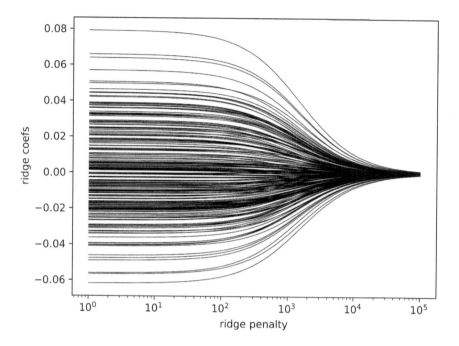

Figure 2.11   Ridge regression coefficients for 200 correlated features. The pattern is different from the lasso regression (Fig. 2.12). The code generating this chart is essentially the same as in Listing 2.5, with `Lasso` changed to `Ridge`.

The case of $p = 2$ is called *ridge regression*. There is a closed-form solution for the ridge regression coefficients:

$$\beta = (\lambda I + X'WX)^{-1}X'WY. \tag{2.84}$$

Eq. (2.84) is different from the OLS weights (2.40) only by a positive diagonal addition to the predictor covariance—which is incidentally equivalent to covariance shrinkage (Sec. 2.4.10). In Eq. (2.84), the diagonal matrix of weights W is normalized to unit trace. Generally, none of the ridge regression coefficients is zero, but they typically decrease with increasing λ (Fig. 2.11). This is the expected behavior in terms of making a "safer" forecast apprehensive of possible out-of-sample surprises, and the out-of-sample performance of a ridge regression can be better than that of a plain OLS. The optimal ridge scale λ is data dependent and is generally growing with the dimension of $\mathbf{x}$.[186] It can be estimated via cross-validation, e.g., using the `sklearn.linear_model.RidgeCV` algorithm from the `scikit-learn` Python library.

Ridge regularization is also used in a more general framework of *kernel ridge regression* (KRR), or just *kernel method*. The kernel method uses a change of independent variables to new, hopefully better, features $\phi = \phi(\mathbf{x})$, which can have a dimensionality D different from $d = \dim(\mathbf{x})$. The result for the regression coefficients is the same as (2.84) up to a change of the independent variables:

$$\gamma = (\lambda I + \Phi' W \Phi)^{-1} \Phi' WY. \qquad (2.85)$$

Here Φ is a $N \times D$ design matrix of the features. For $D > N$, the inversion in (2.85) can use the Woodbury formula (Sec. A2). The forecast at a new point $\mathbf{x}$ is then

$$f(\mathbf{x}) = \phi(\mathbf{x})\gamma = Y(\lambda I + K)^{-1} \kappa(\mathbf{x}),$$
$$K_{ij} = K(\mathbf{x}_i, \mathbf{x}_j), \quad \kappa_i(\mathbf{x}) = K(\mathbf{x}_i, \mathbf{x}). \qquad (2.86)$$

Here $K(\mathbf{x}_i, \mathbf{x}_j) = \Phi'(\mathbf{x}_i) W \Phi(\mathbf{x}_j)$ is the kernel function expressing the covariance, or a degree of similarity, of the features. Note that the features $\phi(\mathbf{x})$ need not be computed or stored; all is needed is the kernel function K of two points. This convenient fact is sometimes called the "kernel trick."

As a generalization of kernel smoothers and Gaussian processes, kernel ridge regression is a powerful framework for nonparametric ML. An interesting application of KRR is for features chosen at random.[187] For N training points, an optimal learning error $O(N^{-1/2})$ can be achieved by using only $O(N^{1/2} \log(N))$ random features.[188]

2.4.11.7 Bandwidth and hypertuning. The K-nearest neighbor, smoothing splines, as well as Nadaraya-Watson, LLR, GP, and KRR

---

[186] I. Johnstone, *Oracle Inequalities and Nonparametric Functional Estimation*, Documenta Mathematica ICM, III, pp. 267–278, 1998.

[187] A. Rahimi and B. Recht, *Random Features for Large-Scale Kernel Machines*, Proceedings of the 20th Int. Conf. on Neural Information Processing, pp. 1177–1184, 2007.

[188] A. Rudi, L. Rosasco, *Generalization Properties of Learning with Random Features*, arXiv:1602.04474 [stat.ML], 2017.

kernel smoothers, all belong to the class of nonparametric *linear smoothers* predicting the target $f(\mathbf{x})$ as a mean of training values y_i with weights $S_i(\mathbf{x})$. The weights are normally nonnegative and add up to one. The choice of the kernel is usually less important than the bandwidth h, which must be chosen based on data or an inductive bias.

Model parameters such as the number of KNN neighbors, the curvature or total variation penalty λ in a spline or TVD, or the bandwidth h in a kernel smoother regulate the complexity of the model. Like any other hyperparameters (Sec. 2.4.7), they are not fitted from the data directly but are subject to domain-specific inductive bias or tuning by cross-validation (CV). A popular approach is leave-one-out (LOO) cross-validation (Sec. 2.4.8). For a linear smoother with the weights $S_i(\mathbf{x})$, the CV score is given by a modified MSE (2.57) penalizing higher (more concentrated) smoothing weights. The shortcut CV formula can be used for an efficient automated tuning of the bandwidth. An example of CV-tuned LLR smoother is given in Fig. 2.9. When kernel smoothing is used for tuning hyperparameters of an ML algorithm, one may want to use an underfit (larger) bandwidth to avoid multiple noisy minima of the ML testing loss function.

2.4.11.8   Lasso regression. The case of $p = 1$ in the regularizing term of Eq. (2.83) is called *lasso regression*.[189] Its behavior is different from the ridge regression by driving some of the coefficients to exact zeros.[190] The larger the lasso penalty, the more zeros there are. This phenomenon is called shrinkage (in a narrow sense) and is used for selection or ranking predictors by importance. Lasso, an animal-catching device, stands here for Least Absolute Selection and Shrinkage Operator. With the curse of dimensionality in mind, using fewer predictors can be better than using them all (Fig. 2.3). Lasso regression coefficients are not written in a closed form, but there is an efficient algorithm that can also scan over the values of λ and compute all points where the number of non-zero solutions changes.[191]

---

[189] T. Hastie, R. Tibshirani, M. Wainwright, *Statistical Learning with Sparsity: The Lasso and Generalizations*, Chapman & Hall/CRC, 2015.

[190] This fact becomes more intuitive upon the exercise of minimizing $ax^2 + bx + |x|$.

[191] B. Efron, T. Hastie, I. Johnstone, R. Tibshirani, *Least angle regression*. The Annals of Statistics, 32(2), pp. 407–499, 2004.

Even though the search of best feature subset has been sped up significantly using modern mixed-integer optimization algorithms,[192] lasso is still much faster. In addition, due to regularization, lasso regression outperforms, out of sample, best subset selection algorithms in the low signal-to-noise ratio regime[193] typical of financial forecasting. There is an interesting connection between the lasso regression and stagewise, or iterative univariate, regression leading to simple and fast learning algorithms with attractive generalization properties.[194]

An example of lasso regression is given in Listing 2.5 and Fig. 2.12.

Listing 2.5 Lasso regression with varying penalty. The result is in Fig. 2.12.

```
import numpy as np
import matplotlib.pyplot as plt
import sklearn
from sklearn.linear_model import Lasso

N = 10000
K = 200 # number of features
signal2noise = 0.003
coefs = np.random.normal(size=K)
alphas = np.exp(np.linspace(np.log(1e-5), np.log(1e-1), 500))
xcor = 0.85
cov = (1 - xcor)*np.diag(np.ones([K])) + xcor*np.ones([K, K])
X = np.random.multivariate_normal(np.zeros(K), cov, size=(N))
y = signal2noise*np.dot(X, coefs) + np.random.normal(size=N)
coefs = np.zeros((len(alphas),K))
for idx, alpha in enumerate(alphas):
    coefs[idx, :] = Lasso(alpha=alpha, precompute=True).fit(X, y).coef_
fig = plt.figure()
for k in range(K):
    plt.plot(alphas, coefs[:, k], '-', lw=0.5)
plt.xlabel('lasso penalty')
plt.ylabel('lasso coefs')
plt.xscale('log')
plt.show()
```

2.4.11.9 Dropout. Large neural networks (Sec. 2.4.4) are both expensive to train and easy to overfit. Despite the evidence of overfit resistance in certain configurations (Sec. 2.4.12), neural networks can

[192] D. Bertsimas, A. King, R, Mazumder, *Best Subset Selection via a Modern Optimization Lens*, arXiv:1507.03133 [stat.ME], 2015.

[193] R. Mazumder, P. Radchenko, A. Dedieu, *Subset Selection with Shrinkage: Sparse Linear Modeling when the SNR is low*, arXiv:1708.03288 [stat.ME], 2017.

[194] R.J. Tibshirani, *A General Framework for Fast Stagewise Algorithms*, arXiv:1408.5801 [stat.ML]. 2015.

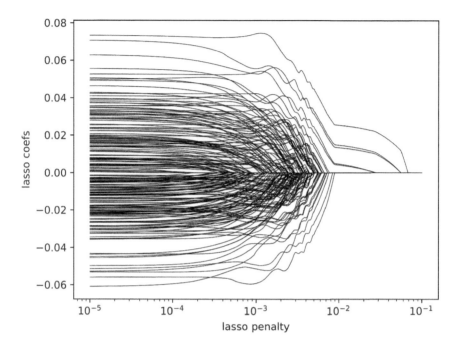

Figure 2.12 Lasso regression coefficients for 200 correlated features. Contrary to the ridge regression (Fig. 2.11), the number of nonzero coefficients decreases with the lasso penalty. The chart is generated with the code in Listing 2.5.

also benefit from a regularization. *Dropout* is an efficient method of regularization whereby a significant random subset of nodes is removed from the network during training.[195,196] Google LLC holds a patent for this method.[197] The validity of the patent appears questioned by the authors of a similar method of *dilution*.[198]

[195] G.E. Hinton, N. Srivastava, A. Krizhevsky, I. Sutskever, R.R. Salakhutdinov, *Improving neural networks by preventing co-adaptation of feature detectors*, arXiv:1207.0580 [cs.NE], 2012.

[196] N. Srivastava, G. Hinton, A. Krizhevsky, I. Sutskever, R. Salakhutdinov, *Dropout: a simple way to prevent neural networks from overfitting*. The Journal of Machine Learning Research, 15(1), pp. 1929–1958.

[197] *System and method for addressing overfitting in a neural network*, US Patent US9406017B2, 2016.

[198] https://en.wikipedia.org/wiki/Dilution_(neural_networks).

2.4.12 Generalization puzzle of deep and overparameterized learning

The Empire State Building has 102 floors. Determine the highest floor from which an egg can be dropped without breaking using the minimum possible number of experiments. There are only two eggs to experiment with.

From a quant interview

The success of large neural networks is both encouraging and mysterious. On the one hand, DNNs are highly expressive in terms of model fitting capacity (Sec. 2.4.4). On the other hand, they have the following troubling properties:

1. DNNs are grossly overparameterized, often with the size (number of fittable weights) K well over the shattering (interpolation) threshold of the training sample. Depending on activation function and topology, the VC dimension of DNNs ranges from $O(K^2)$ to $O(K^4)$.[199] Deep networks easily interpolate, i.e., learn down to zero training error, even randomly labeled image data.[200] The classical learning theory (Sec. 2.3.6) would then predict in no uncertain terms that large DNNs must overfit.

2. The training loss function is high-dimensional and non-convex making the search for a global minimum impossible (NP-hard). In an overparameterized network, though, it is possible to reach the zero bottom of the MSE or similar training loss. However, this will be just one of many such interpolation minima with no reason of it being any better than others.

Despite these arguments, suitably designed DNN learners show a remarkable generalization ability in practice, even without any explicit regularization. With growing network size, both training and test error decrease, and the test error keeps decreasing past the interpolation limit. This surprising behavior is attributed to an implicit regularization,[201]

---

[199] M. Anthony, L. Bartlett, *Neural Network Learning: Theoretical Foundations*, Cambridge University Press, 2009.

[200] C. Zhang, S. Bengio, M. Hardt, B. Recht, O. Vinyals, *Understanding deep learning requires rethinking generalization*, arXiv:1611.03530 [cs.LG], 2017.

[201] B. Neyshabur, R. Tomioka, N. Srebro, *In Search of the Real Inductive Bias: On the Role of Implicit Regularization in Deep Learning*, arXiv:1412.6614 [cs.LG], 2014.

possibly built into the stochastic gradient descent (SGD)[202] almost universally used in neural net training. The dynamics of SGD and its early stopping time were shown to have a regularizing effect, and "redundant" parts of the network remain inactive, when the number of regression network parameters exceeds the size of learning sample size.[203] The smaller the signal-to-noise ratio, the shorter the optimal stopping time. The redundancy of oversized neural networks reminds of the redundancy of the biological brain (Sec. 2.4.5).

The failure of the out-of-sample error to increase with increasing network complexity (size) contradicts the classical bias-variance tradeoff (Sec. 2.3.5) either completely or by adding a second, better minimum of classification generalization error leading to a double descent, or "double dip" dependence of generalization error vs model complexity. Belkin et al.[204] argue that this is due to a minimum-norm regularization implicit in SGD optimization and report a similar overfit resistance behavior in oversized random forests and boosted trees.

On a hand-waving level, additional intuition behind the DNN generalization puzzle could be that a large neural network effectively behaves as an ensemble of learners resisting the curse of dimensionality. The additive nature of the layer-wise composition (2.51) is somewhat similar to additive models (Sec. 2.4.6), which are known to resist overfitting. Multiple paths down the network graph from the input (features) layer to the output (target) layer could interact in a way similar to the cooperation of weak learners in boosting (Sec. 2.4.14), which can be overfit-free for increasing number of learners.

Poggio et al.[205] argue that a deep composition of low-dimensional functions resists the curse of dimensionality due to a *blessing of compositionality*. The relative success of randomized neural networks (Sec. 2.4.5) suggests that deep compositionality along with randomized, by learning or by assignment, network structure somehow has a profound

---

[202] M. Hardt, B. Recht, Y. Singer, *Train faster, generalize better: Stability of stochastic gradient descent*, arXiv:1509.01240 [cs.LG], 2016.

[203] M.S. Advani, A.M. Saxe, *High-dimensional dynamics of generalization error in neural networks*, arXiv:1710.03667 [stat.ML], 2017.

[204] M. Belkin, D. Hsu, S. Ma, S. Mandal, *Reconciling modern machine learning practice and the bias-variance trade-off*, arXiv:1812.11118 [stat.ML], 2018.

[205] T. Poggio, H. Mhaskar, L. Rosasco, B. Miranda, Q. Liao, *Why and When Can Deep—but Not Shallow—Networks Avoid the Curse of Dimensionality: a Review*, arXiv: 1611.00740 [cs.LG], 2016.

regularizing effect resisting the artifacts of overfitting. This observation invokes a vague analogy with the *Anderson localization*, an unintuitive phenomenon in condensed matter physics. Depending on the energy of an electron, its quantum states in a Schrödinger potential can be either bound (with discrete energy levels) or free (with a continuous energy spectrum). However, if the potential has a random component due to a crystalline lattice disorder, even the continuous states become localized.[206] Anderson localization prevents an electron from wondering around to a large distance even when there is no energy obstacle to that. Sinai's random walk[207] is a simplified model of Anderson localization in which a particle is independently moved along the x axis a unit distance to the right with probability p and to the left with probability $1 - p$. If $p = 1/2$, this results in a regular diffusion process with the mean displacement $|x(t)| \sim t^{1/2}$ after t steps. However, if p is a random variable distributed around $1/2$ with $E(\log(p/(1 - p))) = 0$, the random walk slows down to $|x(t)| \sim \log^2(t)$. If propagation of a feature input through a randomized deep neural network can be treated as a random walk, the disorder-induced localization would limit the effect of inputs on the outputs resulting in an implicit regularizing behavior.

Most of the findings of low generalization error in large neural networks are for low-noise (Silicon Valley) settings. It is then natural to ask if the paradox extends to high-noise (Wall Street) settings. To continue the surprise, a similar generalization behavior was reported for simpler kernel regression learners and small to moderate amount of noise,[208,209,210] and even for ordinary least squares.[211] Hastie et al. argue that a strongly overparameterized nonlinear parametric learner, such as a DNN, can be approximated by a linearized model that allows a fairly complete analysis

---

[206] P.W. Anderson, *Absence of Diffusion in Certain Random Lattices*, Physical Review, 109(5), pp. 1492–1505, 1958.

[207] Ya.G. Sinai, *The Limiting Behavior of a One-Dimensional Random Walk in a Random Medium*, Theory of Probability and Its Applications, 27(2), 256-268, 1982.

[208] M. Belkin, S. Ma, S. Mandal, *To understand deep learning we need to understand kernel learning*, arXiv:1802.01396 [stat.ML], 2018.

[209] M. Belkin, A. Rakhlin, A.B. Tsybakov, *Does data interpolation contradict statistical optimality?* arXiv:1806.09471 [stat.ML], 2018.

[210] T. Liang, A. Rakhlin, *Just Interpolate: Kernel "Ridgeless" Regression Can Generalize*, arXiv:1808.00387 [math.ST], 2018.

[211] T. Hastie, A. Montanari, S. Rosset, R.J. Tibshirani, *Surprises in High-Dimensional Ridgeless Least Squares Interpolation*, arXiv:1903.08560 [math.ST], 2019.

Listing 2.6 Double dip of generalization error. The result is in Fig. 2.13.

```
import numpy as np
import sklearn.linear_model as lm
import matplotlib.pyplot as plt
from matplotlib.lines import Line2D


def R2(coef, X, y):  # R-squared
    return np.corrcoef(np.dot(X, coef), y)[0, 1]**2


np.random.seed(3)
N = 500      # total size
T = int(0.5*N) # training size
K = 10000     # max number of features
kk = range(1, K + 1)
signal2noise = 0.003
coefs = np.random.normal(size=K)
fig = plt.figure()
ax = fig.add_subplot()
plt.xscale('log')
for xcor in [0.75, 0.85, 0.95]:
    # correlated features:
    cov = (1 - xcor)*np.diag(np.ones([K])) + xcor*np.ones([K, K])
    X = np.random.multivariate_normal(np.zeros(K), cov, size=(N))
    # noisy target:
    y = signal2noise*np.dot(X, coefs) + np.random.normal(size=N)
    os_r2 = np.zeros(K + 1)
    is_r2 = np.zeros(K + 1)
    for k in kk:
        Xtrain, Xtest = X[0:T, 0:k], X[T:N, 0:k]
        ytrain, ytest = y[0:T], y[T:N]
        reg = lm.LinearRegression(fit_intercept=False).fit(Xtrain, ytrain)
        is_r2[k] = R2(reg.coef_, Xtrain, ytrain)
        os_r2[k] = R2(reg.coef_, Xtest, ytest)
        os_label = f'OS xcor={xcor}: $k^*$={np.argmax(os_r2)}'
        is_label = f'IS xcor={xcor}'
        plt.plot(kk, 1.0 - os_r2[kk], '-', label=os_label)
        plt.plot(kk, 1.0 - is_r2[kk], '--', label=is_lable)
ax.add_artist(Line2D([1, T], [1, 1], linestyle='--', linewidth=0.5))
ax.add_artist(Line2D([T, T], [0, 1], linestyle='--', linewidth=0.5))
plt.text(T*0.78, 0.4, f'$k={T}$', rotation=90)
plt.xlabel('$k$')
plt.ylabel('$1-R^2$')
plt.legend()
plt.show()
```

of the generalization error by using the methods of random matrix theory (Sec. 2.4.10). Interpolation regime in OLS regression does not need an explicit ridge regularization[212] and was characterized as "benign overfitting."[213]

---

[212] D. Kobak, J. Lomond, B. Sanchez, *Optimal ridge penalty for real-world high-dimensional data can be zero or negative due to the implicit ridge regularization*, arXiv:1805.10939 [math.ST], 2020.

[213] G. Chinot, M. Lerasle, *Benign overfitting in the large deviation regime*, arXiv:2003.05838 [math.ST], 2020.

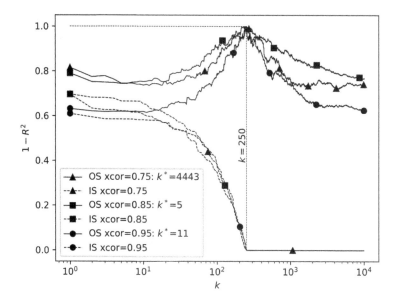

Figure 2.13   Generalization (OS) and training (IS) errors of classical and over-parameterized linear models with 250 training and as many test points vs k correlated OLS predictors. The maximum test error occurs at k equal to the training size (vertical dashed line). Synthetic datasets for three feature correlation levels and the chart are generated by the code in Listing 2.6. Note that `sklearn.linear_model.LinearRegression` uses a minimum norm solution (2.120) for overdetermined problem when $k > 250$. Training (IS) error in this regime is zero.

Recent research provides some theoretical clues into the generalization power of overparameterized kernel ridge regression (Sec. 2.4.11.6) with inputs randomly mapped to a feature space.[214]

The benign overfitting pattern of double-dipping generalization error appears fairly generic and is exhibited by complex and simple learners alike for both low- and high-noise data. An OLS model with high-noise synthetic data similar to the one used in Figs. 2.3 and 2.6 reproduces the effect. Figure 2.13 is generated with Python code in Listing 2.6. It shows a classical bias–variance tradeoff for low to medium model complexity (defined as the number k of OLS predictors).

[214] S. Mei, T. Misiakiewicz, A. Montanari, *Generalization error of random features and kernel methods: hypercontractivity and kernel matrix concentration*, arXiv:2101.10588 [math.ST], January 2021.

With increasing complexity, the generalization error experiences something like a phase transition peaking at the interpolation point (k equal to the training size), followed by a second dip of the test error, which can be lower than that in the classical complexity range. The generalization error pattern depends on the data generation process (via `numpy.random.seed()`), but the double dip feature is stable.

The phenomena discussed in this section remain a subject of active research. A deeper theoretical understanding of the resistance of large neural network to overfitting will undoubtedly result in a more efficient and principled design of deep learners. Financial ML forecasting can also benefit from a large number of predictive features, subject to higher computational costs and limitations of competition-based market efficiency, which is there to stay.

2.4.13   Online machine learning

A large $M \times N$ matrix is stored in memory as a single row-wise array. Give an algorithm transposing the matrix in-place using only a fixed $O(1)$ additional storage.

From a quant interview

Most theoretical foundations and algorithmic implementations of machine learning have been developed for the *batch* setting in which the full training sample is presented for learning and validation. Once new training data become available, the algorithm has to relearn from scratch using the extended or modified sample. Most off-the-shelf ML algorithms available in Python and GNU R libraries operate in the batch mode.[215] When the number of observations and the number of potential predictors usable for forecasting grows beyond a certain point, the batch approach can become impractical due to a large memory footprint and performance issues. In the context of a universe of securities, the data $\{x_{its}, y_{ts}\}$ is indexed by $t = 1, \ldots, T$ (time index), $s = 1, \ldots, N$ (security index), and $i = 1, \ldots, K$ (feature index). When all sizes, N, T, and K are of order 10^3 or greater, we may have a problem.

---

[215] Some of the `scikit-learn` linear model algorithms, including lasso learners, do support preprocessed input in the form of Gram (covariance) matrix updatable incrementally.

Online learning is a possible solution to this problem. In the online setting, a smaller, algorithm-specific "online knowledge" data structure is maintained by inexpensive updates on each new training observation instead of accumulating a growing history of raw observations. The online knowledge data contains information sufficient for predicting y for a new $\mathbf{x}$.

An example of online knowledge is a cumulative covariance matrix C_{ij} for $(K+2)$-dimensional[216] observations

$$\xi = (x[1:K], y, 1). \tag{2.87}$$

The addition of "1" takes care of maintaining the means of $\mathbf{x}$ and y. The covariance is updated daily as follows:

$$C_{ij}(t) = e^{-\gamma} C_{ij}(t-1) + \sum_s w_{ts} \xi_{tis} \xi_{tjs}. \tag{2.88}$$

Here w_{ts} are security-specific observation weights, and γ is a decay rate implementing an exponential moving average (EMA) time weight. Instead of keeping all ξ_{tis} data in an $O(TNK)$ memory to be repeatedly processed later (batch mode), the observations for each time step are accumulated in an $O(K^2)$ data structure and then discarded (online mode). This procedure is similar to the "kernel trick" (Sec. 2.4.11.6).

Weighted means and covariances for either x or y data are then extracted by normalizing by the cumulative observation weight W:

$$\text{Mean}(\xi_i) = \frac{C_{i,K+2}}{W},$$

$$\text{Cov}(\xi_i, \xi_j) = \frac{C_{ij}}{W} - \text{Mean}(\xi_i)\,\text{Mean}(\xi_j), \tag{2.89}$$

$$W = C_{K+2,K+2}.$$

OLS, ridge or lasso regression, and a few other learning algorithms need only covariance data and can therefore be run in an online, as opposed to batch, mode. For example, penalized least square loss of Eq. (2.83) can be equivalently written as minimization of

$$\frac{1}{2} \sum_{ij} \text{Cov}(x_i, x_j)\beta_i\beta_j - \sum_i [\text{Cov}(x_i, y)\beta_i + \lambda|\beta_i|^p]. \tag{2.90}$$

---

[216] One can also add multiple dependent variables $\mathbf{y}$, e.g., for future returns over several horizons to be learned using the same set of predictors in parallel.

For $p \geq 1$, this is a convex problem depending only on the online covariance C with daily update complexity of $O(NK^2)$ and solvable in $O(K^3)$ instructions.

A number of other machine learning algorithms can operate online, or in incremental learning fashion, including gradient methods,[217] Gaussian processes,[218] and certain types of random forests.[219] OLS regression (2.40) can be efficiently updated online using the rank-one inversion update formula (A2.16).

2.4.14   Boosting

Take a handful of dominoes and stack them on top of each other, flat side down and slightly offset along the length, to form an overhang (Fig. 2.14). What is the maximum possible length of the overhang?

From a quant interview

Boosting is a remarkable discovery in statistical learning. Initially posed by Kearns and Valiant,[220,221] the question is how to combine many different weak learners, or ML models $y = f_k(\mathbf{x})$ barely better than pure noise, into a strong learner, or a more accurate forecast $y = F(\mathbf{x})$.

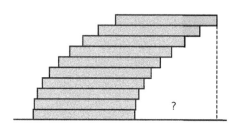

Figure 2.14   Stacked dominoes.

---

[217] D.P. Bertsekas, *Incremental Gradient, Subgradient, and Proximal Methods for Convex Optimization: A Survey*, arXiv:1507.01030 [cs.SY], 2015.

[218] L. Csato, M. Opper. *Sparse on-line Gaussian processes*, Neural Computation, 14(3), pp. 641–668, 2002.

[219] B. Lakshminarayanan, D.M. Roy, Y.W. Teh, *Mondrian Forests: Efficient Online Random Forests*, arXiv:1406.2673 [stat.ML], 2014.

[220] M. Kearns, *Thought of hypothesis boosting*, 1988.

[221] M. Kearns, L. Valiant, *Cryptographic Limitations on Learning Boolean Formulae and Finite Automata*, Proceedings of the twenty-first annual ACM symposium on theory of computing, 1989.

The question was answered in affirmative by Schapire and Freund[222] by formulating the AdaBoost learning meta-algorithm for supervised classification problems, in which the dependent variable y, as well as its predictions f_k, take on only two values, 1 and -1.

The idea of boosting is twofold: learning on someone else's errors and voting by majority. More specifically, AdaBoost manages K weak learners (classifiers) that can be of any type supporting weighted learning.[223] The algorithm involves two sets of weights: voting weights and learning weights. The voting weights α_i are used in the final model

$$F(\mathbf{x}) = \text{Sign}\left(\sum_{k=1}^{K} \alpha_k f_k(\mathbf{x})\right), \tag{2.91}$$

where each learner's prediction $f_k(\mathbf{x}) = \pm 1$. The learning weights w_{ki} for classifier k and observation i depend on in-sample misclassification error of previous learners 1 through $k-1$ combined. In a binary classification with outcomes ± 1, instead of MSE (2.31), it is common to use an exponential loss function

$$L[f_k] = \frac{1}{N} \sum_{i=1}^{N} e^{-f_k(\mathbf{x}_i)y_i} \tag{2.92}$$

penalizing incorrect classifications (e) more than correct ones (e^{-1}). Minimization of the expected exponential loss (2.92) for the combined vote (2.91) gives a closed-form recursive solution for both learning weights w_{ki} and the voting weights α_k. The recursion starts with the first classifier using equal learning weights for all training sample:

$$F_1(\mathbf{x}) = f_1(\mathbf{x}), \quad w_{1i} = 1, \quad i = 1,\ldots,N. \tag{2.93}$$

On each step k, the classification error rate is measured as

$$\varepsilon_k = \frac{1}{2N} \sum_{i=1}^{N} [1 - F_k(\mathbf{x}_i)y_i]. \tag{2.94}$$

[222] Y. Freund, R.E. Schapire, *A decision-theoretic generalization of on-line learning and an application to boosting.* Journal of Computer and System Sciences, 55, pp. 119–139, 1997.
[223] Any learning algorithm, even not supporting weights explicitly, can be fed with duplicate observations with the number of copies proportional to the observation weight.

The error rate is used for setting the voting weight

$$\alpha_k = \frac{1}{2} \log \left(\frac{1 - \varepsilon_k}{\varepsilon_k} \right), \qquad (2.95)$$

a decreasing function of the error. The kth step classification is given by the current weighted majority vote,

$$F_k(\mathbf{x}) = \text{sign} \left(\sum_{k'=1}^{k} \alpha_{k'} f_{k'}(\mathbf{x}) \right). \qquad (2.96)$$

The error rate of this classification is used to adjust the learning weights passed to the next classifier, so more attention is given to previously misclassified items:

$$w_{k+1,i} = w_{ki} \exp(-\alpha_k F_k(\mathbf{x}_i) y_i). \qquad (2.97)$$

If there are infinitely many different weak classifiers, the boosted classifier can theoretically be 100% correct. But wouldn't boosting too many learners amount to overfitting and a large generalization error? To a big surprise, it was found empirically that generalization error often keeps decreasing with the number of AdaBoost iterations, even after the training error reaches zero.

A number of explanations of the AdaBoost lack of overfit was published, including classification margins,[224] additive model view,[225] finite VC dimension of base learners,[226] shrinking properties of linear smoothers,[227] ergodicity of boosting weights in a dynamical system framework,[228] and self-averaging or large interpolating learners.[229]

[224] P. Bartlett, Y. Freund, W.S. Lee, R.E. Schapire, *Boosting the margin: a new explanation for the effectiveness of voting methods*, The Annals of Statistics, 26(5), pp. 1651–1686, 1998.

[225] J. Friedman, T. Hastie, R. Tibshirani, *Additive logistic regression: a statistical view of boosting (with discussion and a rejoinder by the authors)*, The Annals of Statistics, 28(2), pp. 337–407, 2000.

[226] G. Blanchard, G. Lugosi, N. Vayatis, *On the rates of convergence of regularized boosting classifiers*, Journal of Machine Learning Research, 4, pp. 861–894, 2003.

[227] P. Bühlmann, B. Yu, *Boosting with the L_2 loss: Regression and classification*, Journal of the American Statistical Association, 98, pp. 324–339, 2003.

[228] J. Belanich, L.E. Ortiz, *On the Convergence Properties of Optimal AdaBoost*, arXiv: 1212.1108 [cs.LG], 2012.

[229] A.J. Wyner, M. Olson, J. Bleich, D. Mease, *Explaining the success of AdaBoost and random forests as interpolating classifiers*, Journal of Machine Learning Research, 18, pp. 1–33, 2017.

Boosting resistance to overfitting makes it a popular meta-algorithm for classification trees.

There are also regression versions of boosting commonly called *gradient boosting machines* (GBM).[230,231] The simplest formulation of regression boosting is for OLS linear models.[232] If K predictors x_{ki}, $k = 1,\ldots,K$, $i = 1,\ldots,N$, are normalized to zero mean and unit variance, we start with a univariate regression

$$y = \beta_1 x_1 + \varepsilon_1. \tag{2.98}$$

The second predictor x_2 is used to explain the residual error of the first one:

$$\varepsilon_1 = \beta_2 x_2 + \varepsilon_2, \tag{2.99}$$

etc. The iteration proceeds as follows:

$$\beta_1 = \text{Cov}(x_1, y), \quad \varepsilon_1 = y - \beta_1 x_1,$$

$$\beta_{k+1} = \text{Cov}(x_{k+1}, \varepsilon_k) = \text{Cov}(x_{k+1}, y) - \sum_{k'=1}^{k} \beta_{k'} \text{Cov}(x_{k'}, x_{k+1}). \tag{2.100}$$

The boosted linear regression prediction,

$$y = \sum_{k=1}^{K} \beta_k x_k, \tag{2.101}$$

depends on the ordering of the features x_k. Regression boosting is equivalent to the additive model (2.54) with linear $f_k(x)$. As seen from Eq. (2.100), OLS boosting depends only on covariances of the features and the target and can therefore be run on the smaller dataset of online covariances described in Sec. 2.4.13. Gradient boosting can also be used with non-MSE loss functions and nonlinear base learners, regression trees being among most popular. To prevent overfitting, regression

---

[230] J.H. Friedman, *Stochastic Gradient Boosting*, Computational Statistics and Data Analysis, 38, pp. 367–378, 1999.

[231] G. Ke, Q. Meng, T. Finley, T. Wang, W. Chen, W. Ma, Q. Ye, T.-Y. Liu, *LightGBM: A Highly Efficient Gradient Boosting Decision Tree*, In: Advances in Neural Information Processing Systems 30 (NIPS 2017).

[232] R.M. Freund, P. Grigas, R. Mazumder, *A new perspective on boosting in linear regression via subgradient optimization and relatives*, The Annals of Statistics, 45(6), pp. 2328–2364, 2017.

boosting iteration may need an early termination and/or shrinkage modifications.

One way to look at multi-dimensional ML, and boosting in particular, is *sloppy gradient descent* when minimizing training loss. Stochastic gradient descent and early stopping in deep learning (Sec. 2.4.4) are examples of such sloppy minimization. In OLS learning, the loss function

$$L(\boldsymbol{\beta}) = \frac{1}{2}(\mathbf{y} - X\boldsymbol{\beta})^2,$$

$$\frac{\partial L}{\partial \beta_k} = -b_k + \sum_{k'} C_{kk'}\beta_{k'}, \tag{2.102}$$

is minimized by the solution of the linear system $\partial L/\partial \boldsymbol{\beta} = 0$:

$$\beta_k^{(OLS)} = \sum_{k'} C_{kk'}^{-1} b_{k'},$$

$$C_{kk'} = \text{Cov}(x_k, x_{k'}), \tag{2.103}$$

$$b_k = \text{Cov}(x_k, y).$$

Here C is the feature covariance matrix. The OLS solution (2.103) delivers the exact minimum of the training loss. As we saw in Sec. 2.4.10, multivariate OLS regression can overfit due to looking into too much detail beyond bona fide structure. Ridge regression (Sec. 2.4.11.6) shifts learning in the direction of univariate regressions by increasing the diagonal elements of C.

OLS boosting iteration (2.100) is equivalent to minimizing the OLS training loss function (2.102) with an effectively triangular covariance matrix C: $C_{kk'} = 0$ for $k' > k$. Erasing all elements of C above its diagonal is a pretty curious way of shrinkage. In general, multi-dimensional learning must involve some kind of shrinkage or regularization that can be seen as a way of *deterioration* of in-sample loss minimization with potential out-of-sample performance benefits. We don't always want the "correct" minimum of the training loss. There are usually one or just a few exact ways to minimize the training loss function. There are infinitely many inexact or sloppy ways to do so, and this makes ensemble learning by boosting more art than science.

Boosting seems to have better theoretical foundations in classification learning, including more evidence of overfit resistance, than in regression. A good prediction of the sign of future asset return is better than a bad prediction of the actual return, so boosted classification of future returns into positive and negative can be a reasonable alternative to regression learning.

2.4.15 Twicing

In a bag of 1000 coins, 999 are fair and one is fake with tails on both sides. A coin is drawn from this bag and flipped 10 times, landing tails each time. Find the probability that it is the fake coin.

From a quant interview

In the examples of Sec. 2.4.14, boosting was run by iterating multiple learners, such as univariate OLS regressors using distinct features $\mathbf{x}_k$, for predicting the same target y. It is also possible to boost a single learner operating on the same feature space. Let

$$\hat{y}^{(1)} = f(\mathbf{x} | \{\mathbf{x}_i, y_i\}) \qquad (2.104)$$

be the prediction, for feature point $\mathbf{x}$, made by the learner trained on the sample $\{\mathbf{x}_i, y_i\}$. The learner can be used again to explain (or smooth) the residuals

$$\tilde{y}_i^{(1)} = y_i - \hat{y}^{(1)}. \qquad (2.105)$$

Adding such "second-guess" prediction to the first one, we have the model

$$\hat{y}^{(2)} = \hat{y}^{(1)} + f\left(\mathbf{x} | \{\mathbf{x}_i, \tilde{y}_i^{(1)}\}\right). \qquad (2.106)$$

This procedure of learner *twicing* was proposed by Tukey.[233] It is interesting to note other, more famous contributions of John Tukey to the English language which include the words *bit* and *software*.[234] Eq. (2.106) can be further iterated leading to what is known as L_2 boosting.[235]

---

[233] J.W. Tukey, *Exploratory data analysis*, Addison-Wesley, 1977.

[234] D.L. Donoho, *High-Dimensional Data Analysis: The Curses and Blessings of Dimensionality*, Invited lecture at Mathematical Challenges of the 21st Century, AMS National Meeting, Los Angeles, CA, USA, August 6-12, 2000.

[235] P. Bühlmann, J. Gertheiss, S. Hieke, T. Kneib, S. Ma, M. Schumacher, G. Tutz, C.-Y. Wang, Z. Wang, A. Ziegler, *Discussion of "The Evolution of Boosting Algorithms" and "Extending Statistical Boosting,"* Methods of Information in Medicine, 56(3), pp. 436–445, 2014.

The prediction of a linear OLS learner (2.40) is

$$f(\mathbf{x}|\{\mathbf{x}_i, y_i\}) = \mathbf{x}'(X'WX)^{-1}(X'WY), \qquad (2.107)$$

where the uppercase matrices contain the training data and W is a diagonal matrix of weights. Since the residuals of linear regression are orthogonal to the features,

$$X'W(Y - \hat{Y}) = 0, \qquad (2.108)$$

twicing a linear OLS learner results in zero correction to the original prediction.

On the other hand, non-OLS learners can be twiced or boosted in a meaningful way. For example, kernel smoothers described in Sec. 2.4.11 make predictions also linear in the training targets but without the residual orthogonality:

$$f(\mathbf{x}_i|\{\mathbf{x}_i, y_i\}) = S\mathbf{y}, \qquad (2.109)$$

where S is a $N \times N$ row-stochastic smoothing matrix and N is the training sample size. The row-stochastic property means that the sum of each row of S equals 1.[236] Successive single-learner boosting predictions at the training points are built as follows:

$$\hat{\mathbf{y}}^{(1)} = S\mathbf{y},$$
$$\hat{\mathbf{y}}^{(k+1)} = \hat{\mathbf{y}}^{(k)} + S(\mathbf{y} - \hat{\mathbf{y}}^{(k)}). \qquad (2.110)$$

Recursion (2.110) is solved in a closed form,

$$\hat{\mathbf{y}}^{(k)} = S\sum_{j=0}^{k-1} (1 - S)^j \mathbf{y} \qquad (2.111)$$
$$= [I - (I - S)^k]\mathbf{y},$$

where I is the $N \times N$ identity matrix. If, as is often the case for linear smoothers, all eigenvalues of $I - S$ are smaller than 1 by absolute value, infinitely many rounds of boosting converge to an interpolation $\hat{y}_i = y_i$. This is obviously an overfit. Bühlmann and Yu[237] analyze symmetric smoothing splines (Sec. 2.4.11) and provide analytical estimates for the optimal number of boosting rounds k. The weaker the learner, the larger the optimal number of boosting or twicing rounds.

---

[236] This is equivalent to $(1,\ldots, 1)$ being an eigenvector of S with the eigenvalue 1.

[237] P. Bühlmann, B. Yu, *Boosting with the L_2 loss: Regression and classification*, Journal of the American Statistical Association, 98, pp. 324–339, 2003.

2.4.16 Randomized learning

Random numbers should not be generated with a method chosen at random.

Donald Knuth

Several examples of ML algorithms using random inputs in addition to training data have been mentioned earlier. Outside pure math, there is no such thing as a random number or sequence. In physical sciences aka "real life," randomness appears as a result of the Lyapunov exponential sensitivity to initial conditions leading to classical chaos. Quantum-mechanical description of the micro world is intrinsically probabilistic, but it tends to average out to deterministic at the macro level. In computing, a pseudorandom number generator is a deterministic algorithm producing a sequence of bits or numbers that don't repeat over many iterations, tend to be far away from each other, generate a reasonably uniform histogram, and meet some other requirements depending on the application. The more demanding application include Monte Carlo simulation, e.g., for random sampling when computing integrals over a multi-dimensional probability distribution (Sec. 2.3). There are several reasons for machine learning algorithms to use random numbers.

1. Data splitting for cross-validation (Sec. 2.4.8) and bootstrap. Both k-fold and leave-one-out CV can use random samples to guarantee little bias in the test data selection.
2. Hyperparameter optimization. Minimization of the test error, a noisy and expensive-to-evaluate function of hyperparameters, benefits from a combination of exploitation of the regions found to be good so far with randomized exploration of new regions of the hyperparameter space. Reinforcement learning is a branch of ML concerned with an optimal exploration-exploitation tradeoff.
3. Generic initial conditions. Many algorithms need a user-provided initialization. For example, a K-means clustering (Sec. 3.5.2) needs a specification of the initial centroids. Doing this with random numbers all but guarantees that the initial condition is *generic*, meaning without any special symmetry or bias that can potentially affect the algorithm. The outcome of the algorithm is still deterministic, and it can be easily modified by choosing a different random seed to ascertain the algorithm stability. Initial weights in DNNs are also often

chosen randomly and then updated by learning. Global minimization of the DNN training error, a highly non-convex optimization problem, is not usually found, but a random initialization helps find better local minima.[238]

4. Computational cost. When computing resources are limited, it is best to allocate them where they help the most. Other parameters can be filled with generic, or random, values. Randomized neural nets with static weights imputed to most nodes is an example of this approach (Sec. 2.4.5). Design of task-specific neural topology was found to be done much faster by comparing different architectures with mostly random weights,[239] due to the empirical observation that the net topology alone is a major part of the success of feature learning. Stochastic configuration network (SCN) employs incremental addition of randomized hidden layers and OLS learning of the output weights to build an optimal-size neural network.[240]

5. Theoretical tractability. A randomized state of a network is much simpler to describe and to analyze than a trained state. This allows to gain more understanding into the role of different neural architectures in their learning and generalization ability.[241]

6. In some ML models, random numbers are intrinsic to the learning design. Examples include random forest[242] (Sec. 2.4.6) and the restricted Boltzmann machine (RBM) (Sec. 2.4.5).

7. Randomized optimization. Virtually all ML algorithms use a version of minimization of a training loss function. When the function is non-convex, various heuristics are used for a better approximation of a global minimum. Well-known randomized optimization heuristics include stochastic gradient descent (SGD) and simulated annealing.

[238] A. Daniely, R. Frostig, Y. Singer, *Toward Deeper Understanding of Neural Networks: The Power of Initialization and a Dual View on Expressivity*, arXiv:1602.05897 [cs.LG], 2017.

[239] A.M. Saxe, P.W. Koh, Z. Chen, M. Bhand, B. Suresh, A.Y. Ng, *On Random Weights and Unsupervised Feature Learning*, In Proceedings of the 28th Int. Conf. on Machine Learning, Bellevue, WA, USA, 2011.

[240] D. Wang, M. Li, *Stochastic Configuration Networks: Fundamentals and Algorithms*, arXiv:1702.03180 [cs.NE], 2017.

[241] C. Gallicchioa, S. Scardapane, *Deep Randomized Neural Networks*, arXiv:2002.12287 [cs.LG], February 2021.

[242] L. Breiman, *Random Forests*, Machine Learning, 45, pp. 5–32, 2001.

8. Regularization. Stochastic gradient descent was found to have a regularization effect in deep learning (Sec. 2.4.12) and also in a more general context.[243] Dropout (Sec. 2.4.11.9) is an explicit randomized DNN regularization.

2.4.17   Latent structure

> *Prove that $\sum_{n=0}^{\infty} 3^{-n(n+1)/2}$ is irrational.*
>
> From a quant interview

Learning targets observable in the future by currently observed features is not the only paradigm of machine learning. One can also model data that is never observed directly but affects the observables. Examples include:

1. Mixture model is a way of density estimation. Given a dataset $\{z_i\}$ and a hypothesis that it is drawn from a combination of several specific, often Gaussian, distributions, one can estimate the parameters of the components and their weights in the mix. This setting is typically handled using the expectation maximization (EM) algorithm, a version of maximum likelihood estimation (Sec. 2.3.2).

2. Latent semantic analysis (LSA) is a method of NLP seeking to associate text semantics with the distribution of words in documents. Identification of few topics from multiple words involves low-rank approximations for a term-document frequency matrix. Such approximation can be based on singular value decomposition (SVD) or nonnegative matrix factorization (NMF). Similar approaches are used in collaborative filtering (Sec. 3.7) and PLS (Sec. 3.5.1).

3. Hidden Markov Model (HMM) is a method of time series prediction based on a latent structure subject to statistical inference. The HMM postulates the existence of distinct latent states, $x_1, \ldots, x_K$, affecting a time series of outcomes y_i. Transitions between the unobserved states are assumed to form a Markov chain with certain transition probabilities. The observed y is assumed to be a noisy consequence of the current state x. HMM algorithms include estimation of the state transition probabilities $P(x_i|x_j)$, the output probability $P(y|x)$

---

[243] I. Amir, T. Koren, R. Livni, *SGD Generalizes Better Than GD (And Regularization Doesn't Help)*, arXiv:2102.01117 [cs.LG], 2021.

consistent with the observations of ys, the current state x, and, ultimately, the expected next outcome y.

4. Deep neural networks (Sec. 2.4.4) can be also seen as implementing a latent structure by hidden layers. DNN-based learners tend to supersede HMM for speech recognition tasks.[244]

Latent models can be viewed as generative models seeking to recover a low-dimensional structure generating observed data. In the market context, hidden state transitions are meant to model market regime changes with different modes of predictability of future returns.

2.4.18   No free lunch and AutoML

Find the maximum number of pieces a convex pizza can be cut into by 10 straight cuts.

From a quant interview

The list of usable ML learning algorithms is much longer than the OLS regression and nonparametric methods mentioned earlier. Just one class of learners based on neural networks (Sec. 2.4.4) is a subject of research perhaps comparable, by the number of publications, to all combined physics starting with Newton. There is no single best ML technique applicable to all (or most) datasets, a statement sometimes referred to as "No free lunch" (NFL) theorem.[245,246]

The NFL theorem has a tradition of misunderstanding and frivolous interpretation, and this author will be no exception. Loosely speaking, the NFL theorem in the ML context says that any two learners perform, out of sample, identically *on average over all possible datasets*. Without a precise definition of the averaging, however, this statement echoes a situation known under the ML cliché of *Garbage in, garbage out* (GIGO), because an "average" dataset is more likely garbage than it is not.

Alternatively, we can consider one dataset with a meaningful learnability. The NFL theorem then says that whenever a learner performs

[244] A.L. Maas, P. Qi, Z. Xie, A.Y. Hannun, C.T. Lengerich, D. Jurafsky, A.Y. Ng, *Building DNN Acoustic Models for Large Vocabulary Speech Recognition*, arXiv:1406.7806 [cs.CL], 2015.

[245] D.H. Wolpert, *The Lack of A Priori Distinctions Between Learning Algorithms*, Neural Computation, 8(7), pp. 1341–1390, 1996.

[246] D.H. Wolpert, W.G. Macready, *No Free Lunch Theorems for Optimization*, IEEE Transactions on Evolutionary Computation, 1(1), 1997.

well on one set of features, it must perform poorly on some other features. A trivial example is a sample $\{\xi_i, y_i\}$ with $\mathrm{Mean}(\xi) = 0$ and the ground truth $y = \xi^2$. A linear OLS learner will work perfectly for the feature $x_1 = \xi^2$ and badly for the feature $x_2 = \xi$. On the other hand, a nonparametric learner such as a kernel smoother (Sec. 2.4.6) would show an intermediate performance on both x_1 and x_2.

No free lunch in machine learning means we have to pay a meaningful price to learn something meaningful. The price normally goes beyond a pure automatic process and is usually expressed in terms of an inductive bias and educated feature engineering (Sec. 2.4). Once the bill is paid, the researcher need not be concerned with fatalistic interpretations of the NFL theorem.[247,248]

The best suited ML algorithm is data/feature dependent, and it pays to understand both your data and domains of applicability of your learners. For example, more complex learners such as DNNs are better suited for low-noise complex-pattern data such as vision, text, or speech. For high-noise financial data, low-dimensional linear regression learners are good candidates, except when a nonlinearity is expected based on financial reasoning (Sec. 2.4.6). It is also possible that no algorithm will deliver a meaningful out-of-sample prediction due to data nonstationarity (Sec. 2.7) resulting in a GIGO effect.

No free lunch implies that it takes a nontrivial human effort involving rounds of feature engineering, exploratory data analysis (EDA), ML model selection and fitting, validation, and tuning to arrive at the best possible forecast—assuming such thing exists. This makes the job of a quant analyst often frustrating: you never know whether all possible alpha has been extracted from a dataset, so you can move on to the next project, or there is more to it, and how close you are to ruining it by overfitting.

It appears difficult to build a machine learning system performing all necessary research steps, especially EDA and forming inductive biases (Sec. 2.4), automatically and unsupervised. On the other hand, once this job can be done by a rational quant researcher, why not by an AI-powered machine? Given that ML algorithms can be trained

---

[247] C. Giraud-Carrier, F. Provost, *Toward a justification of meta-learning: Is the no free lunch theorem a show-stopper?* in Proceedings of the ICML-2005 Workshop on Meta-learning, Bonn, Germany, 2005.
[248] J. McDermott, *When and Why Metaheuristics Researchers Can Ignore "No Free Lunch" Theorems*, arXiv:1906.03280 [cs.NE], 2019.

to detect internet porn,[249] why not automate the evaluation of "chart porn" in exploratory data analysis? There is indeed an effort underway, both academic[250] and commercial,[251] to create a software layer for automated pipeline of selecting suitable learning algorithms and tuning their hyperparameters in a human-like, or perhaps a bit more systematic, manner. This "learning to learn" framework encroaching on the NFL theorem is called AutoML.[252,253,254,255]

There exists an interesting view[256] that a key to the recent AI/ML progress was the availability of useful training datasets rather than new algorithms. The explosive rise of data in the internet era, while the way people read, speak, and see has been essentially unchanged, could then explain the improvements in the machine processing of text, speech, and image by hypertuning the neural networks and other ML algorithms. On the other hand, noisy and non-stationary financial data, while ample, appear more difficult for automated deep learning.

2.4.19   Computer power and machine learning

People who are more than casually interested in computers should have at least some idea of what the underlying hardware is like. Otherwise the programs they write will be pretty weird.

Donald Knuth

Machine learning uses computational resources, which can be quantified by data storage, network throughput, random access memory

---

[249] Cambridge Consultants, *Use of AI in online content moderation*, Report produced in behalf of the U.K. Office of Communications, 18 July, 2019. Available at https://www.ofcom.org.uk/research-and-data/internet-and-on-demand-research/online-content-moderation.

[250] https://www.automl.org.

[251] https://research.aimultiple.com/auto-ml-software.

[252] T. Elsken, J.H. Metzen, F. Hutter, *Neural Architecture Search: A Survey*, arXiv: 1808.05377 [stat.ML], 2018.

[253] Q. Yao, M. Wang, Y. Chen, W. Dai, Y.-F. Li, W.-W. Tu, Q. Yang, Y. Yu, *Taking Human out of Learning Applications: A Survey on Automated Machine Learning*, arXiv: 1810.13306 [cs.AI], 2018.

[254] E. Real, C. Liang, D.R. So, Q.V. Le, *AutoML-Zero: Evolving Machine Learning Algorithms From Scratch*, arXiv:2003.03384 [cs.LG], 2020.

[255] https://github.com/windmaple/awesome-AutoML.

[256] A. Wissner-Gross, *Datasets Over Algorithms*, https://edge.org/response-detail/26587, 2016.

(RAM), and CPU instructions needed to perform learning tasks. Storage and RAM are measured in bytes, and CPU usage in floating-point operations (FLOPs).[257] There is also an additional cost of data input/output (I/O), which can be significant for non-optimal or non-local data storage.

The time it takes to run an ML task is proportional to the FLOP requirements which can be estimated based on the amount of data and the "Big-O" complexity level of the algorithm. The process time also depends on hardware (CPU, GPU, or TPU) type and any tasks parallelization by multithreading, multiprocessing, or cluster computing. Within a single compute node, the performance can dramatically depend on the process memory management: whether or not memory is accessed in large contiguous blocks and most actively used data fits in the CPU cache. L1/L2 cache access is about two orders of magnitude faster than general RAM access. While the system memory may be ample and cheap, the cache is not, and a process with a larger memory footprint is less likely to hit the cache. Storage order and size of numpy arrays in Python affects the cache efficiency. Compiled languages such as C++ provide more control of memory management and efficient design. While technology and numbers are subject to change, it is useful to visualize a few time scales summarized by Peter Norvig[258] along with other meaningful programming advice:

execute typical instruction	1 ns (nanosecond)
fetch from L1 cache memory	0.5 ns
branch misprediction	5 ns
fetch from L2 cache memory	7 ns
mutex lock/unlock	25 ns
fetch from main memory	100 ns
send 2K bytes over 1 Gbps network	20 μs (microsecond)
read 1MB sequentially from memory	250 μs
fetch from new disk location (seek)	8 ms (millisecond)
read 1MB sequentially from disk	20 ms
send packet US to Europe and back	150 ms

---

[257] Here FLOPs is a plural of FLOP, not to be confused with FLOP/second, a measure of processor speed called FLOPS.

[258] P. Norvig, *Teach Yourself Programming in Ten Years*, available at norvig.com.

The costs of data transmission and storage, I/O, RAM, and arithmetic operations keep changing due to hardware improvement and evolving cloud computing. With new security and legal compliance standards setting foot in the Infrastructure-as-a-Service (IaaS) business, many quant funds are moving their computational infrastructure to commercial cloud platforms. The major cloud providers include Amazon Web Services (AWS), Google Cloud Platform (GCP), Microsoft Azure, and IBM Cloud. Due to the competition among the providers and economies of scale, cloud infrastructure is generally cheaper and more scalable than on-premise computing. Among the difficulties of adopting cloud computing are the cost and latency of moving big data, access to real-time exchange data for high-frequency execution, and legacy information technology. The landscape of cloud computing is changing at a fast pace and shows signs of commoditizing through spot market mechanisms[259] such as those found in the Amazon EC2 pricing model. Computing power is now delivered over the internet pretty much like electrical power is delivered by utilities to consumers over the electrical grid. It is not impossible that, one day, cloud FLOPs, storage terabytes, and ML-as-a-service (MLaaS)[260] will be traded on an exchange like oil and copper are traded now.[261,262]

A typical quant trading business would use data storage on at least a terabyte (10^{12} bytes) scale or much larger, depending on available datasets, time granularity of historical market data, and storage formats. RAM requirements depend on how much of the historical data needs to be loaded in a process memory. RAM needed for a large equity universe is on the order of gigabytes (10^9 bytes) or larger depending on whether the research process supports cross-sectional data loading and online learning (Sec. 2.4.13). Even though it is common to use 64-bit floating-point (`float64` or `double`) data arrays, most (or all) raw

---

[259] S. Shastri, D. Irwin, *Cloud Index Tracking: Enabling Predictable Costs in Cloud Spot Markets*, arXiv:1809.03110 [cs.NI], 2018.

[260] T. Hunt, C. Song, R. Shokri, V. Shmatikov, E. Witchel, *Chiron: Privacy-preserving Machine Learning as a Service*, arXiv:1803.05961 [cs.CR], 2018.

[261] P. De Filippi, M. Said Vieira, *The Commodification of Information Commons: The Case of Cloud Computing* (May 31, 2014). 16 Colum. Sci. & Tech. L. Rev. 102 (2014), Available at SSRN: https://ssrn.com/abstract=2488127.

[262] D.E. Irwin, P. Sharma, S. Shastri, P. Shenoy, *The Financialization of Cloud Computing: Opportunities and Challenges*, Proceedings of 26th International Conference on Computer Communication and Networks (ICCCN), 2017.

numeric data such as asset prices can be stored and loaded in a 32-bit precision while performing all linear algebra, and other arithmetic with potential for error accumulation, in 64 bits.

The amount of computation on data in RAM depends on ML algorithms and can scale well or poorly with the problem size. In a PAC-learnable (Sec. 2.3.6) setting such as image classification, ML accuracy is a growing function of the FLOP budget. Some of the most expensive ML hypertuning sessions can take of the order of 10^{20} FLOPs.[263] This requires specialized massively parallel hardware, as common CPUs perform only of the order of 10^9 FLOPs per core per second. There are efforts[264] to build specialized photonic circuits for neural networks with the goal to speed up learning by 3 orders of magnitude compared with traditional electronic chips.

This author has run 10-year simulations trading $\sim 10^2$ parallel books (Sec. 7.3) on various online ML combinations of $\sim 10^3$ alphas for $\sim 10^4$ stocks taking about 20 GB of RAM and $\sim 10^{15}$ FLOPs. The quality of financial forecasting is fundamentally limited by market efficiency and does not seem to scale with raw computer power very far. Forecasting future asset returns needs ideas more than supercomputers.[265] On the other hand, it is easy to make computation very hard by a poor code design.

In contrast, the role of computer power is central to a different financial endeavor of cryptocurrency mining used as a *proof-of-work* (PoW) in a distributed blockchain.[266] Bitcoin and other cryptocurrencies introduce an artificial or competitive scarcity of new blocks on the distributed ledger making the probability of a successful hash matching of order 10^{-20}.[267] This results in a massive expense of CPU or

[263] E. Real, S. Moore, A. Selle, S. Saxena, Y.L. Suematsu, J. Tan, Q. Le, A. Kurakin, *Large-Scale Evolution of Image Classifiers*, arXiv:1703.01041 [cs.NE], 2017.

[264] M.A. Nahmias, T.F. de Lima, A.N. Tait, H.-T. Peng, B.J. Shastri, *Photonic Multiply-Accumulate Operations for Neural Networks*, IEEE Journal of Selected Topics in Quantum Electronics, 26(1), 2020.

[265] A similar observation was made about computation of turbulence: M.B. Isichenko, *Can computer simulation predict the real behavior of turbulence?* Comments on Plasma Physics and Controlled Fusion, 16(3), pp. 187–206, 1995.

[266] S. Nakamoto, *Bitcoin: A Peer-to-Peer Electronic Cash System*, https://bitcoin.org/bitcoin.pdf, 2009.

[267] A. Gervais, G.O. Karame, V. Capkun, S. Capkun. *Is Bitcoin a Decentralized Currency?*, IEEE Security & Privacy, 12(3), pp. 54–60, 2014.

application-specific integrated circuits (ASIC) power. The worldwide crypto-mining electrical power consumption approaches that of whole Switzerland.[268] The bubbling nature of cryptocurrency trading has been criticized by leading economists.[269,270] There have been proposals to redirect the PoW effort from computing block hashes to more sensible tackling of NP-hard optimization problems.[271]

Computational resources used for deep learning (Sec. 2.4.4) are also substantial when expressed in financial, energy, and environmental costs. Due to progress in hardware design and growing cloud computing infrastructure, the financial costs of computation keep decreasing exponentially, with recent signs of flattening (Fig. 2.15).

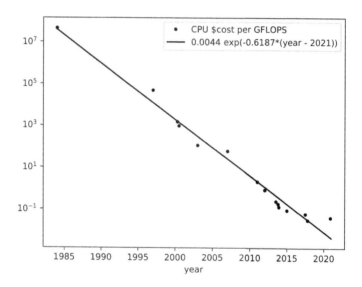

Figure 2.15 Cost of CPU hardware per 10^9 FLOPS speed and OLS linear fit of log cost vs year. Source: https://en.wikipedia.org/wiki/FLOPS data for 1984–2020.

[268] Cambridge Bitcoin Electricity Consumption Index, https://www.cbeci.org.

[269] P. Krugman, *Bubble, Bubble, Fraud and Trouble*, New York Times, Jan 29, 2018.

[270] R.J. Schiller, *Cryptocurrencies and the old allure of new money*, Project Syndicate, May 2018.

[271] C.G. Oliver, A. Ricottone, P. Philippopoulos, *Proposal for a fully decentralized blockchain and proof-of-work algorithm for solving NP-complete problems*, arXiv:1708.09419 [cs.DC], 2017.

Energy consumption per FLOP is also decreasing[272] but not as fast. It is estimated[273] that running a single NLP ML research pipeline results in CO_2 emission twice the one produced by the body of the researcher in her lifetime. Given that a significant amount of ML computing is done in the cloud, tracking the environmental footprint of cloud providers gives a meaningful indication of the global costs of machine learning. Amazon, the world's largest cloud operator, consumes 7×10^{10} KWh per year, or 8 GW on average, which accounts for about 2% of the total electrical consumption in the US.[274]

Data on computational costs incurred by quantitative research and trading are not readily available, but the budgets are known to be significant, even for IT infrastructure outsourced to cloud providers, and are not expected to drop. Instead, quants simply crunch more numbers—or care less about efficient software design—as more memory and processor power become available. Wirth's law reads: *Software gets slower faster than hardware gets faster.*

2.5   Dynamical modeling

A bullet is shot up in the air. What takes longer, its ascent or descent?
From a quant interview

Wouldn't it be nice to discover equations describing time evolution of securities prices, perhaps like Newton's equations predict the orbits of planets in the Solar system? It looks like a long shot, and one can argue that stocks move more like air molecules than planets. Well, even air flows and sound waves have their equations in hydrodynamics and acoustics. In addition, we are talking about just a few thousand securities traded by a few million people, or computer programs for that matter—numbers much smaller than, say, 6×10^{23}.

It is not impossible to formulate reasonable dynamical, and therefore predictive, equations modeling securities and market participants,

---

[272] Y. Sun, N.B. Agostini, S. Dong, D. Kaeli, *Summarizing CPU and GPU Design Trends with Product Data*, arXiv:1911.11313 [cs.DC], 2020.

[273] E. Strubell, A. Ganesh, A. McCallum, *Energy and Policy Considerations for Deep Learning in NLP*, arXiv:1906.02243 [cs.CL], 2019.

[274] G. Synek, *Amazon is one of the largest consumers of electricity but is offloading costs onto others*, Techspot, August 20, 2018.

or "agents." Such equations would necessarily include strong model assumptions and depend on parameters not known from first principles but perhaps fittable from historical data. Even standard statistical forecasting bears a hint of dynamics when we require that features thrown into an ML algorithm *make sense*. A number of stochastic dynamical models were proposed for HFT trading[275,276] and statistical arbitrage.[277]

To demonstrate a general idea, consider the following toy model. There is just one security with log price $p(t)$ in continuous time t and n "quant" traders, each using a momentum view of future price, and generating forecasts proportional to past EMA price increments:

$$f_i(t) = \int_{-\infty}^{t} \frac{dp(t')}{dt'} e^{-\gamma_i(t-t')} \gamma_i dt'. \tag{2.112}$$

To make the forecasts different, and thereby encourage the agents to trade with each other, we assume that their EMA horizons γ_i^{-1} are different. The difference of the ith trader's forecast from the mean drives her asset position P_i as follows:

$$\frac{dP_i}{dt} = \alpha(f_i - \bar{f}), \quad \bar{f} = \frac{1}{n}\sum_i f_i \tag{2.113}$$

Eq. (2.113) guarantees conservation of total shares outstanding: $\sum_i P_i = $ const, but supply/demand forces affect the price in proportion to the mean traders' forecast $\bar{f}$:

$$\frac{dp(t)}{dt} = \lambda \bar{f},$$

$$\bar{f} = \frac{1}{n}\sum_{i=1}^{n} \int_{-\infty}^{t} \frac{dp(t')}{dt'} e^{-\gamma_i(t-t')} \gamma_i dt'. \tag{2.114}$$

The constant λ describes a degree of price impact in response to trades or, rather, demand in this case.

Eq. (2.114) is a deterministic integro-differential equation describing dynamics of an asset driven by traders following a very simple set of rules. If the price has been constant in the past, and there is no new

[275] A. Cartea, S. Jaimungal, *Modeling Asset Prices for Algorithmic and High-Frequency Trading*, Applied Mathematical Finance, 20:6, 512-547, 2013.
[276] T. Chakraborty, M.J. Kearns, *Market Making and Mean Reversion*, Proceedings of the 12th ACM conference on Electronic commerce, June 2011, pp. 307–314.
[277] M.D. Lipkin, M. Avellaneda, *A Dynamic Model for Hard-to-Borrow Stocks*, 2009. Available at SSRN: https://ssrn.com/abstract=1357069.

information, no one wants to trade it. However, a small perturbation can change the situation. Following a standard technique of Fourier analysis for linearized perturbations,[278] assume the log price $p(t) \propto e^{\gamma t}$. Substituting this into (2.114) gives

$$\sum_{i=1}^{n} \left(1 + \frac{\gamma}{\gamma_i} \right)^{-1} = \frac{n}{\lambda}, \qquad (2.115)$$

a polynomial equation of degree n with all real solutions, at most one of them positive. An elementary analysis of (2.115) for $\gamma_i > 0$ shows that a positive solution for γ exists if $\lambda > 1$. In other words, if price is sufficiently impacted by trades, a small price perturbation will generate an exponentially growing trading activity. Of course, nothing in the linear model (2.114) prevents the price perturbation from unlimited growth. Adding stabilizing nonlinear terms will likely make the instability switch to a state of dynamical chaos, whose picture is not foreign to financial markets.[279]

It is not expected that a market caricature with a closed-form solution can describe anything practical. One can try building more complex and realistic agent-based (Sec. 2.6) dynamical models incorporating relevant behavioral aspects, such as greed and fear, trade rules, constraints,

---

[278] For a linear equation like (2.114), the exponential form can be used to work out a general solution by a Fourier ($e^{-i\omega t}$) or Laplace ($e^{\gamma t}$) transform.

[279] This model has earned the author his first financial honorarium of $1,000 while still in academia. Another physicist, who just lost a university research grant and joined a small hedge fund, was thinking where to start. He started with inviting for consultation a few colleagues he knew (all of them are cited in this book). This author was one of those consultants running, at the time, research on plasma instability and turbulence at the University of California and had no clue about trading. So writing up a theory of trading instability on the flight to New York seemed like a natural thing to do. After failing to secure a tenured position in the academia, the author followed in the footsteps of many other scientists heading to the financial industry. It was ridiculously easier to get a full-time quant job in NYC than to get approved for a part-time (or, rather, half-salary) research position at the University of California, San Diego: vetting for the latter was as thorough as if it was a nomination for the Nobel Prize. Available teaching positions were few and far between. An interesting chart in *Physics Today* showed the median age of the US faculty vs year after WWII: almost a straight line with a slope just below 1.0—a stark testimony to the US healthcare success. Soon after starting as a quant analyst at Caxton, the author was offered a visiting position at the Institute for Advanced Study. What would have been a dream job a few months earlier was painfully declined.

and market impact, fit their numerical solutions to historical data—in the hope to predict just a little bit of the future.

2.6   Alternative reality

In a mirror, your right hand becomes left and the left hand becomes right. Why doesn't your head become legs?

From a quant interview

In addition to regularization and cross-validation, another idea for preventing overfitting is running forecasts on "alternative facts," or synthetic market data. Running ML on an ensemble of synthetic prices will likely be unforgiving for models overfit on the single real history.

Depending on inputs used by a model, synthetic data need to include prices and perhaps trading volumes and other fields. Generating meaningful synthetic fundamental or analyst data appears infeasible, but one can introduce exogenous random price shocks modeling arrival of fundamental information. If prices are correctly adjusted for corporate actions, cax are usually unimportant, so synthetic data do not need any.

To provide a meaningful testing field, the synthetic data should resemble real data in some respects. Price time series should be weakly autocorrelated (poorly predictable). Returns should be distributed similarly to real returns, with fat tails corresponding to infrequent material events. Equities should exhibit a degree of collective movement, for example following a factor structure (Sec. 4.2). If a fundamental, that is, not limited to purely technical market and PCA, factor decomposition and residuals are used, synthetic securities need to mimic real ones in the security master. One can generate purely statistical daily returns with a specified covariance.[280]

Agent-based modeling[281,282] was proposed to generate market data by running scenarios of agents interacting with the market. Agent

[280] J. Raimbault, *Second-order control of complex systems with correlated synthetic data*, Complex Adapt. Syst. Model, 7(4), 2019.

[281] Bonabeau, E., 2002, *Agent-based modeling: Methods and techniques for simulating human systems*. Proceedings of the National Academy of Sciences, 99(3), pp. 7280–7287, 2002.

[282] A. Turrell, *Agent-based models: understanding the economy from the bottom up*, Bank of England Quarterly Bulletin, 56(4), pp. 173–188, 2016.

engagement rules, more realistic than those described in Sec. 2.5, were used to generate real-looking synthetic data.[283]

Recently, synthetic markets have been generated[284] using generative adversarial networks (Sec. 2.4.5).

Another, more modest kind of rewriting of the price history makes sense for a portfolio that has been trading for some time at a large size. As described in Sec. 2.1.1, the real prices are "contaminated" by the impact created by this portfolio.[285] Using the portfolio trade history and an impact model (Sec. 5.2), historical prices can be modified to erase the self-impact and thereby remove the unwanted self-fulfilling prophecy effect.

2.7 Timeliness–significance tradeoff

A bus is departing from a bus stop located at (0,0) and goes East (along the x axis). The departure time is uncertain. For a passenger located at (1,-1) it may be too late to go to the bus stop. However, the bus will stop for the passenger anywhere on the x axis once the passenger is already there. If the speed of the passenger is U and the speed of the bus is V > U, how should the passenger proceed to maximize the probability of catching the bus?

From a quant interview[286]

---

[283] N. Raman, J.L. Leidner, K. Vytelingum, G. Horrell, *Synthetic Reality: Synthetic market data generation at scale using agent based modeling*, Simudyne/Refinitiv Technical Paper, 2019.

[284] J. Li, X. Wang, Y. Lin, A. Sinha, M.P. Wellman, *Generating Realistic Stock Market Order Streams*, arXiv:2006.04212 [q-fin.ST], June 2020.

[285] Equity prices can be viewed as a result of net impact made by aggressive traders and absorbed by market makers and passive participants. A portfolio manager generally wants to predict price moves due to all other traders, not herself. The latter, self-impact part belongs to trading costs and portfolio construction (Chapter 6) rather than forecasting.

[286] This question, along with an elegant optics-based solution, is due to Boris Kuvshinov who dealt with exactly this situation when it was a practice in the USSR to send scientists and engineers, seen as non-essential workers, to countryside to help in seasonal agricultural work. The author's early theoretical physics research at the Kurchatov Institute looked indeed relaxed: Our office gatherings involved discussions, tea, chess, and soccer: the barbed-wire-fenced territory of the national lab included a few small soccer fields. The actual work was usually done at home late at night. Later in the US, it took some work habits adjustment to do business in the office.

Bias-variance is not the only tradeoff quants need to handle. The statistical theory of learning relies heavily on the existence of an underlying joint feature-target distribution $F(\mathbf{x}, y)$ with a non-vanishing mutual information (Sec. 2.3.1). In a financial context, this is only an approximation. The reason is that financial markets are nonstationary and statistical distributions keep changing with time, including due to quants learning their models and impacting the markets with trades based on what they learn. Depending on the type of features, and to stay relevant for an immediate future, one may have to limit the training sample to a relatively short recent past, e.g., by exponential moving weighting (Sec. 2.4.13), at the expense of statistical significance. In a low-noise setting, such localized learning leads to a better performance.[287] For financial predictions, a smaller training sample implies a weaker explanatory power (Sec. 2.3.6), often to the extent of making a model unlearnable and useless.

One can think of efficient markets as those where most predictive models for asset prices are unlearnable and useless.

2.8   Grouping

N men and N women are registered at a dating site. Each participant reviews the profiles of opposite-sex participants and ranks them in order of preference. Now the site manager needs to compute a perfect match defined as a list of N heterosexual couples such that no two couples can swap partners without hurting someone's preference. What algorithm can be used to compute the perfect match?

From a quant interview[288]

ML algorithms run on samples of data, which can be selected in many different ways. In the statarb context, one can learn/predict future returns for a single asset, a group of assets, or the whole trading universe.

A single-asset approach is more common for foreign exchange, futures, and other asset classes where the instruments are either few or have little in common.

---

[287] L. Bottou, V. Vapnik, *Local Learning Algorithms*, Neural Computation, 4(6), pp. 888–900, 1992.
[288] A solution to a broader version of this two-sided market problem won a 2012 Nobel Memorial Prize in Economics.

For equities, there are more possibilities depending on features and the forecast horizon. HFT machine learning can be stock-specific due to a large amount of available training data. For more stable learning, data can be aggregated for multiple stocks having similar microstructure characteristics such as *tick size* relative to price and bid-ask spread. Mid- and low-frequency forecasts can be learned in groups by liquidity or industry. Forecasts for a large equity universe can be learned in aggregate, but then it is common to learn future residual (Sec. 4.4), rather than full, returns. For a smoother distribution, these returns can be normalized to unit serial variance, i.e., by stock volatility.

Forecasts based on fundamental and accounting data (Sec. 2.1.3) may be better learnable by industrial sector, defined by the Global Industry Classification Standard (GICS), or another group with relatively uniform capital structure and reporting conventions.

In general, the choice of ML grouping is dictated by the competition of focus (similar assets) with sample size. Suitably selected smaller groups are more statistically homogeneous. Larger groups help statistical significance and lower generalization error (Sec. 2.3.6). This *focus-size tradeoff* is not unlike the bias–variance tradeoff (Sec. 2.3.5).

2.9 Conditioning

Estimate by how much the length of the day will change if the British change their traffic law from left- to right-hand driving.

From a quant interview

Rich financial datasets (Sec. 2.1) pose the problem of using many predictors simultaneously (Sec. 2.4.10). Conditioning is one way of expressing nonlinear interaction of predictors. Given two predictors, x_1 and x_2, a researcher can study a model for $y = f(x_1)$ while *controlling for* x_2. This can mean, for example, building two models, $y = f_\pm(x_1)$, respectively trained and tested on data subsets with $x_2 > 0$ and $x_2 < 0$. For categorical x_2 such as stock industry or sector label, one may wish to run separate model by stock group (Sec. 2.8), especially if industry-specific financials x_1 are involved.

Control, or condition variable can be a macro and not necessarily company specific. For example, one can learn a forecast differently in bull market, during recession, or condition the forecast on a major index or VIX.

Given relatively many available predictors and conditioning variables, there can be exponentially many ways of conditioning, so trying them all is both computationally infeasible and prone to the curse of dimensionality (Sec. 2.4.10). Domain knowledge and inductive bias (Sec. 2.4) are needed to keep conditioning options to a reasonable minimum.

2.10   Pairwise predictors

What is the expected value (both guesstimate and exact formula) of the maximum of one million independent numbers drawn from the normal distribution $\mathcal{N}(0, 1)$?

From a quant interview

Stocks are correlated with each other in both noisy and meaningful ways. Market beta (2.2) is widely used as a measure of sensitivity of an individual security to the broad stock market. It is equally possible to compute sensitivities, either contemporaneous or lagged, of stocks to each other. On a time-lagged basis, such univariate regressions, if statistically meaningful, would provide single name forecasts.

It would probably work better if the researcher had a prior on some stock pairs being leader/follower, for example due to a supply chain or competition relationship (Sec. 2.1.5), or for the dimensionality of the problem reduced by CCA (Sec. 3.5.1) or otherwise. This author attempted to datamine such predictive relationships among all N-choose-two pairs using only prices. The idea failed to generate any meaningful pnl but stayed as an insightful interview question. Given enough datasets, one can find good correlations for bad reasons.[289]

Another way of connecting individual time series is *cointegration*[290] meaning that two time series, up to scaling, are moving roughly together. A natural cointegration of two stocks occurs after an all-stock or cash-and-stock merger announcement of ABC acquiring XYZ for a

---

[289] https://www.tylervigen.com/spurious-correlations.

[290] C.W.J. Granger, P. Newbold, *Spurious regressions in econometrics*, Journal of Econometrics, 2(2), pp. 111–120, 1974.

specified number of ABC shares at some future date, while there is still some uncertainty whether or not the deal will go through (Sec. 2.1.6).

Pairs trading was historically one of the first long-short quantitative strategies not requiring a sophisticated portfolio construction. Any market neutral equity book can be decomposed into overlapping stock pairs. Conversely, multiple pair forecasts, as linear combinations, can be translated into individual asset forecasts as described in Sec. 2.11.

2.11 Forecast for securities from their linear combinations

100 families live in a town of 100 houses. No family likes their house, but there is a moving permutation that would make everyone happy. By town rules, multi-way swaps are not allowed. Any two families can swap their houses, but no family can move more than once a day. Prove that everyone can be made happy in two days.

From a quant interview

The mean reversion example of Sec. 2.2.1 is for residual stock returns. As mentioned in Sec. 2.2.2, factor return forecast can have a different, momentum-type structure. One can choose one or more factor models and generate forecasts for residuals and, optionally,[291] factor returns, which are then put together into full security return forecast as in Eq. (4.9). Both residual and factor returns/forecasts are known combinations of individual stock returns/forecasts.

More generally, a quant researcher can generate multiple forecasts for various linear combinations of stocks, which can be factors, residuals, stock indices, ETFs with known stock composition, or stock pairs. For a meaningful portfolio construction (Chapter 6), however, we need a forecast for each of N individual securities rather than their combinations. Assume that contemporaneous forecasts g_i are available for K groups defined as linear combinations of stocks:

$$g_k = \sum_s A_{ks} f_s, \qquad (2.116)$$

---

[291] Unlike residuals, factor forecasts are less common due to fewer datapoints for factors than for individual stocks.

The $K \times N$ matrix of coefficients A_{ks} is known and possibly sparse. The system can be either under- or over-determined, so we cannot directly solve for stock forecasts f_s. But since we know at least something about future returns, there must be a way to translate this knowledge into individual forecasts. One way to do it is to use the Occam's parsimony principle by looking for the simplest—meaning the smallest—forecasts f_s meeting or approximating Eq. (2.116). We therefore pose a least square loss problem,

$$\mathbf{f} = \text{argmin} \left[\sum_k \left(g_k - \sum_s A_{ks} f_s \right)^2 + \lambda \sum_s f_s^2 \right]. \qquad (2.117)$$

The λ penalty term, even if small, makes sure securities not included in any group end up with zero forecast. Eq. (2.117) is recognized as ridge, or Tikhonov-regularized, regression. In the limit of small regularization, $\lambda \to 0$, the solution is given by the Moore-Penrose matrix inverse, also known as *pseudo inverse*:

$$f_s = \sum_k A_{sk}^+ g_k, \quad A^+ = \lim_{\lambda \to 0^+} (A'A + \lambda I)^{-1} A'. \qquad (2.118)$$

The $N \times K$ pseudo inverse A^+ exists even for rank deficient $A'A$ and can be computed using SVD or eigendecomposition. Hastie et al.[292] remark that the pseudo inverse can be also computed by a gradient descent of Eq. (2.117) for $\lambda = 0$. The iteration goes as

$$\mathbf{f}^{(i)} = \mathbf{f}^{(i-1)} + tA'(\mathbf{g} - A\mathbf{f}^{(i-1)}) \qquad (2.119)$$

and converges to $A^+\mathbf{g}$ for the step size t smaller than the reciprocal maximum eigenvalue of $A'A$.

The pseudo inverse solution (2.118) can be generalized to include weights for groups and/or stocks to express various preferences or conviction levels. For example, if some of the group forecasts g_k are trusted

[292] T. Hastie, A. Montanari, S. Rosset, R.J. Tibshirani, *Surprises in High-Dimensional Ridgeless Least Squares Interpolation*, arXiv:1903.08560 [math.ST], 2019.

more than others, group forecast weights w_k can be introduced in the first sum in (2.117) resulting in the *weighted pseudo inverse*

$$A_W^+ = \lim_{\lambda \to 0^+} (A'WA + \lambda I)^{-1} A'W, \qquad W = \mathrm{Diag}(w_k), \qquad (2.120)$$

which is a generalization of $A^+ = A_I^+$, I being a the identity matrix.

Another example of a linear combination is the forecast itself. Given several reasonably good forecasts ϕ_{ks}, $k = 1, \ldots, K$, a portfolio with positions proportional to ϕ_{ks} is expected to generate a positive return g_k. So one way of combining a set of forecasts ϕ_{ks} into one is given by

$$\mathbf{f} = \boldsymbol{\phi}^+ \mathbf{g}. \qquad (2.121)$$

Other approaches are discussed in Chapter 3.

2.12 Forecast research vs simulation

Out-of-sample MSE or a similar loss function (Sec. 2.3.3) is an important measure of forecast performance, but not the only one used by portfolio managers. In the field where more important quantities are measured in the units of USD, not readily reducible to SI but having a psychological bearing, important consideration is also given to the Sharpe ratio, drawdown, and other nonlinear statistics. There are also trading costs depending on forecast horizon and portfolio turnover. These measures are computed in a simulated trading over historical data.

Even though it is possible (and common) to incorporate forecast learning in a trading simulator (Chapter 7), the complexity of a joint search for optimal forecast and portfolio parameters can be excessive and will require many more simulations than when forecasts and portfolio construction are dealt with separately. Too many simulations over the same history can lead to the trap of overfitting by exhausting the available test sample (Sec. 2.4.2). It is therefore important to separate forecast research (with suitable overfit protection) from portfolio construction that has its own complexities (Chapter 6). In addition, if a forecast is intended for combining with others (Chapter 3), the value of optimizing the forecast, e.g., to beat slippage costs, is limited.

Simulated trading pnl should not be a criterion in forecast research (Sec. 7.2). In the Unix philosophy, complex tasks are divided into small, well-tested programs of minimal scope cooperating via pipes or files. Quantitative portfolio management is a complex program that can also benefit from this philosophy. Feature engineering should generate informative features and pass them on to forecasts. Forecasts should predict future returns over specified horizons as best they can and pass them to forecast combining, finally followed by portfolio construction. Criteria of feature and forecast performance should concentrate on metrics such as mutual information (Sec. 2.3.1), MSE, or MAD (Sec. 2.3.3). Section 3.8 lists additional considerations for forecast research. A trading simulator is just a pipe connecting all the components together.

Chapter 3

Forecast Combining

1. *Alice and Bob own bad watches telling time with independent random errors. Alice's watch says it is 1 pm, and Bob's 2 pm. What time is it?*
2. *Alice and Bob are quant analysts at a hedge fund. They independently develop forecasts from unrelated data sources. Asked about the AAPL stock return for tomorrow, Alice's forecast is 1 bps, and Bob's 2 bps. What is the forecast for AAPL?*

From a quant interview

Given the multiplicity of financial datasets and forecasting ideas, quants soon arrive at a library of forecasts to be used for trading. A "clean" way of trading a separate book for each forecast is more common than one might think, but there are clearly better ways. For example, crossing opposite trades from such books internally will save on trading costs, but this is still suboptimal because individual books would forego many trading opportunities seen as not worth the cost.

Combining weak forecasts into a potentially stronger forecast (when pointing in the same direction) will make more profitable trades possible. In the case of netting (opposite sign) forecasts there is saving in terms of cost of capital, which is often expressed as a limit on the portfolio gross market value (GMV).

Combining alphas for portfolio trading is another kind of alpha. The question of how to combine forecasts has been raised in other fields as well, most frequently in econometrics.[1] Econometric forecast combining almost always means equal-weight or a similar static averaging of individual predictions, which is difficult to improve by more complicated methods.[2] We should note that econometric data such as GDP or unemployment numbers are admittedly better predictable than stock prices, perhaps because it is difficult to trade unemployment.

Static averaging of predictions is one of the most venerable methods of *ensemble learning*. Equal-weight combining should be considered as the baseline benchmark for more flexible and dynamic combining methods.[3]

Forecast combining in portfolio management has not been widely discussed in the literature. An approach of signal weighting or "risk budgeting" has been described in the context of low-turnover asset management with transaction costs modeled by a portfolio's "law of motion" with inertia.[4] As before, our goal is to build a combined prediction of future asset returns without regard to any costs or portfolio construction, whose tasks are best handled separately (Chapters 5 and 6).

---

[1] J. M. Bates and C. W. J. Granger, *The Combination of Forecasts*, Operational Research Quarterly, 20(4), pp. 451–468, 1969.

[2] A. Timmerman, *Chapter 4: Forecast Combinations*, in Handbook of Economic Forecasting, Volume 1, pp. 135–196, 2006.

[3] When the library of forecasts developed for the author's portfolio reached a few dozen items, an "advanced" forecast selection process was implemented as follows. A cron job was set up for daily runs of simulations for (a) the current production forecast mix, (b) for books with each used forecast removed one at a time, and (c) for books with each currently unused forecast added one a time. The marginal pnl of forecasts removed or added were displayed on an internal web portal. The production forecast mix was regularly updated by removing bad used and adding good unused forecasts based on visualization of the marginal pnl charts. The forecast-combining process based on this "chart porn" wasn't particularly systematic and wouldn't consistently beat the static equal-weight benchmark.

[4] R. Grinold. *Signal weighting*, The Journal of Portfolio Management, 36(4), pp. 24–34, 2010.

3.1   Correlation and diversification

A hedge fund has built a thousand strategies such that each two are 10% correlated with each other. Estimate how many effectively independent strategies the fund really has.

For a future quant interview

Among the main goals of combining alphas are diversification of risk and a better Sharpe ratio. A diversification is usually associated with a portfolio of multiple securities. The next logical step is to diversify multiple portfolios driven by different forecasts or use multiple alphas for each of the multiple securities.

The simplest baseline combination is averaging. The fundamental idea of investment diversification takes root in the law of large numbers, which says that the variance of the average of N independent random variables, e.g., portfolio returns, decreases as N^{-1} for large N (Sec. 2.3.4). Independence is important for the risk reduction. If all investments are 100% correlated, all eggs are still in one basket.

What if the correlations are less than 100%? Will adding a large number of moderately correlated alphas or portfolios reduce the risk asymptotically down to zero? The answer is easy to work out under the assumption of normally distributed returns[5] $\mathbf{x} \sim \mathcal{N}(\boldsymbol{\mu}, C)$. The average

$$\overline{x} = \frac{1}{N} \sum_i x_i \qquad (3.1)$$

is then also normal with the mean and the variance given by

$$\text{Mean}(\overline{x}) = \overline{\mu} \equiv \frac{1}{N} \sum_i \mu_i,$$

$$\text{Var}(\overline{x}) = \frac{1}{N^2} \sum_{ij} C_{ij}. \qquad (3.2)$$

If the variables are independent, $C_{ij} = 0$ for $i \neq j$, we have

$$\text{Var}(\overline{x}) = \frac{\text{Var}(x)}{N}, \qquad (3.3)$$

indicating a good diversification by the law of large numbers.

---

[5] The normality assumption is not critical. By the central limit theorem, the sum and the average of many random numbers will be asymptotically normal for large N.

Now assume, for the sake of simplicity, normalized x_i with the variances $C_{ii} = 1$ and an average positive[6] correlation ρ for C_{ij}, $i \neq j$. Then Eq. (3.2) gives

$$\mathrm{Var}(\overline{x}) = \frac{1 + \rho(N-1)}{N} > \rho. \qquad (3.4)$$

No matter how many correlated variables are being averaged, the variance of the result cannot be made smaller than a certain minimum. Averaging the returns of multiple strategies does increase the Sharpe ratio

$$\mathrm{Sharpe}(\overline{x}) = \frac{\mathrm{Mean}(\overline{x})}{\mathrm{Var}^{1/2}(\overline{x})}$$

$$= \overline{\mu}\sqrt{\frac{N}{1 + \rho(N-1)}} < \frac{\overline{\mu}}{\sqrt{\rho}}, \qquad (3.5)$$

but it can't be increased by a factor of more than $\rho^{-1/2}$.

This simple calculation sets a hard limit on static diversification of correlated portfolios. The law of large numbers can be defeated by even modest correlations. For correlations of order ρ, there is no point in having many more than ρ^{-1} portfolios. One can do a little better by dynamic weighting instead of static averaging and implementing asset-level combining, as discussed later in this chapter.

3.2   Portfolio combining

Given two strategies with uncorrelated pnl time series and Sharpe ratios 3.0 and 4.0, what is the maximum possible Sharpe of the combined portfolio?

From a quant interview

It is not uncommon, if suboptimal, to build an equity portfolio with positions proportional to a signal, which can be a one-day forecast or a similar predictive data (Sec. 6.1). To develop an initial intuition into forecast combining, we can think in terms of combining portfolios, or books. Consider two books, $\mathbf{P}_1$ and $\mathbf{P}_2$, defined as vectors of

---

[6] As seen from Eq. (3.2), negative correlations of returns are nice to have, but they rarely happen.

dollar position for each security.[7] We want to combine the two books into one,

$$\mathbf{P} = \alpha_1 \mathbf{P}_1 + \alpha_2 \mathbf{P}_2, \tag{3.6}$$

with an expected better performance than either component. The performance is measured in terms of the pnl,

$$Q_i = \mathbf{P}_i \cdot \mathbf{R}, \tag{3.7}$$

where $\mathbf{R}$ is the (random) vector of realized security returns, and trading costs are ignored for now. We are interested in the mean and the variance of the combined book pnl

$$Q = \alpha_1 Q_1 + \alpha_2 Q_2. \tag{3.8}$$

These mean and variance are:

$$E(Q) = \alpha_1 E(Q_1) + \alpha_2 E(Q_2).$$
$$\text{Var}(Q) = \alpha_1^2 \text{Var}(Q_1) + \alpha_2^2 \text{Var}(Q_2) + 2\alpha_1 \alpha_2 \text{Cov}(Q_1, Q_2). \tag{3.9}$$

Employing the idea of mean-variance optimization (Sec. 6.3), we can maximize expected pnl while controlling for risk in terms of the pnl variance. Using a Lagrange multiplier k, the maximization of the utility

$$U(\alpha_1, \alpha_2) = E(Q) - \frac{k}{2} \text{Var}(Q) \tag{3.10}$$

yields the optimal combining weights

$$\alpha_1 = \frac{1}{k(1 - \rho^2)} \frac{S_1 - \rho S_2}{\sqrt{\text{Var}(Q_1)}},$$
$$\alpha_2 = \frac{1}{k(1 - \rho^2)} \frac{S_2 - \rho S_1}{\sqrt{\text{Var}(Q_2)}}. \tag{3.11}$$

Here additional notation is introduced for the pnl correlation

$$\rho = \frac{\text{Cov}(Q_1, Q_2)}{\sqrt{\text{Var}(Q_1)\text{Var}(Q_2)}} \tag{3.12}$$

---

[7] It is also implied that the books P_{ids} are known historically, so various statistics can be computed. Instead of explicitly using the date index d, we treat the position and the pnl data as random processes with realization by date.

and the (non-annualized) Sharpe ratios

$$S_i = \frac{E(Q_i)}{\sqrt{\mathrm{Var}(Q_i)}}. \tag{3.13}$$

The Lagrange multiplier k, also known as *risk aversion coefficient*, is simply a book size scale in our example. At the optimum of the utility (3.10), the mean is twice the variance term: $E(Q) = k\mathrm{Var}(Q)$, which is typical of linear-quadratic functions. The Sharpe ratio of the optimal combined book is then

$$S = \frac{E(Q)}{\sqrt{\mathrm{Var}(Q)}} = \left(\frac{S_1^2 - 2\rho S_1 S_2 + S_2^2}{1 - \rho^2}\right)^{1/2}. \tag{3.14}$$

Eq. (3.14) has a neat geometric interpretation: if S_1 and S_2 are the sides of a triangle and the correlation ρ is the cosine of the angle between the two sides, then S is the diameter of the circumscribed circle of this triangle[8] (Fig. 3.1).

Expression (3.14) satisfies the inequality $S \geq \max(S_1, S_2)$.[9] When controlling for risk, the combined book is never worse than either component. A book with larger Sharpe and smaller variance gets a larger weight. A losing book with $S_2 < 0$ helps in combination with a negative weight.

What is less intuitive, if the correlation of two performing books gets high enough, $\rho > S_2/S_1 > 0$, the optimal weight α_2 for the lower-Sharpe book gets negative, even though that book is profitable by itself. This observation emphasizes an important role of correlations in combining, and also poses an interesting question of pnl attribution (Sec. 3.8.2) for the purpose of compensation of quants working for a combined portfolio (Sec. 3.8).

Combining portfolios becomes even more interesting when there are many of them, and the curse of dimensionality (Sec. 2.4.10) comes into play. Instead of (3.10) we now want to maximize the multi-dimensional utility

$$U(\boldsymbol{\alpha}) = \boldsymbol{\alpha} \cdot \mathbf{Q} - \frac{k}{2}\boldsymbol{\alpha} C \boldsymbol{\alpha}, \tag{3.15}$$

---

[8] This observation was made by Victor Paskhaver.
[9] Note that the limit $\rho \to 1$ does not result in infinite Sharpe, because in this limit the two books become identical up to scaling so the numerator in (3.14) also goes to zero.

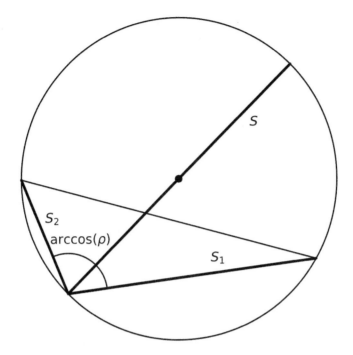

Figure 3.1 Geometric interpretation of the combined Sharpe ratio (3.14) as the diameter of the circumcircle of the triangle formed by component Sharpes. Other things equal, lower correlation ρ (larger angle) results in a higher combined Sharpe ratio.

in which $\mathbf{Q}$ is the K-dimensional vector of the mean book pnls and C is their covariance. The process should be run without lookahead by using, on each time step t, only data observed prior to t, with $\mathbf{Q}_t$ and C_t computed daily on a rolling or EMA basis.

Figure 3.2 presents a basic mathematical experiment of combining 1000 synthetic pnl time series with unit variance $C_{ii} = 1$, unimpressive Sharpe ratios, and significant cross-sectional correlations. The mean-variance utility (3.15) is formally maximized by

$$\alpha^{OLS} = \frac{1}{k} C^{-1} \mathbf{Q}. \tag{3.16}$$

We call this solution OLS by analogy with the simple matrix inversion solving the ordinary least squares (Sec. 2.4.3). Some of the OLS weights can generally be negative. As could be suspected after the examples of

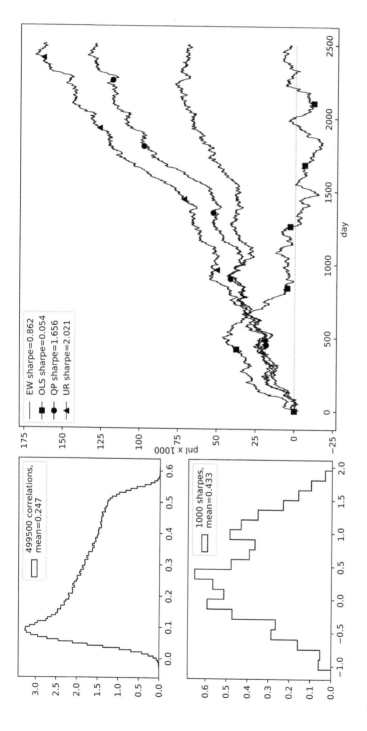

Figure 3.2 Experimental study of combining $K = 1000$ synthetic correlated pnl time series. Left: distributions of $K(K-1)/2$ pairwise daily pnl correlations (top) and K Sharpe ratios (bottom) of the components. Right: combined pnls for equal-weight (EW) benchmark with $\alpha_i \equiv 1$, OLS weights (3.16), QP solution with non-negative weights (3.17), and one with an undisclosed regularization (UR). On any given day, only a few dozen QP or UR weights end up non-zero on average. All weights are dynamically scaled to match the rolling variance of the EW book.

Sec. 2.4.10, the multi-dimensional OLS combining should not fare well out-of-sample in dimensions $K \gg 1$. Figure 3.2 indeed shows that the OLS solution (3.16), which is supposed to handle all correlations correctly, is inferior to the naive equal-weight benchmark (EW), once again showing the curse of dimensionality.

One way to regularize the mean-variance combining is to constrain the weights α_i to be nonnegative. This is also a form of inductive bias based on the idea that we are dealing with mostly performing, albeit mediocre, books, which are not intended for shorting. Maximizing (3.15) subject to $\alpha_i \geq 0$ gives a quadratic programming (QP) solution[10]

$$\alpha^{QP} = \underset{\alpha_i \geq 0}{\operatorname{argmax}} \left[\alpha \cdot \mathbf{Q} - \frac{k}{2} \alpha C \alpha \right]. \qquad (3.17)$$

The experiment of Fig. 3.2 shows that the QP approach is more fruitful, by almost doubling the EW benchmark Sharpe ratio and lowering the drawdown by about a third. Other, data-dependent types of regularization can further improve portfolio combining.

The results of both static and dynamic pnl combining in this exercise are still less than stellar despite operating on a thousand pnl time series. As noted in Sec. 3.1, this many books are excessive given the mean correlation $\rho = 0.25$ used in our experiment. The EW Sharpe of 0.86 is about twice the mean Sharpe of the components, which is consistent with formula (3.5). Smarter combining can improve things by a factor of two or more, but surely not by a factor of $\sqrt{1000}$.

Success of online mean-variance portfolio combining depends on the underlying data and has its correlation-diversification limits, perhaps less stringent than those of static weighting (Sec. 3.1), but apparently in the same scaling ballpark. The NFL theorem (Sec. 2.4.18) rules out a single best ML approach or type of regularization. There are multiple methods for both portfolio-level and asset-level (Sec. 3.3) forecast combining.

---

[10] QP solving algorithms are discussed in the context of portfolio construction in Sec. 6.1.

3.3   Mean-variance combination of forecasts

As argued in Sec. 2.12, combining forecasts by analyzing pnl time series may be not the best idea. Forecasting (including forecast combining) should focus on the best possible prediction of returns and leave portfolio construction alone.[11] Incorporating in the process stock-level returns, as opposed to portfolio-level pnls, also looks like a harder work more likely to pay off.

A first idea is to look for a linear combination of K forecasts minimizing the mean square prediction error:

$$\mathbf{f}(\boldsymbol{\alpha}) = \sum_{i=1}^{K} \alpha_i \mathbf{f}_i,$$

(3.18)

$$\boldsymbol{\alpha} = \texttt{argmin } \texttt{Var}(\mathbf{f}(\boldsymbol{\alpha}) - \mathbf{R}).$$

Eq. (3.18) is recognized as an OLS linear regression of realized returns $\mathbf{R}$, as targets, vs K forecasts $\mathbf{f}_i$ as predictors.[12] If there are just a few forecasts to combine, this is a reasonable approach. But beyond that we expect to hit the curse of dimensionality once again. To minimize the generalization error, one can use constrained regression, ridge or lasso regularization, or overfit-resistant versions of boosting. Note that boosting is not a combination of independent forecasts but rather a framework for their inter-dependent learning (Sec. 2.4.14).

If regularization is broadly viewed as a tighter control over ML output, imposing direct constraints on α_i is just another kind of regularization. Like in Sec. 3.2, one can minimize (3.18) subject to all $\alpha_i \geq 0$. OLS regression with inequality constraints is a QP problem that can be solved about as efficiently as an unconstrained OLS (Sec. 6.1). One can constrain the weights even further by requiring them to sum up to one: $\sum_i \alpha_i = 1$, as is often done in econometric forecast combining.[13] This, together with non-negativity of the weights, would mean a weighted

---

[11] Even though some portfolio construction ideas may bear consequences for forecasting, for example via liquidity-dependent statistical weights to designate more and less important securities.

[12] Eq. (3.18) is a simplified notation for the implied rolling regression that can have both security and date weights.

[13] C.W.J. Granger, R. Ramanathan, *Improved Methods of Combining Forecasts*, Journal of Forecasting, 3, pp. 197–204, 1984.

mean of the pooled forecasts resulting in a likely underestimate[14] of the overall forecast scale. Combined forecast needs to be scaled correctly for optimization balancing expected pnl vs costs (Chapter 6). After all, one of the motivations for combining multiple weak forecasts is to beat trading costs by a stronger combination.

3.4   Combining features vs combining forecasts

Consider K forecasts $\mathbf{f}_i$, $i = 1, \ldots, K$, for the same horizon, all aiming to predict the same future return $\mathbf{R}$. Here again we treat the forecasts and the return as random N-vectors, N being the universe size, with realization by date. From a probabilistic viewpoint, knowing that each $\mathbf{f}_i$ is an expectation, conditional on some features, of $\mathbf{R}$, does not immediately help us to formulate the "combined expectation," a concept sadly missing from probability theory. Instead, we can use the forecasting method recursively and treat the forecasts as a dataset usable as new features. The difference of the forecasts from regular features is that bona fide forecasts—fruits of laborious research—are *better features*. This is a useful prior indicating that the forecasts should probably appear in the combination with nonnegative weights, although some exceptions are possible (Sec. 3.2).

It is natural to ask the following question. If there are K forecasts, each learned on M features, why not just learn a new single forecast on all the KM features combined? The answer lies in the curse of dimensionality (Sec. 2.4.10), a theoretical concept that keeps demonstrating itself empirically, e.g., in the simple examples of Figs. 2.6 and 3.2.

If the number of features n is large, it is better, for reasons of dimensionality reduction (and also maintenance logistics), to split them up among independent learners and then combine the forecasts produced by these learners. Many questions remain. Should there be $n^{1/2}$ learners, each running on $n^{1/2}$ features, or some other feature allocation, e.g., the better the features, the more of them can be fed in one learner? Is feature overlap across learners a good idea? For a very large n, such as 10^6, should one use a deeper hierarchy of forecasts-turned-features (Sec. 3.5.3)?

---

[14] This can be seen from the extreme example of combining K uncorrelated forecasts. In this case the OLS combination is a sum, rather than a mean, of the components.

The answers are unknown and generally data-dependent. There is no free lunch (Sec. 2.4.18).

3.5 Dimensionality reduction

A group of quant analysts receive their end-of-year bonuses. Each analyst wants to know the average bonus without disclosing her own to the group. How can the group figure out the average bonus?

From a quant interview

Approximate low-dimensional representations of high-dimensional data is a popular technique in many data-driven fields.[15] There are several approaches to reduce an unacceptably high dimension in forecast combining. They are based on the idea that, given unavoidable[16] correlations among the forecasts, a thousand forecasts is not really a thousand, but maybe effectively just 20 (Sec. 3.1). After all, how many independent financial data sources are there? A way of combining 10^9 alphas has been reported.[17]

3.5.1 PCA, PCR, CCA, ICA, LCA, and PLS

A physicist took a picture of a decorative street light fixture in Nice, France (Fig. 3.3). The fixture has a square base with sides of length 60 cm and several bulbs inside. The sheet metal walls are perforated in a regular pattern. Find the distance between the light fixture and the physicist.

From a quant interview

---

[15] C.O.S. Sorzano, J. Vargas, A.P. Montano, *A survey of dimensionality reduction techniques*, arXiv:1403.2877v1 [stat.ML], 2014.

[16] Some shops running a centralized alpha pool impose a limit on correlation for any new alpha vs existing alphas, which appears a good practice. However, some quants may have handled this requirement by adding carefully crafted noise to their alphas. This is not much different from a "cobra effect" described in S.D. Levitt, S.J. Dubner, *Freakonomics: A Rogue Economist Explores the Hidden Side of Everything*, William Morrow, New York, 2005.

[17] Z. Kakushadze, W. Yu, *How to Combine a Billion Alphas*, arXiv:1603.05937v2 [q-fin.PM], 2016.

Figure 3.3   Photo and 2003 Estonia Physics Olympiad problem by Prof. Jaan Kalda.

Here we briefly describe a few related acronyms for statistical transformation of predictors and/or targets often used for dimensionality reduction.

Principal component analysis (PCA)[18] is perhaps the most popular dimensionality reduction approach based on the eigendecomposition of the covariance matrix $C_{ij} = \text{Cov}(\mathbf{f}_i, \mathbf{f}_j)$. The idea behind PCA is that K forecasts can be equivalently replaced by K independent linear combinations, while the eigenvectors of C_{ij} provide coefficients hopefully discriminating between more and less "useful" combinations. Upon retaining only the most useful linearly combined forecasts one can hope that few PCA components carry all the important information while avoiding the curse of dimensionality (Sec. 2.4.10). This is essentially a necessary bias-variance tradeoff.

---

[18] J. Shlens, *A Tutorial on Principal Component Analysis*, arXiv:1404.1100 [cs.LG], 2014.

Starting with the largest eigenvalue, the corresponding unit–norm eigenvector gives a linear combination of forecasts having the largest variance possible. Geometrically, if a realization of the K forecasts is treated as a point in a K-dimensional Euclidean space and their distribution as a scatter-plot cloud, the eigenvectors (PCA components) are the semi-axis directions of the cloud approximated as an ellipsoid, and the eigenvalues are the squared semi-axes of the ellipsoid. Smaller eigenvalues correspond to "squeezed" directions of lower data variability and are therefore deemed less useful. Weighted PCA, in the context of security returns rather than forecasts, is discussed in more detail in Sec. 4.5.

Principal component regression (PCR) is a regression of the y target against few, $k \ll K$, principal components of the $\mathbf{x}$ predictors used as new features. In addition to the dimension reduction, the PCR features are orthogonal thereby reducing out-of-sample instability of regression coefficients stemming from collinearity of regressors.

Canonical correlation analysis (CCA)[19] seeks scalar linear combinations of two sets of random variables, for N-dimensional $\mathbf{x}$ and M-dimensional $\mathbf{y}$, maximizing their correlation. The first pair of the *canonical components* is defined by

$$(\mathbf{a}_1, \mathbf{b}_1) = \texttt{argmax}\, \texttt{Cor}(\mathbf{a} \cdot \mathbf{x}, \mathbf{b} \cdot \mathbf{y}). \qquad (3.19)$$

The rest of the pairs are defined similarly under the constraint of

$$\texttt{Cor}(\mathbf{a}_i \cdot \mathbf{x}, \mathbf{a}_j \cdot \mathbf{x}) = \texttt{Cor}(\mathbf{b}_i \cdot \mathbf{y}, \mathbf{b}_j \cdot \mathbf{y}) = 0 \quad \text{for} \quad i \neq j. \qquad (3.20)$$

The CCA components can be computed from the singular value decomposition (SVD) of the $N \times M$ covariance matrix $\texttt{Cov}(\mathbf{x}, \mathbf{y})$.

Independent component analysis (ICA)[20] provides another kind of linear combinations targeting their maximum independence rather than variance. This makes ICA closer to clustering (Sec. 3.5.2) except the similarity between components is minimized rather than maximized. Formally, given a sample of K-dimensional observations $\mathbf{x}$, ICA seeks to represent the data as a linear mixture of statistically independent, in the sense of zero mutual information (Sec. 2.3.1),

---

[19] H. Hotelling, *Relations between two sets of variates*, Biometrika, 28(3-4), pp. 321–377, 1936.

[20] J.V. Stone, *Independent component analysis: a tutorial introduction*. Cambridge, MIT Press, 2004.

k-dimensional components **s**: $\mathbf{x} \sim A\mathbf{s}$ where A is a $K \times k$ mixing matrix. The case $k < K$ gives a dimensionality reduction, although ICA is more general. One can think of a *cocktail party problem* when you are trying to tune into one of several interesting conversations happening in the same room. For Gaussian data, ICA reduces to PCA.[21] ICA is most effective for non-Gaussian components by employing transformation of data maximizing the non-Gaussianity. ICA can be seen as a way of recovering a hidden latent structure.

Latent class analysis (LCA) seeks to represent a distribution of correlated categorical, as opposed to numerical, variables as a combination of a few independent latent classes. Similar to collaborative filtering, solving an LCA problem can involve a nonnegative matrix factorization (NMF) (Sec. 3.7).

Partial least squares (PLS)[22] is an iterative algorithm seeking low-dimensional latent structure as projections from the feature space maximizing covariances with targets. In contrast to PCA or ICA seeking components emphasizing variability or independence only among features, PLS targets both shrinkage of multiple predictors **x** and explanatory power for the target y. The $N \times K$ design matrix X is approximated as

$$X = TP',\qquad(3.21)$$

where P is a $K \times k$ (latent) loadings matrix and the $N \times k$ orthonormal matrix T is chosen to maximize the covariance with the target Y. Similarly to PCA, PCS also involves eigenvectors, but of the matrix $X'YY'X$[23] rather than $X'X$. One can think of the K-vector

$$\mathbf{Q} = Y'X\qquad(3.22)$$

as mean "pnls" generated by the K forecasts used for signal-based portfolio allocation (Sec. 6.1). The matrix

$$X'YY'X = \text{Cov}(\mathbf{Q}, \mathbf{Q})\qquad(3.23)$$

---

[21] J. Shlens, *A Tutorial on Independent Component Analysis*, arXiv:1404.2986 [cs.LG], 2014.

[22] S. Wold, M. Sjöström, L. Eriksson, *PLS-regression: a basic tool of chemometrics*, Chemometrics and Intelligent Laboratory Systems, 58(2), pp. 109–130, 2001.

[23] K.S. Ng, *A Simple Explanation of Partial Least Squares*, 2015.

is the $K \times K$ covariance of the pnls considered in Sec. 3.2. A multi-pass regression method of Kelly and Pruitt[24] is similar to PLS in some respects.

Solving PCA, CCA, and PLS problems can all be implemented as a search for extremal points of the *Rayleigh quotient*

$$\mathcal{R}(\mathbf{w}) = \frac{\mathbf{w} \cdot \mathbf{A}\mathbf{w}}{\mathbf{w} \cdot \mathbf{B}\mathbf{w}} \qquad (3.24)$$

or, equivalently, solving the generalized eigenvalue problem $\mathbf{A}\mathbf{w} = \lambda\mathbf{B}\mathbf{w}$, for suitably chosen matrices $\mathbf{A}$ and $\mathbf{B}$.[25] For high-dimensional data, gradient-based optimization of the Rayleigh quotient can be numerically more efficient than linear algebra.

3.5.2 Clustering

In the US, every fifteenth libertarian is a vegetarian, and every thirteenth vegetarian is a libertarian. Are there more vegetarians or libertarians?

From a quant interview

Once we expect not that many "really independent" forecasts, groups of similar forecasts can be identified as "clusters" and collapsed into their representative means. Clustering is a collection of generic algorithms handling abstract objects along with a measure of their similarity or distance between the objects. There are many clustering algorithms designed for fixed or variable number of clusters, unique or multi-cluster attribution, hierarchical or flat structure, and so forth. What matters the most for forecast combining is the definition of similarity between two forecasts. A similarity function can include a combination of correlation between the forecasts or their pnl time series, co-location of drawdowns, or other patterns.

Clustering can be formulated as an optimization problem,[26] such as minimization of the sum of distances from objects to cluster centroids.

---

[24] B. Kelly, S. Pruitt, *The three-pass regression filter: A new approach to forecasting using many predictors*, Journal of Econometrics, 186(2), pp. 294–316, 2015.

[25] M. Borga, T. Landelius, H. Knutsson, *A Unified Approach to PCA, PLS, MLR and CCA*, Linköping University, Department of Electrical Engineering, 1998.

[26] D. Bertsimas, A. Orfanoudaki, H. Wiberg, *Interpretable clustering: an optimization approach*. Machine Learning, August 2020.

This kind of optimization is typically NP-hard and is solved with approximate heuristic algorithms. Such algorithms include Lloyd, K-means, Gaussian mixture, affinity propagation, correlation clustering, and many others. Some algorithms go beyond heuristics and achieve provable proximity to the exact result.[27]

3.5.3 Hierarchical combining

Q: *Am I correct that 1 stands for True and 0 for False?*
A: *1.*

From a programming discussion forum

When the number of forecasts K becomes too large to be handled with existing algorithms, such as $\propto O(K^3)$ complexity for regularized OLS, or (more importantly) fails out-of-sample due to the curse of dimensionality, the following procedure can help.

Split the forecasts into G groups, each group containing K/G forecasts. $G = K^{1/2}$ is a balanced choice. Alternatively, the groups can be based on clustering. Combine each group independently. Then combine G combined forecasts. This process is related to the interplay of features vs forecasts (Sec. 3.4).

The uncertainty of how to split the forecasts into groups could be turned into advantage by running many, potentially random, splits and bagging combined results.

3.6 Synthetic security view

Another view of a forecast is that of a synthetic ETF-like instrument. The instrument can be defined as \$1 (GMV or Euclidean norm) invested in the underlying universe in proportion to the forecast values f_{ds}. Unlike equities, holding such instrument involves a cost of carry—trading costs of the dynamically rebalanced underlying portfolio. Costs are generally irrelevant for the purpose of forecast combining.

---

[27] S. Chawla, K. Makarychev, T. Schramm, G. Yaroslavtsev, *Near Optimal LP Rounding Algorithm for Correlation Clustering on Complete and Complete k-partite Graphs*, arXiv:1412.0681 [cs.DS], 2014.

A forecast combination is a portfolio, presumably long-only, of such synthetics. The expected return of a forecast can be approximated with its past return or perhaps predicted using time-series analysis.[28] Optimizing a portfolio of synthetics involves their covariance matrix. Applying a mean-variance optimization to this portfolio directly would lead to a high-dimensional problem similar to (3.18), which is to be avoided.

Similar to stock factor models, one could introduce risk factors for the synthetics[29,30] and only then do the mean-variance. Risk factors for securities are interpreted as common themes of group movements (Sec. 4.2). In the case of the synthetics, these groups can be identified in terms of underlying datasets, learning styles, or technical approaches using PCA or clustering.

Another use of the forecast view as a synthetic instrument was mentioned in Sec. 2.11 where a single forecast is extracted from forecasts for multiple linear combinations.

3.7   Collaborative filtering

A middle school class of 42 students is arranged in 6 rows with 7 students in each row. The tallest student in each row is called a "giant", and the shortest in each column is called a "dwarf". Who is taller: the shortest giant or the tallest dwarf?

From a quant interview[31]

Among other approaches to combined, or collaborative, forecasting are the methods of *collaborative filtering* (CF).[32] CF algorithms are used in

---

[28] R.J. Hyndman, G. Athanasopoulos *Forecasting: principles and practice*, OTexts, 2018.

[29] Z. Kakushadze, *Combining Alphas via Bounded Regression*, Risks, 3(4), pp. 474–490, 2015.

[30] Z. Kakushadze, W. Yu, *Decoding Stock Market with Quant Alphas*. Journal of Asset Management 19(1) 38-48, 2018.

[31] A middle school student attending the Math-M-Addicts problem solving program found it difficult to answer this question and turned to learning a programming language for an experimental math approach.

[32] F. Meyer, *Recommender systems in industrial contexts*, arXiv:1203.4487 [cs.IR], 2012.

Netflix movie picks, Amazon product recommendations, and Google's PageRank search algorithm, to name a few.

The basic idea is that two different users, if known to like or dislike certain items the same way, could predict each other's preference for previously unseen items. Formally, given an $I \times J$ sparse matrix of preferences A_{ij} of user i for item j, the problem is to fill in the blanks. If forecasts are treated as users and stocks as items then CF could provide data for stocks not covered by all forecasts or deemed unreliable.

There are two main approaches to solving the CF problem. One is based on neighborhood methods, or clustering of users by similarity of their taste. The other approach is based on hidden or latent variables, often in the form of fitting the preference matrix as a product of two low-rank matrices,

$$A_{I \times J} = U_{I \times K} V_{K \times J}, \quad K \ll I, J. \tag{3.25}$$

The intuition behind the low-rank factorization is search for a simple underlying structure or, in ML language, low model complexity to prevent overfitting. Low-rank modeling of covariance matrices used for factor risk models (Sec. 4.2) is based on a similar intuition. Eq. (3.25) is not unlike a singular value decomposition (Sec. 4.5) constrained to K largest eigenvalues. In the context of movie ratings, the related PCA- or LCA-like factors (Sec. 3.5.1) turn out to reflect movie genres such as comedy, romance, or drama. A limitation of CF methods is that they can't rate movies not yet seen by anyone.

The approximate factorization (3.25) is often performed under additional constraints. Requiring that all elements of the matrices U and V be nonnegative leads to a nonnegative matrix factorization (NMF) problem. The standard formulation of NMF is minimizing the Frobenius norm error $||A - UV||$ over nonnegative matrices U and V and a given intermediate size K. This problem is known to be NP-hard,[33] but there are iterative algorithms converging to an acceptable local minimum.[34] A useful feature of the latent structure

---

[33] S.A. Vavasis, *On the complexity of nonnegative matrix factorization*, arXiv:0708.4149 [cs.NA], 2007.

[34] D.D. Lee, H.S. Seung, *Learning the parts of objects by non-negative matrix factorization*, Nature, 401, pp. 788–791, 1999.

solved by NMF is its interpretability,[35] including due to an equivalence of NMF to the K-means clustering problem[36] (Sec. 3.5.2).

3.8   Alpha pool management

If the correlation between A and B is 90% and the correlation between B and C is 90%, what is the correlation between A and C?

From a quant interview

Earlier in this chapter, the case was made for a portfolio driven by a combined forecast based on the effort of multiple quant researchers operating in a collaborative or silo environment. An extension of this logic is *alpha capture* (Sec. 2.1.12), or *alpha pool* framework applicable to a broader class of contributors including discretionary traders. Maintaining a diversified alpha pool and running a smart centralized forecast combining algorithm and cost-aware portfolio optimization is perhaps the most efficient quant business model used by the more advanced quantitative funds like Renaissance Technologies. For better or for worse, the No free lunch theorem (Sec. 2.4.18) suggests there is no simple way to know if your alpha combining is the best possible. This makes large alpha pool operators run multiple forecast combining books. By some accounts,[37] the cost of alpha combining can be 30% of the cost of developing the alphas in the first place.

There are two sides to forecast combining. The first one is a win–win synergy when individual forecasts are not strong enough to beat trading costs (Chapter 5) but the combination is above the threshold. Netting of positions and trades and reduced alpha risk (Sec. 4.9) for weakly or negatively correlated forecasts is also a major plus of combining. The other side is adversarial: positively correlated forecasts compete for weight in the mix. Many weights can end up zero or even negative

---

[35] X. Fu, K. Huang, N.D. Sidiropoulos, W.-K. Ma, *Nonnegative Matrix Factorization for Signal and Data Analytics: [Identifiability, Algorithms, and Applications]*, arXiv:1803.01257 [eess.SP], 2018.

[36] C. Ding, X. He, H.D. Simon, *On the Equivalence of Nonnegative Matrix Factorization and Spectral Clustering*, Proceedings of the 2005 SIAM International Conference on Data Mining.

[37] Z. Kakushadze, W. Yu, *Decoding Stock Market with Quant Alphas.* Journal of Asset Management 19(1) 38–48, 2018.

(Sec. 3.2). Either way, forecasts contribute to the optimal bottom line in a complicated, nonlinear way, and the sum of the contributions, however computed, does not normally add up to the total. Depending on which effect, synergistic or adversarial, dominates, the forecasts contributions to the pnl can be either super- or subadditive.

Alpha researchers, who may not be directly involved in portfolio trading, are best provided with meaningful guidelines and feedback.

3.8.1 Forecast development guidelines

Unless sourcing alphas as-is, e.g., from existing portfolios, contributions to the alpha pool should follow certain conventions for better downstream results. These conventions can include the following.

3.8.1.1 Point-in-time data. As any other datafeed, forecast records must be timestamped historically with the same intraday time, trading or not, as it would be in real-time production. Universe selection for the forecasts should be also PIT and free of survival bias (Sec. 2.1.2). The time of forecast submission, upon which the contributor gives up write access to the forecast generating process, is an important metadata marking the start of the forecast's true out-of-sample period.

3.8.1.2 Horizon and scaling. A forecast should represent expected return over a specified horizon and be scaled accordingly. This information is naturally available for ML-based forecasts but can be implicit for rule-based trade signals and strategies. Event-based forecasts, e.g., those around earnings announcements or other isolated dates, can have variable horizons. The best horizon and forecast scale can be inferred by regression of future returns vs the signal, but this additional inference step can result in extra noise, especially during periods of forecast underperformance. For better coverage of the horizon spectrum, forecasts can be solicited for a set of standardized horizons such as $h_i = 3^i$ days for $i = 0, 1, 2, ...$, and similarly for any intraday horizons. To generate real long-horizon ML forecasts free of easier shorter-term findings, researchers can exclude shorter returns by learning, on day d, return targets such as

$$y_d^{(i)} = \sum_{d'=d+h_{i-1}}^{d+h_i} R_{d'}. \tag{3.26}$$

Forecast combining can be independently run for each horizon range, and the full "term structure" of the combined forecast can be extracted to feed a multi-period portfolio optimizer (Sec. 6.5).

3.8.1.3 Type of target return.
A forecast should indicate the type of future return being predicted. This can be an actual return, a market-neutral return, a residual return per factor model (Sec. 4.4), or a factor-specific return. Discarding factor returns at the alpha research level is not totally unreasonable but foregoes potentially useful factor exposures. Any residualization can be performed at the portfolio construction stage. For longer horizons, it is also useful to specify whether linear or log returns (Sec. 1.3) were used.

3.8.1.4 Performance metrics.
An alpha researcher needs criteria of quality of forecasts he or she is working on. A single forecast is not required to successfully trade a portfolio with transaction costs. Its goal is to predict future returns of indicated type over a stated horizon. Correspondingly, relevant performance metrics can include MSE or MAD loss and correlation with future return (Sec. 2.3.3). Other statistics include skewness of errors and their distribution by time. For example, high autocorrelation of misprediction can result in prolonged drawdowns making the alpha liable to be discarded, lacking benefit of hindsight, as likely bubbled or arbed out (Sec. 4.9).

MSE and other statistics are best weighted to encourage better predictions for more liquid assets. More flexibly though, forecasts can be developed separately by asset group such as liquidity, index membership, or industrial sectors (Sec. 2.8). Traditional, portfolio-based performance data such as rate of return, Sharpe ratio, turnover, and factor exposure computed by a cost-free trading simulation (Sec. 7) with proportional allocation (Sec. 6.1) is also a possibility, but not as granular as forecasting performance by stock group, return type, and horizon.

3.8.1.5 Measure of forecast uncertainty.
If forecast learning process supports confidence intervals, e.g., computed by cross-validation (Sec. 2.4.8), this information can be carried through the forecast-combining process and used in portfolio construction (Sec. 6.8).

3.8.1.6 Correlation with existing forecasts. It is certainly best if any new forecast is not too collinear with existing forecasts in the pool. This requirement can be difficult to meet consistently if researchers work on a limited collection of raw datasets. Setting a rigid upper bound on the correlation, especially under formulaic compensation rules, could lead to researchers gaming the system as mentioned in Sec. 3.5 and is therefore best avoided. Low or negatively correlated forecasts will stand a better chance of higher weight in a combined book thus automatically elevating the visibility of such contributions. A possible way of limiting correlations is rationing researchers' access to raw datasets for lower overlap, but such constraints can have their downsides too.

In general, it is best if the forecast-combining algorithm handles forecast correlations, small or large, automatically. Another useful feature of a combining algo is automatic garbage detection, so non-performing or pure noise forecasts do not affect the combining process other than by taking some additional resources handling the useless data.

3.8.1.7 Raw feature library. For a standardized ML datafeed, raw data may need a preprocessing by generating large read-optimized derived data potentially usable as ML features. While useful for a big data research pipeline (Sec. 2.4.18), this stage can also incorporate analytics and financial insight or just a hunch potentially making a difference at later stages. The raw features can include, for example, various moments of the price level population in a limit order book, which would make sense based on the market microstructure theory.[38] It is expected that most items in the raw feature library will not survive a closer examination, and many will be highly correlated by effectively implementing a parameter grid search. The raw feature library can also be used to optimize coverage of available raw data by analysts to make sure no stone is left unturned.

3.8.1.8 Overfit handling. An alpha pool is a dynamic framework with daily updates of existing forecasts and a stream of new forecasts

---

[38] J.-P. Bouchaud, J. Bonart, J. Donier, M. Gould, *Trades, Quotes and Prices. Financial Markets Under the Microscope*, Cambridge University Press, 2018.

regularly submitted and only occasionally removed. This means that at any point in time a sizable number of alphas in the pool will be recent additions with a very short out-of-sample track record. More often than not, forecast performance is miraculously better before the submission date than thereafter. The combining process should be aware of the forecasts' out-of-sample start dates, so recent additions be handled with a systematic grain of salt as possibly overfit until proved otherwise. Among other approaches, in-sample forecast periods can be artificially degraded by noise or an intermittent "poison pill" component anticorrelated with future returns. Such a negative lookahead compensating for a suspected positive lookahead might help to avoid training the combining algorithm on "science fiction."

3.8.2   Pnl attribution

> *Prof. M. Berry once formulated the following two principles:*
>
> - *The Arnold Principle. If a notion bears a personal name, then this name is not the name of the discoverer.*
> - *The Berry Principle. The Arnold Principle is applicable to itself.*
>
> Vladimir Arnold[39]

As mentioned in Sec. 3.2, the question of pnl attribution of a combined portfolio is a nontrivial one: a forecast performing well in isolation may be best shorted in combination with others. The problem is further complicated by the portfolio construction layer involving risk, costs, and the corresponding utility optimization. Those complexities are best kept out of forecasting (Sec. 2.12) but are clearly relevant to the firm-wide pnl. There are a few ways to estimate the pnl attribution of forecasts in a pool. None is perfect.

3.8.2.1   **Marginal attribution.** The most straightforward pnl attribution to a forecast is based on a historical simulation (Sec. 7) combining

---

[39] Consistent with this principle, the continent hosting Wall Street is aptly called America. Quoted from V.I. Arnold, *On teaching mathematics*, https://dsweb.siam.org/The-Magazine/All-Issues/vi-arnold-on-teaching-mathematics.

(a) all alpha pool forecasts and (b) all but the forecast in question. This approach is similar to the ML leave-one-out cross-validation (Sec. 2.4.8). Any (negated) marginal deterioration of the resulting simulated pnl can be treated as the forecast contribution. Due to the combining nonlinearity, such marginal contributions will not sum up to the total pnl, but they can be used on a relative basis.

A possible problem with the marginal attribution is the cost of simulation, which needs to be run as many times as there are forecasts in the pool. Some ML algorithms, e.g., those based on the online covariance (Sec. 2.4.13), support an efficient leave-one-out prediction thereby making it possible to run the attribution study inexpensively in a single process. Alternatively, if one is interested in a pnl attribution by groups of forecasts, e.g., by contributor, there will be fewer simulations to run.

Needless to say, it is expected that a historical simulation can reproduce production results reasonably well (Sec. 7.1).

3.8.2.2 Regression-based attribution. Another type of attribution inference is based on statistical relationships between individual forecasts and combined portfolio positions or pnl. This can be easily implemented in the production process without running off-line simulations. Let f_{ids} be the K forecasts ($i = 1, \ldots, K$) generated on day d for security s and P_{ds} the dollar position taken as a result of forecast combining and portfolio construction. Daily regression weights w_{di} can be solved from "explaining positions by forecasts" as follows:

$$\mathbf{w}_d = \underset{w_{di} \geq 0}{\mathrm{argmin}} \sum_s \left(P_{ds} - \sum_{i=1}^{K} w_{di} f_{ids} \right)^2 \tag{3.27}$$

$$= \mathrm{QP}^+(\mathrm{Cov}(\mathbf{f}_i, \mathbf{f}_j), \mathrm{Cov}(\mathbf{f}_i, \mathbf{P})).$$

Here $\mathrm{QP}^+(\mathbf{A}, \mathbf{b})$ denotes the solution of the quadratic programming problem

$$\mathbf{x} = \mathrm{argmin} \left(\frac{1}{2} \mathbf{x} \cdot \mathbf{A} \mathbf{x} - \mathbf{b} \cdot \mathbf{x} \right) \quad \text{subject to } x_i \geq 0. \tag{3.28}$$

Alternatively, one can regress the next-day pnl

$$Q_{d+1,s} = P_{ds} R_{d+1,s}, \tag{3.29}$$

instead of the position target P_{ds}, vs the forecasts. The constrained regression (3.27) can be run over multiple days for smoother attribution weights w_i. If the forecasts $\mathbf{f}_i$ differ by horizon or coverage, they should be brought to an "effective" form like (6.29) and normalized to cross-sectional unit variance, so $\sum_s f_{ids}^2 = 1$.

Although the forecast weights α_i in the combination (3.18) and the pnl-attribution weights w_i will be correlated, it is possible to have $w_i > 0$ for $\alpha_i = 0$ and vice versa. This is due to portfolio construction effects including costs and risk: contributions of shorter-horizon and factor exposed forecasts will be more likely suppressed by the portfolio optimizer.

Chapter 4

Risk

In this business it's easy to confuse luck with brains.

Jim Simons

n the context of quantitative portfolio management, risk is understood as variability of portfolio pnl and ways to control it. Variance of the pnl is perhaps the simplest risk measure but not the only one used in the financial industry. But even the plain variance has certain complexities and may need further simplification (shrinkage) as described below.

4.1   Value at risk and expected shortfall

Value at Risk (VaR) provides a fairly detailed view of portfolio risk in the form of a function $VaR(p)$ expressing the lower bound of worst expected daily losses vs probability p of such losses. A useful companion risk measure is *expected shortfall*, or *conditional value at risk* (CVaR), expressing the expected loss conditioned on crossing the VaR threshold.

VaR and CVaR are usually reported at a fixed probability p such as 1% or 5%.

Let $F(Q)$ be the probability density of the daily portfolio pnl Q. If

$$\sigma^2 = \text{Var}(Q) \tag{4.1}$$

is a measure of the overall width of the distribution F (a number), then $\text{VaR}(p)$ and $\text{CVaR}(p)$ are functions characterizing the left ($Q < 0$) tail of the distribution. A fatter left tail means higher absolute values of VaR and CVaR. The functions $\text{VaR}(p)$ and $\text{CVaR}(p)$ are defined by

$$p = \int_{-\infty}^{\text{VaR}(p)} F(Q)dQ,$$
$$\text{CVaR}(p) = \frac{1}{p} \int_{-\infty}^{\text{VaR}(p)} QF(Q)dQ, \tag{4.2}$$

and shown in Fig. 4.1. For mathematical convenience, Eq. (4.2) defines VaR and CVaR as bad-tail, normally negative, pnl values. A more conventional definition negates these values. For a normal distribution,

$$F = \mathcal{N}(0, \sigma^2), \tag{4.3}$$

the absolute values of $\text{VaR}(p)$ and $\text{CVaR}(p)$ equal the standard deviation σ at $p = 16\%$ and $p = 38\%$, respectively, and increase for smaller (more catastrophic) p. If either function $\text{VaR}(p)$ or $\text{CVaR}(p)$ is known, one can infer the full pnl distribution $F(Q)$.

If VaR is the best case scenario in the worst p-quantile of losses, then CVaR is seen as more conservative (mean) loss in the same quantile. In addition, CVaR satisfies an important condition of *subadditivity* and VaR does not.[1] The subadditivity, or convexity, property of a risk metric $V(X)$ for portfolios X and Y requires $V(X + Y) \leq V(X) + V(Y)$, or that the risk of a combined portfolio be lower than the sum of two risks expressing the effect of diversification.[2]

Computing (C)VaR requires a hard-to-measure distribution of portfolio returns, especially for rare bad events. The distribution can be

---

[1] P. Artzner, F. Delbaen, E. Jean-Marc, D.D. Heath, *Coherent Measures of Risk*, Mathematical Finance, 9(3), pp. 203–228, 1999.

[2] This also implies a risk metric linearity, $V(\alpha X) = \alpha V(X)$, or measuring risk in the units of USD rather than USD^2. The latter, variance-based risk is common in mean-variance optimization (Sec. 6.3).

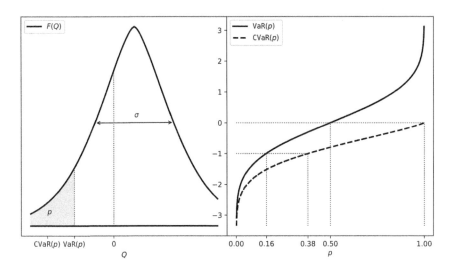

Figure 4.1 Left: a graphical definition of CVaR and VaR based on the pnl probability density $F(Q)$. The area of the shaded region equals the quantile level p. CVaR is the mean Q over that region. As defined in Eq. (4.2), the risk metrics satisfy the inequality $CVaR(p) < VaR(p) < 0$. The standard deviation $\sigma = Var^{1/2}(Q)$ is shown schematically. Right: $VaR(p)$ and $CVaR(p)$ functions computed for normal $F(Q)$ with zero mean and $\sigma = 1$.

skewed when combined over multiple correlated assets or portfolios. VaR has been criticized as an error-prone regulatory metric.[3]

For the purpose of quantitative portfolio optimization (Chapter 6), a variance-based risk metric is typically used leading to variants of quadratic programming (QP) utilities. There is also an approach to portfolio optimization based on expected shortfall[4,5] leading to a linear programming (LP) problem. Unlike mean–variance optimization, CVaR-based optimization emphasizes asymmetry of risk by penalizing losses rather than the general pnl variability. This can be also done in mean–variance by using a one-sided (loss-only) variance. The one-sided variance of returns is not necessarily proportional to the

[3] N.N. Taleb, *The Black Swan: The Impact of the Highly Improbable*, Random House, 2007.
[4] R.T. Rockafellar, S. Uryasev, *Optimization of conditional value-at-risk*, Journal of Risk, 2(3), pp. 21–41, 2000.
[5] D. Bertsimas, G.J. Lauprete, A. Samarov, *Shortfall as a risk measure: properties, optimization and applications*, Journal of Economic Dynamics & Control, 28, pp. 1353–1381, 2004.

regular variance. This is seen from time series of many assets that tend to grow slow and fall fast indicating a greed-fear asymmetry.

In the context of pnl data perception by human investors and risk managers, risk does not reduce to the variability of daily portfolio pnl alone. Also important are serial correlations of daily pnls, specifically the *drawdown* statistic, or maximum peak-to-trough drop on the cumulative pnl chart and its duration. It is not straightforward to include drawdown in an optimizer utility (Sec. 6.3), but it can be approximated by the covariance or the expected shortfall of multi-day returns: a large correlation of monthly returns across assets makes a month-long portfolio drawdown more likely. Note that VaR and CVaR defined via the distribution of daily returns reflect on rare single-day losses rather than multi-day drawdowns.

4.2   Factor models

Let R_s be a random daily return of security s, with realization by date. Then a portfolio with dollar positions P_s generates a random pnl $Q = \mathbf{P} \cdot \mathbf{R}$, assuming no trading costs for now. The expectation and the variance of the portfolio pnl are

$$E(Q) = \sum_s f_s P_s,$$

$$\mathrm{Var}(Q) = \sum_{s,s'} P_s P_{s'} \mathrm{Cov}(R_s, R_{s'}), \tag{4.4}$$

where the forecast f_s is used in place of the expected return $E(R_s)$.[6]

The covariance of security returns $C_{ss'} = \mathrm{Cov}(R_s, R_{s'})$ appearing in Eq. (4.4) is easier to write mathematically than measure historically, let alone forecast for the future. For a universe of, say, 2000 stocks over a ten-year history, the covariance matrix of about 2 million independent entries is to be estimated from some 5 million stock × date observations, which is not a great statistical coverage. Given the finite sample size uncertainty, one can expect a significant noise in the covariance and a high probability of unexpected pnl moves.

---

[6] In practice, a forecast is not exactly the expectation of return, but rather an approximation of varying quality. This distinction is unimportant for our current purposes, but bears on *alpha risk* (Sec. 4.9).

As discussed in Sec. 2.4.10 in the forecast context, a covariance matrix is best cleaned of noise and/or simplified by shrinkage. It also helps if its inverse, which appears in OLS regression and also in mean-variance optimization (Sec. 6.3), be less noisy. In portfolio risk, another kind of shrinkage known as *factor models*, is common. Unlike shrinkage by suppression of off-diagonal stock covariances, a factor model replaces the covariance matrix by something else, Eq. (4.7), by postulating that stocks interact (co-vary) with each other only indirectly, via so-called *risk factors*. A risk factor for equities is a linear combination of stocks expressing a certain theme of collective stock movement. The vector of coefficients in this linear combination is called *factor loading*. Identifying common themes of multi-asset returns is not unlike looking for hidden structure in collaborative filtering or recommender systems (Sec. 3.7). One can look for the risk factors using both technical approaches (Sec. 4.5) and relying on the domain knowledge of financial markets leading to various *style factors* (Sec. 4.3).

4.3   Types of risk factors

A hunter walks one mile South and one mile East. He spots a bear, gets scared, runs one mile North, and ends up right back where he started. What color is the bear?

From a quant interview

The simplest, and often most important, risk factor is the market factor with loadings of market betas defined in Eq. (2.2). This factor expresses the herding effect of stocks moving together due to macroeconomic or political news. Additional factors can include:

1. Industrial sectors or industry groups, e.g., by GICS, with Boolean loadings of 1 if stock belongs to the group and 0 otherwise.
2. Principal components (Sec. 4.5). These are not totally independent of market and sectors and can be used as their proxy. PCA factors are also useful for futures and other asset classes where style factors (listed below) are not easily defined.
3. Geography/country factors are usable for a global equity portfolio or for US-traded universe including American Depository Receipts (ADRs).

4. Style factors:

- Growth: a combination of earnings per share (actual and predicted), company assets and capital structure, etc.
- Value: based on book-to-price ratio.
- Company size, possibly under a nonlinear transformation like $\log^3$(market_cap).
- Volatility: based on historical price variability and/or option-implied volatility.
- Momentum: measure of persistence of stock returns relative to the market, aka *relative strength*.
- Earnings: earnings-to-price ratio, analyst predicted or actual.
- Leverage: based on debt-to-total assets ratio, or implicitly derived from stock sensitivity to interest rates or bond prices.
- Dividend yield: historical or predicted dividend payout.

5. Stock return sensitivity to macroeconomic time series such as foreign exchange rates, interest rates, and some commodity prices.

Several vendors, notably MSCI Barra and Northfield Information Services, provide various factor model data for different universes and systematic trading styles. Shrinkage and other adjustments are made for stability and explanatory power of some factor loadings.[7]

Risk factors are generally interpreted as directions $\mathbf{L}_i$ in the linear space of portfolio positions, which are to be avoided because of the possibility of large correlated return movements in those directions. Avoiding such exposures reduces correlations across portfolio returns in different assets resulting in better diversification (Sec. 3.1) and lower risk. The simplest form of risk management is building a portfolio with the vector of dollar positions P_s orthogonal to the loadings:

$$\mathbf{P} \cdot \mathbf{L}_i = 0. \tag{4.5}$$

Given a space of securities much larger than the subspace spanned by few risk factors, the exact factor neutrality (4.5), as a linear constraint for portfolio construction (Sec. 6.1), is fairly mild. However, if risk factors are correlated and/or their returns are predictable, an optimal portfolio allocation is not exactly factor neutral (Sec. 6.3).

---

[7] Y. Liu, J. Menchero, D. J. Orr, J. Wang, *The Barra US Equity Model (USE4): Empirical Notes*, MSCI research paper, September 2011. Available at msci.com.

In the case of the market factor, the loadings are market betas, numbers of order one. Given some differences in methodology of evaluating market betas, a much simpler dollar neutrality is often used where betas are replaced by ones giving a dollar-neutral portfolio with

$$\sum_s P_s = 0. \tag{4.6}$$

Dollar neutrality is broadly recognized by stock brokers as a lower-risk portfolio qualifying for a margin trading account with higher leverage. Ability to buy and sell securities using borrowed funds, and thereby enhance expected return on capital (ROC), can be a more important motivation for market-neutral and long-short strategies than risk itself. Approaches to choosing an optimal leverage level are discussed in Sec. 6.9.

4.4 Return and risk decomposition

As long as the number of chosen risk factors K is much smaller than the number of securities in the universe N, a factor model provides a compressed (or shrunk) and interpretable representation of the security covariance:

$$C_{ss'} = \sigma_s^2 \delta_{ss'} + \sum_{ij} U_{ij} L_{is} L_{js'}, \quad \text{or}$$

$$C = \mathrm{Diag}(\sigma_s^2) + L'UL. \tag{4.7}$$

In this equation, the first term σ_s^2 is the residual variance of stock s, $\mathbf{L}_i$ are the loadings for the K risk factors, and U is the $K \times K$ covariance matrix of factor returns. The factor returns ρ_i are extracted from daily OLS regression for stock returns R_s vs loadings as predictors:[8]

$$\rho = \mathrm{argmin} \sum_s w_s \left(R_s - \sum_i L_{is} \rho_i \right)^2$$

$$= (LWL')^{-1} LWR, \tag{4.8}$$

---

[8] It is also possible to run stagewise regression by groups of risk factors, e.g., by applying the market factor first, then explaining market-free residuals by industrial sectors, etc. In addition to somewhat better interpretability, orthogonal stages such as industries can be run more efficiently.

where w_s are the current statistical security weights and $W = \mathtt{Diag}(w_s)$. This regression aims at explaining stock returns $\mathbf{R}$ by the factors $\mathbf{L}_i$ as far as it goes; the rest is the *residual* return r_s:

$$R_s = \sum_i L_{is}\rho_i + r_s. \tag{4.9}$$

Note that the regression (4.8)-(4.9) is run for *contemporaneous* returns and risk loadings. In this sense, a factor model is an "explanation", rather than prediction, of asset returns. R-squared of the factor model regression can be of order 30%. The explanatory power of risk models is not subject to trading arbitrage and is therefore not as tiny as for prediction of future returns (Sec. 2.3.3). It is said that you can't make extra money by running fancy risk models,[9] but they can save you some pain.

Getting back to Eq. (4.7), the historical residual volatility

$$\sigma_s^2 = \mathtt{Var}(r_s) < \mathtt{Var}(R_s) \tag{4.10}$$

and the factor covariance

$$U_{ij} = \mathtt{Cov}(\rho_i, \rho_j) \tag{4.11}$$

are computed over a rolling window of dates or using EMA date weights. Formally, Eq. (4.7) follows from the decomposition (4.9) and the assumption of uncorrelated residuals:

$$\mathtt{Cov}(r_s, r_{s'}) = \mathtt{Diag}(\sigma_s^2). \tag{4.12}$$

This assumption is not really based on data, but rather introduces a special kind of shrinkage constraint on the large covariance of asset returns (Sec. 2.4.10).

4.5   Weighted PCA

While well constructed fundamental industrial and style factors are expected to add price-independent value, pure technical/statistical factors have their established place in risk management. In non-equity

---

[9] With a possible exception of better mean-reversion alpha when using better residuals (Sec. 2.2.1).

asset classes such as futures or foreign exchange (FX), technical risk factors may be the only available option.

Principal component analysis (PCA) was mentioned in Sec. 3.5.1 in the context of dimensionality reduction. When applied to stock returns, PCA gives the principal directions of return variability and serves as perhaps the best pure technical source of risk factors. In this section we provide the algebra needed for computing PCA factors generalized to a framework in which securities are assigned statistical weights similar to those used in forecasting.[10]

Let R_{ds} be a "fat" $n \times N$ matrix of returns with number of days n smaller than the number of stocks N, a situation common for large equity universes. We can think about the rows of this matrix as realizations of a random N-vector of cross-sectional returns $\mathbf{R}$. The daily observations can be optionally assigned a historical weight u_d, e.g., larger for more recent observations. Consider a random vector $\tilde{\mathbf{R}}$ of serially centered returns with historical trends subtracted:

$$\tilde{R}_{ds} = R_{ds} - \sum_{d' \leq d} u_{d'} R_{d's}. \tag{4.13}$$

The date weights are assumed normalized, so

$$\sum_{d' \leq d} u_{d'} = 1. \tag{4.14}$$

The covariance matrix of the detrended returns is

$$\tilde{C}_{ss'} = \mathrm{Cov}(\tilde{R}_s, \tilde{R}_{s'}) = \sum_d u_d \tilde{R}_{ds} \tilde{R}_{ds'}$$
$$= \tilde{R}' U \tilde{R}, \quad U = \mathrm{Diag}(u_d). \tag{4.15}$$

We now switch from N stocks to K ETF-like synthetic instruments with underlying stock composition vectors $\mathbf{e}_i$. The returns of the synthetics is a random K-vector $\boldsymbol{\rho}$:

$$\rho_i = \sum_s e_{is} \tilde{R}_s \tag{4.16}$$

with the $K \times K$ covariance matrix

$$\Gamma_{ij} = \mathrm{Cov}(\rho_i, \rho_j) = \sum_{ss'} e_{is} e_{js'} \tilde{C}_{ss'}. \tag{4.17}$$

---

[10] The weight matrix w_{ds} can also be used to define a dynamic universe of stocks by the condition $w_{ds} \neq 0$.

We now want to choose the vectors $\mathbf{e}_i$ to make the synthetics covariance diagonal and to maximize the variances Γ_{ii} subject to a fixed norm of each synthetic composition. This is where stock weights w_s come into play. The weights are meant as scales of dollar positions. For the synthetic weights e_{is} to reflect this scaling, we introduce the w_s^{-1} factor in the norm so, other things equal, the components e_{is} will end up suppressed for smaller w_s. Using Lagrange multipliers λ_i, the maximization of the synthetics variance,

$$\max_{\mathbf{e}_i} \left(\sum_{ss'} \tilde{C}_{ss'} e_{is} e_{is'} - \lambda_i \sum_s w_s^{-1} e_{is}^2 \right), \qquad (4.18)$$

gives an eigenvalue problem:

$$\tilde{C} \mathbf{e}_i = \lambda_i W^{-1} \mathbf{e}_i, \quad W = \mathtt{Diag}(w_s). \qquad (4.19)$$

Upon left-multiplying (4.19) by $W^{1/2}$ we observe that

$$\mathbf{f} = W^{-1/2} \mathbf{e} \qquad (4.20)$$

is an eigenvector of the matrix

$$\hat{C} = W^{1/2} \tilde{C} W^{1/2} = \hat{R}' \hat{R}, \qquad (4.21)$$

where we define the weight-adjusted returns

$$\hat{R} = U^{1/2} \tilde{R} W^{1/2}, \quad \text{or} \quad \hat{R}_{ds} = \tilde{R}_{ds} w_{ds}^{1/2}. \qquad (4.22)$$

Here

$$w_{ds} = u_d w_s \qquad (4.23)$$

is the weight of an individual date-asset observation. The weight adjustment of returns in (4.21)-(4.22) takes care of the PCA weighting.

Out of N eigenvectors of the covariance $\hat{R}'\hat{R}$ we need $K \ll N$ with the largest eigenvalues $\lambda_1 > \lambda_2 > \dots > \lambda_K$. If the number of days n is smaller than the number of stocks N, there are at most n non-zero eigenvalues.

4.6   PCA transformation

Write an efficient C program printing all permutations of its command-line arguments.

From a quant interview

One can solve the eigenproblem for the $N \times N$ asset-wise covariance matrix (4.21) directly, which can be computationally expensive requiring $O(N^2)$ memory and $O(N^3)$ FLOPs. If the number of days is smaller than the number of assets, $n < N$,[11] there is a more efficient way. Left-multiplying the eigenvalue problem

$$\hat{R}' \hat{R} \, \mathbf{f} = \lambda \mathbf{f} \tag{4.24}$$

by $\hat{R}$ we have

$$\hat{R} \hat{R}' \mathbf{g} = \lambda \mathbf{g}, \quad \mathbf{g} = \hat{R} \mathbf{f}, \tag{4.25}$$

which is a smaller, $n \times n$ eigenvalue problem for the day-wise covariance $\hat{R} \hat{R}'$. Left-multiplying (4.25) by $\hat{R}'$ once again,

$$\hat{R}' \hat{R} (\hat{R}' \mathbf{g}) = \lambda (\hat{R}' \mathbf{g}), \tag{4.26}$$

we arrive at the original $N \times N$ eigenvalue problem (4.24) that is solved by

$$\mathbf{f}_i = \lambda_i^{-1/2} \hat{R}' \mathbf{g}_i, \quad \hat{R} \hat{R}' \, \mathbf{g}_i = \lambda_i \mathbf{g}_i. \tag{4.27}$$

The factor $\lambda_i^{-1/2}$ was added for a normalization so, if $\mathbf{g}_i$ are orthonormal ($\mathbf{g}_i \cdot \mathbf{g}_j = \delta_{ij}$), so are $\mathbf{e}_i$. Finally, the weighted PCA loadings are given by

$$\mathbf{e}_i = \lambda_i^{-1/2} W^{-1/2} \hat{R}' \mathbf{g}_i, \tag{4.28}$$

where λ_i are K largest eigenvalues, and $\mathbf{g}_i$ the corresponding eigenvectors of the $n \times n$ matrix

$$(\hat{R} \hat{R}')_{dd'} = \sum_s (w_{ds} w_{d's})^{1/2} \tilde{R}_{ds} \tilde{R}_{d's}. \tag{4.29}$$

So the cost of PCA computation for an n-day history and N securities is $O(\min(n^3, N^3))$.

---

[11] The universe size N has to be larger than the actual number of tradable stocks because during a multi-year simulation history (Sec. 7), stocks come in and out of existence, so at any given day perhaps half of the securities have zero weight but must be maintained in the covariance.

4.7   Crowding and liquidation

Why do sausages, when cooked, break along their length and never across?

From a quant interview

Given about the same financial data (Sec. 2.1) available to all quants and somewhat common rational research process, quants often arrive at similar forecasts. For example, in the early 2000s, when the *dot-com bubble* was deflating and fundamental valuation of companies was back on the table, a few quant funds performed exceptionally well with forecasts using novel fundamental data more suited for a quantitative process (Sec. 2.1.3). These forecasts were apparently soon rediscovered by more quant shops rushing money into similar alphas. This created a quantamental bubble not unlike the dot-com bubble—recall the synthetic security view of a forecast (Sec. 3.6). There were some painful drawdowns in 2003 when the quantamental bubble deflated. It appears that many quant alphas are subject to such bubbling dynamics, causing periods of strategy losses and portfolio liquidation events.

Some quant liquidation events, August 2007[12] being among the most dramatic, may have been started by closing a portfolio for reasons not related to its alpha performance. Still, losses suffered by similar portfolios due to the impact (Sec. 5.2) created by the culprit produced an avalanche of liquidation as a matter of self-fulfilling panic during August 6-9, 2007.[13] Bank-run-style liquidation moved stock prices significantly in the direction opposite to common quant long-short alphas, especially those with longer horizons used for building larger portfolios. Fire-sale liquidation of such portfolios, including one managed by this author, created a painful price impact over a few days. By the end of the week, Renaissance Technologies reported 8.7% loss for the month of August,[14] which was one of the better performances in the market-neutral space.

---

[12] A. Khandani, A.W. Lo, *What Happened to the Quants in August 2007? Evidence from Factors and Transactions Data*, October 2008. Available at SSRN: https://ssrn.com/abstract=1288988.

[13] From an August 6 phone call with a colleague working for a friendly competitor: "Are you guys fucked up too?" "That would be an understatement."

[14] G. Zuckerman, J.R. Hagerty, D. Gauthier-Villars, *Impact of Mortgage Crisis Spreads*, The Wall Street Journal, August 10, 2007.

Many quant groups went out of business. It took some others years to get out of the drawdown.[15] The dislocation did not affect broad market indices as dramatically and went largely unnoticed by diversified long-only investors.

A similar but slower pattern of "quant crash" occurred in March 2020 amid a broad market slump due to the COVID-19 pandemic.[16]

The *flash crash* on May 6, 2010 lasted under an hour and affected both long-short and long-only portfolios.[17] The reasons for the flash crash, while still disputed, seemed mostly of a technical nature. To avoid such instability in the markets, US Securities and Exchange Commission (SEC) instituted additional circuit breaker rules for US exchanges based on return data for S&P500, Russell 1000, and PowerShares QQQ indices, but not any market-neutral indices.

The quant dislocations of 2007 and 2020 were painful to primarily market-neutral funds and did not result in new regulatory actions. Market-neutral strategies are employed by hedge funds serving sophisticated, or *accredited investors*, who presumably understand their risks and do not need additional government protection. In addition, most hedge funds accept investments only from institutions or high-net-worth individuals and require a minimum investment of $1M or more. Pension funds do invest in hedge funds, but their exposure to market-neutral strategies is usually limited and can be regulated depending on jurisdiction.[18] Unlike the broad stock market affecting savings of the general public, the market-neutral space is a zero-sum game, so losses of some quants are gains of other quants or market makers.

In most extreme quant dislocation events, sharp losses were followed by a regime change with a period of abnormally high performance.

---

[15] The author's portfolio recovered its pre-August'07 pnl level within days due to reopening positions early following an impressive performance reversal shown by a real-time paper trading system (Sec. 7.4). Many other PMs were not given such an opportunity because of automatic drawdown-based risk management rules.

[16] Incidentally, it was this event that afforded the author free time for writing this book.

[17] *Findings regarding the market events of May 6, 2010*, Report of the staffs of the CFTC and SEC to the joint advisory committee on emerging regulatory issues, September 30, 2010. https://www.sec.gov/news/studies/2010/marketevents-report.pdf.

[18] The Organisation for Economic Co-operation and Development (OECD) publishes regular reports on investment regulation of pension funds. A survey for 2020 is available at http://www.oecd.org.

However, due to prevalent non-quantitative risk management practices, portfolio deleverage is normally imposed after a certain level of loss, and the post-crash performance is often left unrealized.

Attempts to mitigate such events by introducing additional "catastrophic" risk factors were made by different teams. It appears that any such factors are aligned with most popular quant alphas and, as such, kill the alphas when used in the normal course of business. During liquidation events, correlations among alphas significantly increase, defeating any alpha diversification (Sec. 3.1).

Optimization of the total expected portfolio manager payout subject to termination upon a certain drawdown is an interesting dynamic programming problem not unlike Merton's optimal consumption.[19]

4.8   Liquidity risk and short squeeze

Markets can remain irrational a lot longer than you and I can remain solvent.

John Maynard Keynes

A long stock position can lose up to 100% of its value if the stock price goes down to zero. On the other hand, a loss on a short position is theoretically unlimited, because there is no limit on stock appreciation, especially for cheap or illiquid equities subject to news shocks or manipulation. The asymmetry of long vs short risk is further amplified by leverage (Sec. 6.9). Short positions in penny stocks are best avoided or at least penalized at a level higher than the normal variance penalty (Sec. 6.3).

Liquidity is another risk factor affecting a portfolio that lost its value and needs to be reduced or closed to avoid further losses, including through a *margin call*. Selling a long position, or covering a short in an illiquid asset moves its price in a way amplifying the loss (Sec. 5.2). For this reason, portfolio managers often introduce asset-level constraints on the absolute position size proportional to the asset liquidity expressed as the recent average or median dollar volume (ADV or MDV). Accounting for trading costs of just acquiring the target position (Sec. 6.3) is not enough.

---

[19] R.C. Merton, *Lifetime Portfolio Selection under Uncertainty: the Continuous-Time Case.* The Review of Economics and Statistics, 51(3), pp. 247–257, 1969.

The adverse effect of liquidity applies to both long and short positions, but the losses can be more dramatic for shorts, as reflected by the term *short squeeze*. In addition to the natural volatility and material news, a short squeeze can be due to market manipulation. During the last week of January 2021, an apparently intentional short squeeze was initiated by a large group of retail investors in several US stocks including GameStop Inc. (GME), AMC Entertainment Holdings Inc. (AMC), and other "meme stocks." Over the month of January, GameStop and AMC stocks rose respectively 1,780% and 560% without material fundamental company news. Several hedge funds holding sizable short positions in these stocks, including Melvin Capital, suffered steep losses. Financial institutions on the other side of the trade recorded equally abnormal profits, albeit with a lesser news coverage.[20] It has been suggested[21] that retail buyers used social media to orchestrate an appreciation of stocks with a significant short interest, which is primarily attributable to large hedge funds (Sec. 2.1.8), as a way of "populist insurgency" against the hedge fund industry.

There is little hope to quantitatively forecast such price moves in this brave new world. Whether or not socially driven stock bubbles or financial flash mobs constitute market manipulation, and what to do about it, yet remains to be sorted out by the industry and its regulators.

4.9 Forecast uncertainty and alpha risk

A well sharpened pencil was placed upright, lead down, on a desk and did not fall down for 5 seconds. Prove that the pencil was glued to the desk.

From a quant interview

An important kind of risk is the risk of forecast underperformance. Recall that forecast is meant as an expectation of the random future return, and most ML algorithms can also predict its variance or confidence bands, either in a closed form (Sec. 2.4.3) or by cross-validation

---

[20] As a general non-quantitative observation, mainstream news media appear fairly asymmetric. Assuming rational management of media outlets, the larger emphasis on bad news implies that good news is harder to sell.

[21] N. Kulwin, *Reddit, the Elites and the Dream of GameStop 'To the Moon'*, The New York Times, Jan 28, 2021.

(Sec. 2.4.8). If the confidence band is large, it can result in a significant variance of portfolio performance.

For a linear regression forecast

$$\mathbf{f} = X'\beta \tag{4.30}$$

with K regression coefficients β and a $K \times N$ feature matrix X, the $K \times K$ coefficients estimation covariance (2.44) gives the $N \times N$ forecast uncertainty covariance

$$\mathrm{Cov}(\mathbf{f}, \mathbf{f}) = X'\mathrm{Cov}(\beta, \beta)X, \tag{4.31}$$

whose diagonal contains the forecast error bars by asset. This risk can be approximately handled in portfolio construction (Sec. 6.8).

More importantly, forecasts also have their life cycles and tend to work better after initial discovery and/or new data availability, then decay and can periodically revert due to crowding. This risk is harder to measure using statistical methods. One idea to handle this is considering forecasts as tradable instruments (synthetics) and build a portfolio, presumably long-only, of these synthetics. A difficulty with this approach is prediction, or forecasting the forecasts.[22] Unlike equities having both technical and fundamental data and often learnable in aggregate (Sec. 2.8), forecasts are products of feature engineering, ML fitting, and one-off ideas. There is little reason to expect that the lessons of one forecast are instructive for others.

Portfolios running on just a few, even strong, forecasts are expected to underperform sooner or later. The only obvious way to handle alpha

---

[22] Predictions of forecasts performance using scalar time series analysis are usually unreliable due to a small size of daily pnl data. While the hope is that past forecast performance is an indication of future performance, and visualization of pnl charts makes an impression of predictability, attempts to time the forecast performance described in footnote 3 on p. 130 were unsuccessful. Another test of the power of human visualization, in which this author and a diligent analyst served as two mechanical Turks, involved a laborious effort of visual classification of trailing one-year pnl charts generated for weekly cut-off dates, with lookahead data erased, into "more promising" and "less promising" for the near future. The initial result of using such classification recorded PIT was a nice improvement of a dynamic forecast selection. However, after finding a bug of one-day (!) lookahead not properly removed from the one-year charts and repeating the eye-straining classification, all the improvement was gone. Perhaps outsourcing "chart porn" watching to a DNN classifier would do a better job than mechanical turking.

risk is continuous generation of new forecasts and systematic management of a growing library of alphas (Sec. 3.8). There is an important
balance between improving existing models and searching for new ones,
which is not unlike the exploration-exploitation tradeoff in reinforcement learning.

Alpha risk factors are not limited to quantitative competition and
rediscovery. Financial forecasts are based on the notion of somewhat
rational, and therefore stable, underlying market dynamics providing
some signal on top of the larger ambient noise. When these dynamics
change abruptly, for example, due to liquidation events (Sec. 4.7) or
social meme themes (Sec. 4.8), forecasts learned on historical data are
due for potentially serious underperformance. Risk management for
such situations is challenging and should be based on market-wide
pattern recognition or latent variables.

Chapter 5

Trading Costs and Market Elasticity

T rading financial securities involves several types of costs that can be both explicit, such as a broker fee, or implicit. The latter means that the actual trade price ends up different from the market price at the time when the trade is planned. More generally, the cost of a stock trade is the difference between the price paid or received per share traded and a benchmark price. The cost depends on the benchmark definition. Common benchmarks include arrival price, all-day or rest-of-day volume weighted average price (VWAP), or daily closing price. Brokers routinely offer VWAP-tracking execution services. In this context, the cost is the trade price deterioration with respect to the VWAP.

The benchmark price must be consistent across the portfolio management process. The forecast predicts a future price change from the benchmark and thereby an expected profit to be earned on a trade. The cost is subtracted from the profit and thus plays an important role in deciding whether or not the trade is worth the cost.

As we shall see, trading costs are uncertain, just as forecasts are. In an efficient market, the predictability of returns is close to the costs of trading. For a ballpark estimate, one can forecast stock returns at the level of the order of 1 bps per day (Sec. 2.3.3), and the cost of trading is of the same order of magnitude. It takes a better than average skill in both forecasting and execution to keep the difference between the two numbers consistently positive.

For a meaningful portfolio construction process (Chapter 6), one needs to distinguish, at least mathematically, between two kinds of trading costs per share or dollar traded: those independent of the trade size and those increasing with the trade size. These two kinds are usually referred to as *slippage* and *impact* costs, respectively.

5.1   Slippage

The average Parisian has 150,000 hairs on his or her head. Prove that there are at least two persons in Paris who have exactly the same number of hairs.

From a quant interview

One can think of slippage as half the cost of a roundtrip trade per share, when the trade size is too small to move the stock price. Slippage depends on the bid-ask spread, the stock's liquidity and volatility, and the execution algorithm used by the portfolio. Slippage also depends on the evolving market ecology, meaning the number and the types of market participants and their trading algorithms.[1] Slippage is a noisy instrument-dependent quantity that needs periodic recalibration by trading cost analysis (TCA). For backtest and portfolio optimization, an approximation like

$$\text{slippage} = c_1 \times \text{mean\_spread} + c_2 \qquad (5.1)$$

is usually used, with coefficients fitted from production data.

Broker fees, exchange liquidity fees/rebates, and any transaction taxes are normally fixed amounts per share traded and can be treated as components of slippage.

---

[1] J.D. Farmer, *Market force, ecology and evolution*, arXiv:adap-org/9812005, 2000.

5.2   Impact

A billiard ball at rest is hit by an identical moving ball. Assuming elastic collision and no friction, find the angle between the trajectories of the two balls after the collision.

From a quant interview

Impact costs, per share traded, increase with the trade size due to impacting the stock price. The price impact is a result of demand/supply forces playing out in the exchange order book. Market microstructure[2,3] studies how exchange rules and different kinds of trade orders affect price formation. Market impact is a serious consideration for mid-frequency statistical arbitrage US portfolios starting with GMV size of $100M or less, depending on turnover and distribution of alpha by liquidity.

Price impact, as an effect with meaningful underlying mechanisms not foreign to physicists, has been a subject of active theoretical and empirical research.[4] Starting with Kyle,[5] various theoretical models of price impact have been proposed predicting linear or sublinear dependence of impact I vs trade size T. Impact $I(T)$ is defined as part of security return following, and *attributable to*, a trade of size T. This general definition is extremely vague, requires clarification, and raises a few important questions.

1. First, one must specify time scales for (a) the trade, which can be a single market order of 100 shares executed instantly or a large block processed by an execution algo over the whole day, and (b) the post-trade horizon over which the impact is measured. It is more or less a consensus that impact, once caused by a trade, will decay over time.[6] If a trade is broken up into multiple small trades spread in time, one has to deal with trade and impact overlapping in time.

---

[2] M. O'Hara, *Market Microstructure Theory.* Wiley, 1998.
[3] J.-P. Bouchaud, J. Bonart, J. Donier, M. Gould, *Trades, Quotes and Prices. Financial Markets Under the Microscope*, Cambridge University Press, 2018.
[4] J.-P. Bouchaud, *Price Impact*, arXiv:0903.2428v1 [q-fin.TR], 2009.
[5] A.S. Kyle, *Continuous Auctions and Insider Trading*, Econometrica, 53(6), pp. 1315–1336, 1985.
[6] It is plausible, if immeasurable, that a trade's price impact decays down to a certain level, with a small persistent component explaining long-term evolution of asset prices driven by the forces of supply and demand. See Sec. 5.4.

2. Next comes the question of attribution. If the price has gone up after Alice bought 1000 shares of CAT, did it go up because of the trade or because the machine maker stock would go up anyway, as Alice skillfully predicted? There is no way to know for sure, because there are no two realities in one of which Alice traded and in the other she did not. The only relatively inexpensive[7] way to connect trade and price change is by running statistical inference on a large dataset of trades vs price returns immediately following the trades, while also controlling for broad market moves and forecasts. More on this below.

3. The next good question is *whose* trades are we looking at. In the grand market picture, each trade has two sides, a buyer and a seller, who are matched anonymously via broker intermediaries at an exchange. Without distinguishing the sides, any impact would cancel out because all trades come in pairs, T and $-T$. For impact study, trade aggression level, or whether liquidity is taken or provided, is more relevant than the trade sign. An aggressive liquidity taker is expected to make a positive (negative) price impact by a buy (sell). A market maker, the likely other side of the trade, will have it the other way around. Impact study is further complicated by more advanced quant portfolios trading with a mix of aggressive and passive orders.[8] In short, impact models cannot be universal. Impact is portfolio-specific and depends on its algorithmic execution capabilities.

4. When analyzing trade data of a mature quant portfolio for price impact, there is a chance that other quant portfolios have been generating similar trades at the same time due to alpha crowding (Sec. 4.7). This effect would lead to an overestimate of impact by the subject portfolio.

That said, one could hope there is a reasonably universal impact formula for most actively managed portfolios, with a few portfolio-specific

---

[7] There are also costly ways to measure costs. Some large quant funds are rumored to periodically generate random, i.e., unrelated to forecasts, trades of various sizes in multiple securities for unbiased TCA studies. On several bug-related occasions, this author had also created, and then analyzed, shock impact by unintended large trades. One order management system incident (Sec. 7.5) involved a 15-minute-long roundtrip in AAPL sized at a significant portion of ADV. It showed a clear price response well outside normal intraday volatility. That TCA cost the portfolio an estimated $5M.

[8] F. Guilbaud, H. Pham, *Optimal High Frequency Trading with limit and market orders*, arXiv:1106.5040 [q-fin.TR], 2011.

parameters to be calibrated by the portfolio manager. While the Kyle model predicts linear impact $I \propto T$, a sublinear dependence was reported more frequently, especially for smaller trades. A square root impact $I \propto T^{1/2}$ was proposed based on order book dynamics[9], empirical data,[10,11] and even pure dimensional analysis.[12]

5.2.1 Empirical observations

High tide in Montauk, NY was at 6 am today. When will it be there next time?

From a quant interview

This author has run empirical studies of price impact specific to his portfolios. The studies were run on large datasets of direct market access (DMA) limit orders, each resulting in a series of executions filling the order partially or in full, often followed by a cancel for the remaining volume. An important observation is that impact is created not only by fills, but also by orders,[13] even by those never filled. This is understandable from the viewpoint of HFT traders or market makers running their trading algorithms on the full view of the order book (Sec. 6.10.3). In general, the more buy orders are sitting on the order book, the more likely the market is driven by buyers—a bullish HFT signal.[14]

If a portfolio execution algo is set up in a way to buy more (less) if the price goes down (up), then running TCA on executions only can result in a negative impact, because buy trades more likely executed on a downtick can be followed by more price drops due to a momentum.

---

[9] J. Donier, J. Bonart, I. Mastromatteo, J.-P. Bouchaud, *A fully consistent, minimal model for non-linear market impact*, arXiv:1412.0141v4 [q-fin.TR], 2014.

[10] R. Almgren, C. Thum, E. Hauptmann, H. Li, *Direct Estimation of Equity Market Impact*, doi:10.1.1.146.1241, 2005.

[11] B. Tóth, Y. Lempérière, C. Deremble, J. de Lataillade, J. Kockelkoren, J.-P. Bouchaud, *Anomalous price impact and the critical nature of liquidity in financial markets*, arXiv:1105.1694 [q-fin.TR], 2018.

[12] M. Pohl, A. Ristig, W. Schachermayer, L. Tangpi, *The amazing power of dimensional analysis: Quantifying market impact*, arXiv:1702.05434v2 [q-fin.TR], 2017.

[13] R. Cont, A. Kukanov, S. Stoikov, *The Price Impact of Order Book Events*, arXiv: 1011.6402 [q-fin.TR], 2011.

[14] M. Avellaneda, J. Reed, S. Stoikov, *Forecasting Prices from Level-I Quotes in the Presence of Hidden Liquidity*, Algorithmic Finance, Vol. 1, No. 1, 2011, Available at SSRN: https://ssrn.com/abstract=1691401.

A way out of this, and let me be vague here, could be replacing cancel in the order-trade- ... -trade-cancel chain by a hypothetical fill, even at unfavorable price, instead of the cancel. Running thus modified TCA gives more reasonable results that are roughly in agreement with abnormal shock impact, which was observed after occasional erroneous trades mentioned on p. 175. Another, more lightweight approach used by this author as a supplemental sanity check was a poll of several professional non-quant traders on expected price change if they were to execute sizable trades in a few familiar names of varying liquidity.[15] A recent poll of financial economists about permanent price impact in a macro setting of moving funds from bonds to stocks resulted in a larger variance and a stronger bias.[16]

Price impact data is very noisy and should also be adjusted for broad market moves explaining a good part of stock variance, as well as handling a forecast-based trade bias. In the simplest form, this means subtracting from stock returns contemporaneous market return and any short-term forecast used in contemplating the trade. In the experience of this author, it is difficult to separate slippage from impact and to distinguish between various exponents ψ in the impact model $I(T) \propto |T|^{\psi}$. Measuring the rate of impact decay is even more difficult and can result in an estimate off by an order of magnitude.

5.2.2 Linear impact model

> The price $p(t)$ of a stock is known in advance for all $t \in [0, T]$. You can trade the stock without restriction using unlimited capital but your broker charges you a fee, per second, proportional to the square trading rate. What maximum pnl can be made starting with zero position at $t = 0$ and liquidating by $t = T$?
>
> From a quant interview[17]

---

[15] Before order management was fully automated, larger trades would be placed by human traders over the phone. Ensuring good execution required advanced communication skills. These professionals cheerfully exposed ESL-educated quants like this author to the intricacies of the English language you won't hear on NPR.

[16] X. Gabaix, R.S.J. Koijen, *In Search of the Origins of Financial Fluctuations: The Inelastic Markets Hypothesis*, Swiss Finance Institute Research Paper No. 20-91, Available at SSRN: https://ssrn.com/abstract=3686935, 2021.

[17] A self-assured quant candidate worked out an explicit answer to this question. When asked why his formula gives a non-zero pnl for $p(t) = $ const, the candidate challenged the author to find an error in his math.

It is not inconsistent with data, as far as this author's TCA is concerned, to use a simple linear impact model with an exponential decay. Written in continuous time,[18] the model reads

$$\dot{I} = \lambda \dot{P} - \nu I, \quad \text{or}$$

$$I(t) = \int_0^t \lambda \dot{P}(t') e^{-\nu(t-t')} dt', \tag{5.2}$$

assuming zero position and impact for $t < 0$. Here $I(t)$ is the impact part of the stock return $R(t)$, $P(t)$ is the portfolio position in this stock, and dot stands for time derivative so $\dot{P}$ is trading rate. The impact coefficient λ is inversely proportional to the stock's average or median dollar volume (ADV or MDV) and is possibly a function of stock volatility. The impact decay time ν^{-1} can be anywhere between a few hours and a few days.

In this simple model, if a trade T is made over time much shorter than impact decay, the cost of the trade is

$$\text{Cost}(T) = \frac{\lambda T^2}{2}. \tag{5.3}$$

It is due to buying the asset at an increased price, and the cost can be undone (in the absence of slippage) by immediately making an opposite trade. Otherwise, the cost is realized later (but can be booked in a simulator immediately) as the impact wears out and the price reverts back.

The combined effect of fixed slippage and linear impact makes trade cost per dollar traded a concave nonlinear function of the trade size $T \geq 0$:

$$\frac{\text{Cost}(T)}{T} = c \, \text{Sign}(T) + \frac{\lambda}{2} T, \tag{5.4}$$

which, given low TCA accuracy, is not that different from a square root function (Fig. 5.1).

---

[18] Continuous time is an approximation for multiple trades smoothed over time. The fact that time t includes both trading and non-trading hours while impact decays overnight can be accounted for by introducing an effective time, or *horizon*, coordinate measured in days. The effective time changes faster during trading hours, slower otherwise, and increases by 1 when moving from an intraday time point to the same point on the next trading day. Impact model in the effective continuous time is more concise than the case of discrete trades, which is also straightforward.

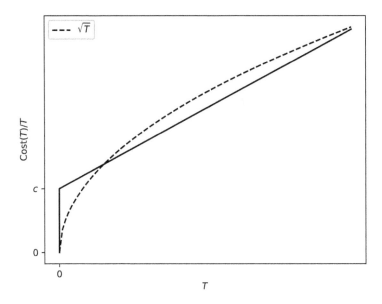

Figure 5.1   Linear impact cost plus slippage vs square root impact cost.

Adoption of the linear structure of price impact response and its exponential decay makes it possible to solve a multi-period optimization problem for a single security in a closed form (Sec. 6.4), which, other things equal, is a significant advantage over nonlinear impact models.

For position $P(t)$ evolving in continuous time, the impact cost is

$$\mathsf{Cost}(0, t) = - \int_0^t P(t')\dot{I}(t')dt'. \tag{5.5}$$

Integrating (5.5) by parts, we have

$$\mathsf{Cost}(0, t) = -P(t)I(t) + \int_0^t \dot{P}(t')I(t')dt'$$

$$= -P(t)I(t) + \frac{\lambda}{2} \iint_0^t \dot{P}(t')\dot{P}(t'')e^{-v|t'-t''|}dt'\,dt''. \tag{5.6}$$

This formula expresses the fact that a trade made at one time t' affects the cost of a trade made at a later time t''. This is due to the finite post-trade impact life time.

5.2.3   Instantaneous impact cost model

In the limit of a fast impact decay, $v \to \infty$, which is relevant for a portfolio turnover rate much slower than v, we can approximate the exponential impact kernel in (5.6) by a delta function:

$$e^{-v|t'-t''|} \to \frac{2}{v}\delta(t' - t'').   \tag{5.7}$$

Assuming a finite ratio

$$\mu = \frac{\lambda}{v},   \tag{5.8}$$

we arrive at the simplified impact model with an instantaneous cost of trading:

$$I = \mu\dot{P}, \quad \frac{d\text{Cost}}{dt} = \mu\dot{P}^2(t).   \tag{5.9}$$

This time-local impact cost model is useful for developing multi-period optimization intuition (Sec. 6.4.1).

5.2.4   Impact arbitrage

It is useful to differentiate functions and to solve differential equations.
Isaac Newton[19]

The first term in (5.6) is the terminal loss sustained by the final position $P(t)$ after the impact $I(t)$ decays. As a function of time, this term is bounded. The second term grows linearly with time t and describes interaction of trades made at different times. As a quadratic form with Laplacian kernel, it is positive definite (Sec. A3), so *impact arbitrage*, i.e., generating a consistent pnl by affecting stock price by trading, is impossible.

If the impact coefficient λ is a function of time, e.g., due to fluctuating intraday trading activity levels (which tends to be higher near

---

[19] A know-how considered by Newton as his most valuable secret. As a proof of priority, an encrypted anagram "6accdae13eff7i3l9n4o4qrr4s8t12ux," for Latin *Data aequatione quotcunque fluentes quantitae involvente fluxiones invenire et vice versa*, was sent to G.W. Leibniz, considered as a competitor, in 1677.

the market open and just before the market close), an impact arbitrage becomes theoretically possible by moving up the price by a buy during an illiquid period and selling back during a liquid period. Expressing from (5.2) the trading rate

$$\dot{P} = \frac{\dot{I} + vI}{\lambda}, \tag{5.10}$$

impact cost can be rewritten by repeatedly integrating by parts and omitting boundary values:

$$\int P\dot{I}dt = -\int I\dot{P}dt = -\int I\frac{\dot{I} + vI}{\lambda}dt$$
$$= -\int \frac{I^2}{2\lambda^2}(\dot{\lambda} + 2v\lambda)dt. \tag{5.11}$$

A negative impact cost can be generated during time periods when

$$\dot{\lambda} < -2v\lambda, \tag{5.12}$$

and could be potentially exploited by a portfolio.

Trying to benefit from impact arbitrage would be risky and possibly illegal.[20] We will assume that λ is (nearly) constant.

5.3 Cost of carry

Finally, just holding a position can involve its own cost known for physical commodities as cost of carry. For equities traded on a margin, this is interest on borrowed funds minus interest proceeds on stock sold short. For a market-neutral portfolio this is expressed in terms of a fixed cost of capital, which is usually insignificant in comparison with trading costs. An exception are hard-to-borrow equities, whose shorting involves additional broker fees.

---

[20] Theoretically, active management of price impact could be construed as market manipulation. The U.S. Securities Exchange Act of 1934 prohibits transactions affecting the price of a publicly traded security "for the purpose of inducing the purchase or sale of such security by others."

5.4   Market-wide impact and elasticity

Theocritus and Homer he disparaged,
but read, in compensation, Adam Smith,
and was a deep economist:
that is, he could assess the way
a state grows rich,
what it subsists upon, and why
it needs not gold
when it has got the simple product.

Alexander Pushkin[21]

The market impact of trades (Sec. 5.2) is not just a cost to a portfolio manager. It is the very reason why asset prices evolve, something the PM would very much like to understand and predict. Given that each stock is subject to the price impact, it is logical to ask what drives the equity market at a macro scale—in case the PM wants to manage exposures to SPY or other broad indices. The question is also of interest to economists, central bankers, regulators, and IRA account holders, to name a few.

One could argue that the trade impact, or supply and demand market pressure exerted by *homo economicus* investors, is ultimately motivated by rational fundamental analysis or the value of future dividend streams attached to equity holdings. Rational investing is neither the only nor the main effect driving the markets. There are also political, environmental, and public health events, government monetary policies, and *fads and fashions* of investing as a social activity.[22]

Another important part of the supply and demand landscape includes *liquidity traders*, i.e., those who trade not because they have specific bullish or bearish views of the assets but because they must. Pension plans and mutual funds continuously allocate participants' contributions according to their mandates and prospectuses. Payment of annuities and lump sum distributions requires selling assets regardless of any forecast. Holdings of pension and mutual funds account for a large portion of outstanding equity shares, and they are often positioned as liquidity traders. Over 50% of global pension

---

[21] A.S. Pushkin, *Eugene Onegin*, 1833. Translated by Vladimir Nabokov (1964).

[22] R.J. Shiller, Stock Prices and Social Dynamics, Brookings Papers on Economic Activity, 1984(2), pp. 457–510, 1984.

fund holdings are in equities,[23] even though the Social Security Trust Fund, the world's largest pension fund managing 2.9×10^{12} in assets,[24] invests only in government bonds.

Public and private pension funds, mutual funds, and insurance companies are the biggest institutional investors.[25] When large institutions manage flows of funds under certain constraints, there are market-wide consequences. An influential recent paper[26] analyzes the effect of institutional fixed equity share mandate on the aggregate market price elasticity. *Price elasticity* is defined as the sensitivity of a tradable item's supply or demand to its price. The trade curve of Sec. 6.10.1 is an example of real-time elastic supply or demand for shares of stock. The inverse of the elasticity describes the price sensitivity to demand or supply and has a meaning similar to market impact. Gabaix and Koijen estimate that an inflow of $1 into the stock market results in an aggregate market value increase of about $5, an illustration of what they term the *inelastic market hypothesis*.

The author, by no means an expert in macroeconomics, will take a risk of offering a simple explanation of the inelastic market effect. Let's assume that there is only one publicly traded stock with N shares outstanding, currently at price p, and only one institutional fund, *Incumbent Investments Inc.*, holding all (or most) of those shares.[27] The fund has a mandate to maintain a certain percentage α, e.g., 80%, of its total assets A in stock and the rest, $(1 - \alpha)A$, in cash. To meet the requirement, the fund's cash holdings must be

$$C = \frac{1 - \alpha}{\alpha} Np. \tag{5.13}$$

Now there is an inflow of funds to the market: a new fund, *The Surplus Group*, wants to buy δN shares of the stock. If Incumbent sold the shares to Surplus at the current price p, Incumbent's stock holdings percentage would drop below α, which is unacceptable. But Incumbent would agree

---

[23] https://www.oecd.org/pensions/Pension-Funds-in-Figures-2020.pdf.

[24] https://www.swfinstitute.org/profile/598cdaa60124e9fd2d05beb4.

[25] A. De La Cruz, A. Medina, Y. Tang, *Owners of the World's Listed Companies*, OECD Capital Market Series, Paris, 2019.

[26] X. Gabaix, R.S.J. Koijen, *In Search of the Origins of Financial Fluctuations: The Inelastic Markets Hypothesis*, Swiss Finance Institute Research Paper No. 20-91, Available at SSRN: https://ssrn.com/abstract=3686935, 2021.

[27] The idea being that a large institutional investor is the likely ultimate counterparty for any net market flow.

to sell at a higher price. If the after-trade price is $p + \delta p$, and the average trade price is in the middle, $p + \delta p/2$, the Incumbent's holdings mandate,

$$\frac{\text{stock}}{\text{stock} + \text{cash}} = \frac{(N - \delta N)(p + \delta p)}{(N - \delta N)(p + \delta p) + C + \delta N(p + \delta p/2)} = \alpha, \tag{5.14}$$

is solved by the price increase

$$\frac{\delta p}{p} = \frac{\delta N}{(1 - \alpha)N - (1 - \alpha/2)\delta N} \approx \frac{1}{1 - \alpha}\frac{\delta N}{N}. \tag{5.15}$$

The factor $(1 - \alpha)^{-1} > 1$ indicates a permanent market-wide impact due to the flow of funds. For $\alpha = 0.8$, the total market value increase, $N\delta p = 5p\delta N$, is a large multiple of the additional investment.

Conversely, if Incumbent faces an outflow of funds, the fund must initiate a sale in the market with few willing buyers, thus driving the stock price down until the holdings mandate is met again. The algebra for this case is the same as above up to the change of sign of δp.

In this simplified, *spherical-cow*-type model, the aggregate stock market value would behave like a bubble inflated by pension and other investible savings and deflated by redemptions and accelerated retirement of the workforce. Imagine a magic $5 bill in your wallet which turns into $1 when you want to actually spend the money.

The inelastic market impact of equity sales needed to fund growing pension payments could be one of the reasons for the crash of Japan's stock market.[28] The crash was followed by the *Lost Decade* (1991–2001) of economic stagnation amid an aging population and increasing number of retirees, a distinctive feature of Japan's demographics.[29] A *liquidity trap*[30] and a unique inefficiency of common fiscal policies[31] are cited as being among the causes of the Lost Decade(s).

Notwithstanding performance and solvency concerns,[32] it may be good, after all, that the U.S. Social Security Trust Fund stays away from the stock market.

---

[28] Vladimir V. Yankov pointed out this possible connection.

[29] https://data.worldbank.org/indicator/SL.TLF.CACT.NE.ZS?locations=JP.

[30] P.R. Krugman, *It's Baaack: Japan's Slump and the Return of the Liquidity Trap*, Brookings Papers in Economic Activity, 1998(2), 1998.

[31] N. Yoshino, F. Taghizadeh-Hesary, *Japan's Lost Decade: Lessons for Other Economies*, Asian Development Bank Institute Working Paper No. 521, 2015.

[32] B.F. Huston, *Social Security: The Trust Funds and Alternative Investments*, Congressional Research Service report R45709, 2019. Available at https://crsreports.congress.gov.

Chapter 6

Portfolio Construction

To trade a profitable portfolio, one generally wants to buy low and sell high. To systematically follow through on this, we need a forecast of future returns, a risk model, a trading cost model, and a portfolio construction algorithm using all of the above.

6.1   Hedged allocation

Ms. Three, Ms. Five, and Ms. Eight are making a cake. For this project Ms. Three contributes 3 lbs of flour, Ms. Five contributes 5 lbs of flour, and Ms. Eight, who has no flour, pays $8 cash. If the deal is fair, how much cash do Ms. Three and Ms. Five get back?

From a quant interview

Perhaps the simplest, and therefore fairly popular, portfolio construction method is signal-based allocation. A "signal" is either a forecast or a number proportional to, or altogether replacing, the forecast.

Given signals f_s, one computes portfolio positions P_s proportional to f_s. If there is only one risk factor to avoid, such as the market, one adds to the portfolio a *hedge*, a liquid ETF instrument such as SPY for US equities, as a market proxy with beta close to 1, in the amount computed to kill the market exposure of the portfolio. If there are industrial sector risk factors, they can be handled likewise by hedging by several broad sector ETFs such as XLK for technology, XLV for healthcare, XLU for utilities, and so forth. Signal-based allocation largely ignores trading costs, whose effect is then tested by a trading simulation (Chapter 7).

For more general risk factors specified by their loadings $\mathbf{L}_i$, $i = 1, \ldots, K$, one can orthogonalize the raw position $\mathbf{P} = a\mathbf{f}$ with respect to the risk factors,

$$\mathbf{P} = \mathbf{P}_{\|} + \mathbf{P}_{\perp}, \quad \mathbf{P}_{\perp} \cdot \mathbf{L}_i = 0. \tag{6.1}$$

This decomposition is unique and given by standard linear algebra. Equivalently, we could orthogonalize the signals WRT risk factors, $\mathbf{f} \rightarrow \mathbf{f}_{\perp}$, to start with.

In practice, the position vector $\mathbf{P}$ cannot be arbitrary and must be confined in a box $P_s \in B_s = [P_s^{min}, P_s^{max}]$. The constraints can include both firm-wide legal requirements and self-imposed limits, such as maximum daily trade size and position in terms of percentages of each name's ADV. Trade size is constrained to control impact costs (Sec. 5.2). Position size is constrained for potentially better portfolio diversification (Sec. 3.1) and to limit time to liquidate if necessary (Sec. 4.8). Linear algebra does not fit in a box. Constrained allocation can be handled using penalties by maximizing a utility function such as

$$F(\mathbf{P}) = \mathbf{f} \cdot \mathbf{P} - \frac{1}{2a}\mathbf{P}^2 - k \sum_i (\mathbf{L}_i \cdot \mathbf{P})^2, \quad \mathbf{P} \in \mathbf{B}. \tag{6.2}$$

In the absence of risk factors and constraints, this results in $\mathbf{P} = a\mathbf{f}$. Maximizing (6.2) subject to applicable box constraints and high enough factor exposure penalty k will result in a position almost orthogonal to all risk factors, and the regularizing scale a can be chosen iteratively to meet desired portfolio size. This is a convex *quadratic programming* (QP) optimization problem, which can be handled efficiently with many available QP solvers. Among those, the Barzilai-Borwein algorithm[1] is one of the easiest to implement. By empirical observations, it converges in $O(N^2 \log(N))$ FLOPs.

Alternatively, one can use a QP algorithm with K linear equality constraints $\mathbf{P} \cdot \mathbf{L}_i = 0$. There is no guarantee these are compatible with the box constraints, so one should be prepared to handle infeasible QP exceptions.

6.2   Forecast from rule-based strategy

Some event-based trading strategies (Sec. 2.1.7) may not use forecasts explicitly. Instead, there are trade rules specifying conditions for entering and exiting positions. A trade-rule-based strategy is formulated in terms of a target position as a prescribed function of time:

$$\mathbf{P} = \mathbf{P}^*(t). \tag{6.3}$$

To combine such strategy with other, forecast-based strategies, the trade rules need to be translated into a forecast, a process opposite to portfolio construction. One way to do so is to form a utility function penalizing for deviations from the strategy target $\mathbf{P}^*$. We can also include in the utility a penalty for risk factor exposure and apply constraints:

$$F(\mathbf{P}) = -A(\mathbf{P} - \mathbf{P}^*)^2 - k \sum_i (\mathbf{L}_i \cdot \mathbf{P})^2, \quad \mathbf{P} \in \mathbf{B}. \tag{6.4}$$

Up to a constant independent of the position $\mathbf{P}$, Eq. (6.4) is equivalent to (6.2) with the forecast

$$\mathbf{f}(t) = 2A\mathbf{P}^*(t). \tag{6.5}$$

The constant A (or, generally, a vector $\mathbf{A}$) needs to be suitably normalized for a correct forecast scale. This is required for comparing expected portfolio returns with trading costs, as discussed later in this chapter. A possibly complicated term structure of the trade-rule-based forecast $\mathbf{f}(t)$,

---

[1] J. Barzilai, J.M. Borwein, *Two-Point Step Size Gradient Methods*, IMA Journal of Numerical Analysis, 8(1), pp. 141–148, 1988.

either in isolation or combined with other forecasts, can be handled by a multi-period optimizer (Sec. 6.5).

6.3   Single-period vs multi-period mean-variance utility

A singly linked list is a data structure defined by its head node containing a pointer to the next node or null if the node is the tail of the list. What algorithm, linear in list size and with fixed memory, can be used to determine whether the list has a tail?

From a quant interview

Allocation utility (6.2), while reflecting forecast and risk loadings, still appears somewhat arbitrary. It would be better if the utility expressed our goals and preferences more explicitly. If the forecast f_s is meant as an expectation of the stock's daily return, then $\mathbf{f} \cdot \mathbf{P}$ is the expectation of daily pnl. This pnl term appears in Eq. (6.2) and makes sense for a utility function. A regularization term can be made more precise by expressing risk aversion as a penalty for the expected pnl variance. With a factor risk model, the covariance matrix (4.7) is positive definite and takes care of both regularization and factor risk. The expected pnl should be also adjusted for trading costs associated with transitioning from the current position $\mathbf{P}_0$ to the new position $\mathbf{P}$. With slippage c_s and impact cost (5.4), the portfolio utility is

$$F(\mathbf{P}) = \mathbf{f} \cdot \mathbf{P} - \mathbf{I} \cdot \mathbf{T} - \mathbf{c} \cdot |\mathbf{T}| - k\mathbf{P}C\mathbf{P}, \qquad (6.6)$$

where

$$I_s = I_{0s} + \frac{\lambda_s}{2} T_s \qquad (6.7)$$

is the trade impact in security s and

$$\mathbf{T} = \mathbf{P} - \mathbf{P}_0 \qquad (6.8)$$

is the vector of trades. In Eq. in (6.6), the absolute value of a vector is understood component-wise and C is the return covariance matrix such as in Eq. (4.7). To use impact cost as written, the time period must be shorter than the impact decay time v^{-1}.

Eq. (6.6), as a single-period utility, is insufficient for nonlocal impact costs when earlier trades affect the cost of later trades (Sec. 5.2.2). To tackle multi-period, aka multi-horizon or multi-step, optimization, it is convenient to use continuous time. Let the current time point at which the forecast is produced and portfolio optimization is run be $t = 0$. Instead of a one-day forecast, we use forecast $\mathbf{f}(t)$ a function of horizon. This combined forecast can include shorter technical and longer fundamental forecasts. The function $f_s(t)$ starts with $f_s(0) = 0$, is not monotone in general, but it will approach a constant at $t \to \infty$, i.e., beyond the longest available prediction. We are looking for the position path $\mathbf{P}(t)$ maximizing a time-integrated utility as a *functional* of $\mathbf{P}(t)$:

$$F[\mathbf{P}(t)] = \int_0^\infty (\mathbf{P} \cdot \dot{\mathbf{f}} - \mathbf{c} \cdot |\dot{\mathbf{P}}| - \dot{\mathbf{P}}\Lambda\dot{\mathbf{P}} - k\mathbf{P}C\mathbf{P})dt. \tag{6.9}$$

In Eq. (6.9), Λ is a linear integral operator appearing in the impact model (5.2). It appears quite plausible[2] that trades in one stock cause impact in other stocks as well, so $\Lambda_{ss'}$ is a matrix integral operator. Since fitting a cross-impact matrix to execution data looks difficult, we normally assume this matrix diagonal.[3] The impact operator is defined by

$$I_s(t) = \Lambda\dot{P}_s(t) = \lambda_s \int_0^t e^{-\nu_s|t-t'|}\dot{P}_s(t')dt'. \tag{6.10}$$

Finite-life-time impact couples each asset position serially (by time) and requires optimizing for position paths $P_s(t)$—functions rather than numbers.

The last, variance-penalty term in (6.9) consists of risk aversion by asset (*residual*, or *idiosyncratic*, risk) and factor exposure risk:

$$\mathbf{P}C\mathbf{P} = \sum_s \sigma_s^2 P_s^2 + \sum_{ij} U_{ij}(\mathbf{L}_i \cdot \mathbf{P})(\mathbf{L}_j \cdot \mathbf{P}) \tag{6.11}$$

The factor risk couples assets cross-sectionally via the loadings $\mathbf{L}_i$ and requires optimizing for all assets simultaneously. Given some estimation uncertainty in the factor covariance U_{ij}, even after asset covariance shrinkage by the factor model (Sec. 4.2), it is not unreasonable to use

---

[2] M. Benzaquen, I. Mastromatteo, Z. Eisler, J.-P. Bouchaud, *Dissecting cross-impact on stock markets: An empirical analysis*, arXiv:1609.02395v2 [q-fin.TR], 2016.

[3] A more general symmetric $\Lambda_{ss'}$ matrix is considered in Sec. 6.5.1.

different penalties for the diagonal and the factor risk in (6.11) instead of the single risk aversion coefficient k.

Any costs of carry (Sec. 5.3) are linear in the dollar position and can be absorbed in the forecast $\hat{f}$, along with the projected decay of the initial impact $I_0 e^{-vt}$.

Utility (6.9) must be maximized with respect to all possible position paths $P(t)$ starting with the current position $P(0) = P_0$. Given that $\hat{f}(\infty) = 0$ (no forecast beyond a max horizon), the position must go to zero as $t \to \infty$ to avoid risk with no reward. After the optimal path $P(t)$ is solved for, much of the solution will be discarded though because after trading down the initial part of the path, new information becomes available, forecasts are updated, and the process repeats.[4] One can optionally discount future utility (6.9) by an exponential factor $e^{-\Gamma t}$.

Numerical maximization of the multi-period utility (6.9) or its discrete versions is challenging due to the additional time dimension, but there are ways to simplify it by doing part of the work analytically. In the following sections this is demonstrated in several special cases.

6.4   Single-name multi-period optimization

If the off-diagonal (factor) part is omitted from the stock covariance (4.7), portfolio optimization splits into optimizations by individual stock. Single-name optimization, a useful building block of the full portfolio optimization, is the subject of this section.

6.4.1   Optimization with fast impact decay

If you ever stirred tea with a teaspoon, you may have noticed that pieces of tea leaves accumulate at the center of the bottom of the cup. Why aren't they drawn to the outside by centrifugal force?

From a quant interview

If trading rate is much slower than impact decay, we can use the local trading cost limit (5.9). Single name utility with this cost and no slippage is

$$F[P(t)] = \int_0^\infty (\dot{f}P - kP^2 - \mu\dot{P}^2)dt. \qquad (6.12)$$

---

[4] Alternative approaches explicitly accounting for the forecast revision are discussed in Sec. 6.7.

The variation[5] of the utility,

$$\delta F = \int_0^\infty (\dot{f}\delta P - 2kP\delta P - 2\mu\dot{P}\delta\dot{P})dt, \qquad (6.13)$$

upon integrating by parts gives the optimality condition

$$(\partial_t^2 - \omega^2)P = \frac{\dot{f}}{2\mu}, \quad \omega = \left(\frac{k}{\mu}\right)^{1/2}, \qquad (6.14)$$

which is somewhat similar to the dynamics of a body of mass μ immersed in a viscous fluid and acted upon by an external force $\dot{f}$. Rewriting this as

$$(\partial_t + \omega)P = (\partial_t - \omega)^{-1}\frac{\dot{f}}{2\mu}$$

$$= \frac{1}{2\mu}\int_0^\infty \dot{f}(t)e^{-\omega t}dt, \qquad (6.15)$$

we obtain the initial trading rate

$$\dot{P}(0) = -\omega P_0 + \frac{1}{2\mu}\int_0^\infty \dot{f}(t)e^{-\omega t}dt. \qquad (6.16)$$

The full path can also be written in a closed form, but the knowledge of just $\dot{P}(0)$ is sufficient to start trading. The first term in (6.16) reflects risk aversion. The second term is an exponential moving average of expected future price changes with time constant $\omega^{-1} \propto \mu^{1/2}$ and plays the role of an *effective forecast*. The time constant is shorter (longer) for more (less) liquid stocks, expressing an inertia–like behavior. The result is intuitive in that liquid names can be traded on shorter signals and illiquid ones should only react to longer forecasts.

Solution (6.16) can be also written in the form of future position target P^* and the optimal rate ω of trading toward the target:

$$\dot{P}(0) = \omega(P^* - P_0),$$

$$P^* = (2k\mu)^{-1/2}\int_0^\infty \dot{f}(t)e^{-\omega t}dt. \qquad (6.17)$$

[5] A.R. Forsyth, *Calculus of Variations*, Dover, 1960.

Result (6.17) is easy to generalize to an exponentially discounted future utility introduced by an addition time weight $e^{-\Gamma t}$ in Eq. (6.12). As expected, discounting of future pnl results in an increased forecast EMA rate ω:

$$\omega = \frac{\Gamma}{2} + \left(\frac{\Gamma^2}{4} + \frac{k}{\mu}\right)^{1/2}. \qquad (6.18)$$

6.4.2 Optimization with exponentially decaying impact

A parallel light beam is passing through a hollow pipe filled with suspended dust, so the total cross-sectional area of all dust particles in the pipe equals its cross-section. How much of the light energy will pass through the pipe?

From a quant interview

The model of Sec. 6.4.1 is a special limit, for large λ and v and finite $\mu = \lambda/v$, of the exponentially decaying impact. Here we consider the more general single-name utility

$$F[P(t)] = \int_0^\infty (\dot{f}P - kP^2 - I\dot{P})dt, \qquad (6.19)$$

$$\dot{I} = \lambda\dot{P} - vI.$$

Introducing the new variable[6]

$$Q = P - I/\lambda, \qquad (6.20)$$

the position and the impact are expressed as

$$P = Q + \dot{Q}/v, \quad I = (\lambda/v)\dot{Q}. \qquad (6.21)$$

Then the utility (6.19) transforms to

$$F[Q(t)] = \int_0^\infty \left(gQ - kQ^2 - \frac{k}{\omega^2}\dot{Q}^2\right)dt, \qquad (6.22)$$

where

$$g(t) = \dot{f}(t) - v^{-1}\ddot{f}(t),$$

$$\omega = \alpha v, \qquad (6.23)$$

$$\alpha = \left(1 + \frac{\lambda v}{k}\right)^{-1/2}.$$

---

[6] An elegant solution using this variable is due to Andrei Johansen (unpublished, 2005). Originally, the results of this section were obtained using a Laplace transform.

The utility functional (6.22) is identical to (6.12) up to relabeling and can be maximized by a similar variational procedure. The optimal path for $Q(t)$ is

$$Q(t) = Q_0 e^{-\omega t} + \frac{\omega^2}{2k} \int_0^\infty g(t') Q_{t'}(t) dt',$$ (6.24)

where

$$Q_{t'}(t) = \frac{1}{2\omega}(e^{-\omega|t-t'|} - e^{-\omega(t+t')})$$ (6.25)

is the Green's function of the operator $\omega^2 - \partial_t^2$, or bounded solution of the linear equation

$$(\omega^2 - \partial_t^2)Q_{t'}(t) = \delta(t - t'), \quad \text{s.t.} \quad Q_{t'}(0) = 0.$$ (6.26)

Transforming back to

$$P = Q + \frac{\dot{Q}}{v},$$ (6.27)

we observe that the optimal position path generally starts with a discontinuity, or a finite size trade, from the initial P_0 to the target

$$P^* = (1 - \alpha)Q_0 + \frac{\alpha^2 v}{2k} f_\omega^{\text{eff}}.$$ (6.28)

The *effective forecast* introduced in (6.28) depends on the security liquidity relative to risk aversion:

$$f_\omega^{\text{eff}} = \int_0^\infty g(t) e^{-\omega t} dt$$

$$= \begin{cases} \dot{f}_0/v + f_\infty, & k \ll \lambda v, \\ \dot{f}_0/v, & k \gg \lambda v. \end{cases}$$ (6.29)

Just like in the local impact model (6.16), the effective forecast is sensitive to shorter (longer) horizons for more (less) liquid names. Unlike the local impact cost model (6.12), a finite trade in model (6.19) incurs finite cost and is therefore allowed. If (6.17) gives an optimal rate of trading to a target, (6.28) indicates an optimal position to take immediately. In the limit $v \gg k/\lambda$ the targets (6.17) and (6.28) are the same.

As a common feature of linear-quadratic functions, the optimum is reached at the point where quadratic penalties amount to one-half the linear term. This means that it is optimal to give away half of the forecast-driven gross pnl to impact cost and risk penalty.

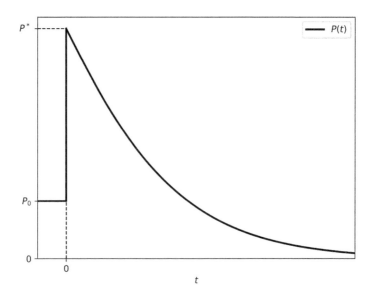

Figure 6.1   Schematic of optimal position path with impact decay.

After the initial trade $T^* = P^* - P_0$, the optimal position path $P(t)$ is continuous (Fig. 6.1). One can show that the continuous part is consistent with (6.28) applied to infinitesimal changes of the forecast $f(t)$ due to time shifts.

6.4.3   Optimization conditional on a future position

Having in mind portfolio optimization with factor risk introducing interaction among stocks, we need to consider single-stock solutions away from the optimum (6.28), so a deterioration in single-name utility (6.19) could be counterbalanced by a beneficial reduction of multi-asset factor risk. One way to introduce a single-name non-optimality is a constraint on a future position P_f. For intraday optimization, P_f could be an end-of-day position target, but that constraint would be too rigid near the market close. Given an abundance of exponentials in the solution of Sec. 6.4.2, it is convenient to introduce, instead of a fixed point in time, a constraint in terms of the future EMA position

$$P_f = \int_0^\infty P(t)e^{-\gamma t}\gamma \, dt, \qquad (6.30)$$

with a horizon γ^{-1} suitable for imposing factor risk penalties on P_f.

Incorporating condition (6.30) in the utility (6.19) with a Lagrange multiplier m just redefines the forecast as

$$\dot{f} \to \dot{f} + m\gamma e^{-\gamma t}, \tag{6.31}$$

without changing algebra. The maximum of the utility subject to the P_f constraint works out to a quadratic:

$$F^*(P_f) = \max_{P:\ \text{EMA}(P) = P_f} F[P(t)] = -aP_f^2 + bP_f + c, \tag{6.32}$$

with the coefficients

$$a = \frac{2k(\omega + \gamma)^2}{\gamma(\omega + \alpha\gamma)^2},$$

$$b = \frac{4k(1 - \alpha)(\omega + \gamma)}{(\omega + \alpha\gamma)^2}Q_0 - \frac{2\omega(\omega + \gamma)}{\omega + \alpha\gamma}\frac{f_\omega^{eff} - f_\gamma^{eff}}{\omega - \gamma}, \tag{6.33}$$

and f_x^{eff} given by Eq. (6.29). Under the EMA constraint (6.30), the optimal solution $P(t)$ also starts with a finite trade to the target

$$P^*(P_f) = (1 - \alpha)\frac{\omega - \alpha\gamma}{\omega + \alpha\gamma}Q_0 + \frac{\alpha^2 v}{2k}f_\omega^{eff}$$

$$- \frac{\alpha\omega\gamma(\omega + \gamma)}{k}\frac{f_\omega^{eff} - f_\gamma^{eff}}{\omega^2 - \gamma^2} + 2\alpha\frac{\omega + \gamma}{\omega + \alpha\gamma}P_f. \tag{6.34}$$

The maximum of (6.32) is reached at

$$P_f^* = \frac{b}{2a} = \frac{\gamma(1 - \alpha)}{\omega + \gamma}Q_0 - \frac{\gamma\omega(\omega + \alpha\gamma)}{2k}\frac{f_\omega^{eff} - f_\gamma^{eff}}{\omega^2 - \gamma^2}, \tag{6.35}$$

which is a "harmless" constraint on (6.19). Correspondingly, in the immediate future limit $\gamma \to \infty$, P_f^* equals the optimal position P^* (6.28) as it should. The conditional single-name utility (6.32) for $P_f \neq P_f^*$ will be used in Sec. 6.5.3.

6.4.4   Position value and utility leak

Given a steel pipe with an audible water flow, what would be the simplest nondestructive measurement of the direction of the flow?

From a quant interview

A utility function

$$F[P(t), \dot{f}(t)] = \int_0^\infty \left((\dot{f} + \dot{I})P - kP^2 - c|\dot{P}|\right)w(t)dt \tag{6.36}$$

can be used for more than just portfolio construction. Here a time discount factor $w(t)$ (e.g., an exponential $w(t) = \Gamma e^{-\Gamma t}$) is introduced to keep the utility finite. Consider a forecast consisting of two components,

$$\dot{f} = \dot{f}_1 + \dot{f}_2, \tag{6.37}$$

the second one with a very long horizon so $\dot{f}_2$ is almost constant. Then the slow forecast can be eliminated by observing that

$$F[P(t), \dot{f}_1 + \dot{f}_2] = F\left[P(t) - \frac{\dot{f}_2}{2k}, \dot{f}_1\right] + \int_0^\infty \frac{w(t)\dot{f}_2^2}{4k} dt. \tag{6.38}$$

The second term is independent of position and can be omitted. So when adding a very slow forecast f_2, the position should be shifted by a constant $\dot{f}_2/(2k)$. This is a simple way of combining forecasts with disparate horizons at the portfolio construction level. The opposite case of utilizing a fast forecast is considered in Sec. 6.10.2.

Some broker-dealers offer basket trading services to clients. A client may want to acquire or sell a sizable portfolio of securities,[7] or *basket*, without worrying about a potentially lengthy execution and associated risks and transaction costs. The broker's trading desk can take the basket on its balance sheet at the basket's current market price and charge a fee for the trouble of unwinding the basket. Depending on existing position at the desk and possibly available forecasts, the basket can be more or less attractive to the desk manager thus affecting the fee she would charge the client.

A measure of attractiveness of a position is *position value* expressed as the utility function assuming optimal execution:

$$F^*(P_0; \dot{f}(t)) = \max_{P(t): \ P(0) = P_0} F[P(t), \dot{f}(t)]. \tag{6.39}$$

The *ansatz* (6.21) suggests that, in the absence of slippage, the value of an initial position P depends on P and impact I only in the combination

$$Q = P - \frac{I}{\lambda}, \tag{6.40}$$

meaning that position-impact states (P, I) and $(P + T, I + \lambda T)$ are equally valuable. This is seen from the fact that a trade T can be

---

[7] These can be actual shares or swap-like derivatives.

reversed, and its impact undone, if the impact was given no chance to decay. This reversibility will disappear if we impose a time delay.

Position value offers another view of a single-name solution away from the optimum. If trade to the optimal position (6.28) is not done immediately, and position $P \neq P^*$ is held for a short period time δt, working out a second variation of the utility functional (6.19) indicates the utility, and position value, loss:

$$\delta F = -(k + \lambda v)(P - P^*)^2 \delta t. \tag{6.41}$$

We can therefore associate non-optimality of a single-name position with a *utility leak* at the rate

$$\dot{f}(P) = -(k + \lambda v)(P - P^*)^2, \tag{6.42}$$

where the optimum P^* is given by Eq. (6.28). Formula (6.42) will be used in Sec. 6.5.4.

6.4.5   Optimization with slippage

Find the center of a given circle using only a compass.

From a quant interview

We now analyze the effect of slippage with impact cost omitted. Single-name utility in this limit is

$$F[P(t)] = \int_0^\infty (\dot{f}P - kP^2 - c|\dot{P}|)dt. \tag{6.43}$$

Integration by parts gives

$$F[P(t)] = \int_0^\infty (-\dot{P}\big[f + c\,\mathtt{sign}(\dot{P})\big] - kP^2)dt, \tag{6.44}$$

indicating that slippage c is added to or subtracted from the forecast. A constant addition to $f(t)$ would not affect the basic solution

$$P(t) = \frac{f(t)}{2k}. \tag{6.45}$$

However, due to changes in trading direction the problem is more complicated and depends on the initial condition and the shape of the forecast curve. It is more or less clear that the optimal solution consists of intervals

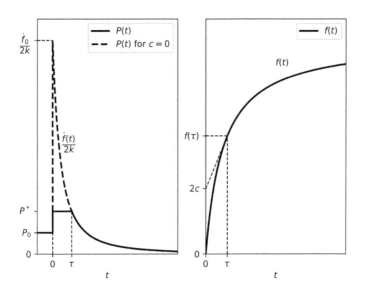

Figure 6.2 Left: Optimal position path with slippage (solid line). Right: Geometric solution of Eq. (6.47) for the plateau width τ. The dashed line starting at $(0, 2c)$ and tangent to the graph of $f(t)$ is used to determine τ. A rational forecast shape (6.49) was used for generating the chart.

of constant position and trading according to (6.45). In fact, Eq. (6.43) is equivalent to the total variation denoising (TVD) of the slippage-free target (6.45) subject to the cost of round trips (Sec. 2.4.11.2).

To be specific, assume an initial condition with $0 < P_0 < \dot{f}_0/(2k)$ and optimize for the single parameter τ, a holding period after the initial trade $P^* - P_0$, as shown in Fig. 6.2. Eq. (6.44) gives utility as a function of τ. Dropping constants, we have

$$F(\tau) = \frac{\dot{f}(\tau)}{2k}\left(f(\tau) - 2c - \frac{\tau}{2}\dot{f}(\tau)\right) + \int_\tau^\infty \frac{\dot{f}^2(t)}{4k}dt. \qquad (6.46)$$

This function is maximized at

$$f(\tau) - \tau\dot{f}(\tau) = 2c. \qquad (6.47)$$

A graphical solution to (6.47) is shown in the right Fig. 6.2. For a positive concave $f(t)$, the solution exists if the total forecast exceeds the cost of a roundtrip:

$$f(\infty) > 2c. \qquad (6.48)$$

For $c \to 0$, we have $\tau \to 0$, and the optimal position path follows (6.45). The larger the slippage, the larger τ and smaller the trade. For $P_0 > \dot{f}_0/(2k) > 0$, the optimal solution is to trade to position $\dot{f}_0/(2k)$ and then follow the path (6.45).

For a closed-form example, let forecast be a rational function of the horizon:

$$f(t) = \frac{f_\infty \gamma t}{1 + \gamma t}.$$ (6.49)

Then, for $f_\infty > 0$ and $P_0 < P^*$, the optimal position and the time to hold it are given by

$$P^* = \frac{\gamma f_\infty}{2k}\left(1 - \sqrt{\frac{2c}{f_\infty}}\right)^2,$$

$$\tau = \gamma^{-1}\frac{(2c)^{1/2}}{f_\infty^{1/2} - (2c)^{1/2}}.$$ (6.50)

For a monotone $\dot{f}(t)$, all other cases can be similarly written in a closed, if implicit, form. If forecast $f(t)$ has inflection points, analysis along these lines is also doable but quickly gets complicated. The complexity is due to the non-analytic (absolute-value) nature of the slippage term in the utility functional (6.43).

A general feature of optimal trading with slippage costs can be described in terms of a *comfort range* $[P^*_{\min}(t), P^*_{\max}(t)]$ such as if position P is within the range, it should not be traded. If current position is outside the range, it should be traded to its nearest boundary. The boundaries $P^*_{\min,\max}$ depend on the slippage and on the forecast profile $f(t)$. The larger the slippage, the wider the comfort range and more likely it includes zero position. A similar pattern of "No Trade" zone was described for optimal trading with slippage under a diffusive price process.[8,9]

In the geometry of Fig. 6.2, the comfort range is $[P^*, \dot{f}_0/(2k)]$. For $\dot{f}(t)$ changing sign one or more times, the range is wider due to potential cost of multiple roundtrips.

[8] J. de Lataillade, C. Deremble, M. Potters, J.-P. Bouchaud, *Optimal Trading with Linear Costs*, arXiv:1203.5957 [q-fin.PM], 2012.
[9] R.J. Martin, *Universal trading under proportional transaction costs*, arXiv:1603.06558 [q-fin.TR], 2016.

6.5 Multi-period portfolio optimization

In mathematics you don't understand things. You just get used to them.

John von Neumann

The problem of optimizing a portfolio of correlated assets is solved, one way or another, by multiple portfolio managers on a daily basis and is clearly an important part of the trading business, quantitative and discretionary alike. The problem has been studied extensively starting with Markowitz,[10] whose treatment did not include transaction costs or time-dependent return expectation. The problem becomes more difficult, both analytically and computationally, when there is future time structure and non-local impact costs requiring a multi-period treatment. There are two principal directions to handle: cross-sectional (same time, different assets) and serial (same asset, different times). They need to be combined in a portfolio construction procedure.

If trading costs are period-specific (localized in time), the periods decouple and the portfolio can be cross-sectionally optimized for each time period sequentially.[11] In the presence of a multi-period price impact, all periods must be optimized simultaneously. In this section we discuss several ways to do it. We use a continuous-time approach adopted in Sec. 6.4. Discrete time algorithms also exist[12] but are not covered here.

6.5.1 Unconstrained portfolio optimization with linear impact costs

Here we apply the single-asset reasoning of Sec. 6.4.2 to the multi-asset utility (6.9) with slippage costs omitted. Switching from scalar notation

[10] H. Markowitz, *The optimization of a quadratic function subject to linear constraints*, Naval Research Logistics, 3(1–2), pp. 111–133, 1956.

[11] S. Boyd, E. Busseti, S. Diamond, R.N. Kahn, K. Koh, P. Nystrup, J. Speth, *Multi-Period Trading via Convex Optimization*, arXiv:1705.00109v1 [q-fin.PM], 2017.

[12] N.B. Gârleanu, L.H. Pedersen, *Dynamic trading with predictable returns and transaction costs*, The Journal of Finance, 68(6), pp. 2309–2340, 2013.

to vectors and matrices, we write

$$F[\mathbf{P}(t)] = \int_0^\infty (\dot{\mathbf{f}}\mathbf{P} - k\mathbf{P}C\mathbf{P} - \mathbf{I}\dot{\mathbf{P}})dt,$$

$$\mathbf{I} = \Lambda\dot{\mathbf{P}} - \nu\mathbf{I}.$$

(6.51)

Here the impact matrix $\Lambda_{ss'}$ may include non-diagonal elements describing cross-impact of assets, but the impact decay rate ν is assumed the same for all securities, an assumption that would be easy to relax. An arbitrage argument[13,14] suggests that the the cross-impact matrix $\Lambda_{ss'}$ is symmetric. A recent analysis[15] questions the causality of empirical cross-impact estimation and suggests the impact matrix may as well be considered diagonal. For a symmetric or diagonal $\Lambda_{ss'}$, integration by parts leads to a utility functional quadratic in $\mathbf{Q}$:

$$F[\mathbf{Q}(t)] = \int_0^\infty (\mathbf{g}\mathbf{Q} - k\mathbf{Q}C\mathbf{Q} - k\dot{\mathbf{Q}}\Omega^{-2}\dot{\mathbf{Q}}) \, dt,$$

$$\mathbf{g} = \dot{\mathbf{f}} - \frac{1}{\nu}\ddot{\mathbf{f}}.$$

(6.52)

Here $\mathbf{Q}$ is defined similarly to (6.21):

$$\mathbf{P} = \mathbf{Q} + \frac{\dot{\mathbf{Q}}}{\nu},$$

$$\mathbf{I} = \frac{1}{\nu}\Lambda\dot{\mathbf{Q}}.$$

(6.53)

The symmetric positive definite matrix Ω appearing in Eq. (6.52) via

$$\Omega^{-2} = \frac{1}{\nu^2}\left(C + \frac{\nu}{k}\Lambda\right)$$

(6.54)

[13] I. Mastromatteo, M. Benzaquen, Z. Eisler, J.-P. Bouchaud, *Trading Lightly: Cross-Impact and Optimal Portfolio Execution*, arXiv:1702.03838v3, 2017.

[14] M. Schneider, F. Lillo, *Cross-impact and no-dynamic-arbitrage*, arXiv:1612.07742 [q-fin.TR], 2017.

[15] F. Capponi, R. Cont, *Multi-Asset Market Impact and Order Flow Commonality*, Available at SSRN: https://ssrn.com/abstract=3706390, October 6, 2020.

can be computed using an $N \times N$ eigendecomposition or Denman-Beavers iteration.[16] A matrix-form (portfolio) generalization of the result (6.28) for the optimal position is then

$$\mathbf{P}^* = \left(1 - \frac{1}{v}\Omega\right)\mathbf{Q}_0 + \frac{1}{2kv}\int_0^\infty \Omega^2 e^{-\Omega t}\mathbf{g}(t)dt. \qquad (6.55)$$

The matrix exponential appearing in (6.55), as well as any other well-behaved function of a real symmetric matrix A, is computable via its eigendecomposition:[17]

$$A = X\Lambda X' \implies f(A) = Xf(\Lambda)X', \qquad (6.56)$$

where $\Lambda = \mathrm{Diag}(\lambda_i)$ is the diagonal matrix of the eigenvalues of A, X is a unitary matrix whose columns are the eigenvectors of A, and

$$f(\Lambda) = \mathrm{Diag}(f(\lambda_i)). \qquad (6.57)$$

A closed-form matrix solution (6.55) for the optimal portfolio positions is nice to have, but its practicality is limited by the assumed lack of constraints, no obvious way of adding slippage, and the $O(N^3)$ complexity of eigendecomposition for a universe of N securities. However, if the impact matrix Λ is diagonal and the covariance C is factor-modeled as (4.7), the special diagonal plus low rank matrix structure allows eigendecomposition in $O(N^2)$ FLOPs.[18,19]

Below we provide a few approximations for multi-period portfolio optimization that are more flexible than the "final answer" (6.55).

---

[16] E.D. Denman, A.N. Beavers Jr, *The matrix sign function and computations in systems*, Applied Mathematics and Computation, 2(1), pp. 63–94, 1976.

[17] N.J. Higham, *Functions of Matrices: Theory and Computation*, University of Manchester, 2008.

[18] P. Benner, S. Dolgov, V. Khoromskaia, B.N. Khoromskij, *Fast iterative solution of the Bethe-Salpeter eigenvalue problem using low-rank and QTT tensor approximation*, arXiv: 1602.02646v1 [math.NA], 2016.

[19] R. Liang, *Fast and Stable Low-Rank Symmetric Eigen-Update*, Ph.D. thesis, University of California at Berkeley, 2018.

6.5.2 Iterative handling of factor risk

Iterate over all vertices of a 32-dimensional cube so that each step is made along an edge and each vertex is visited exactly once.

From a quant interview

Given ways of solving a single-name multi-period optimization, one could try to account for asset interaction iteratively. Using the covariance structure (4.7), utility (6.9) can be written as

$$F[\mathbf{P}(t)] = \sum_s \int \left(\tilde{f}_s P_s - k\sigma_s^2 P_s^2 - I_s \dot{P}_s - c_s |\dot{P}_s| \right) dt, \qquad (6.58)$$

with forecasts for stock s adjusted for the "risk pressure" from other stocks:

$$\tilde{f}_s = \dot{f}_s - k \sum_{ijs'} U_{ij} L_{is} L_{js'} P_{s'}. \qquad (6.59)$$

Using positions from previous iteration in the risk adjusted forecast (6.59), one can repeatedly optimize each single-asset term in (6.58). The convergence of such iterations depends on the initial approximation ((6.55) being a good candidate), adaptive scaling of k in (6.59), the spectrum of the matrix $L'UL$, and several data-dependent factors, slippage being a stabilizing one.

6.5.3 Optimizing future EMA positions

Among methods not subject to convergence concerns there is one based on a single-asset optimization conditional on future EMA positions $\mathbf{P}_f$ described in Sec. 6.4.3. A factor risk penalty $\mathbf{P}'L'UL\mathbf{P}$, instead of the instantaneous position $\mathbf{P}(t)$, could as well be applied to a future position $\mathbf{P}_f$ smoothed over a suitable horizon γ^{-1}. In addition to mathematical convenience, this smoothing can also decrease portfolio turnover.

So we use the utility function (6.32) with the addition of the future factor risk:

$$F(\mathbf{P}_f) = \sum_s (-a_s P_{fs}^2 + b_s P_{fs})$$

$$- \frac{k}{\gamma} \sum_{ijss'} U_{ij} L_{is} L_{js'} P_{fs} P_{fs'}. \qquad (6.60)$$

Without constraints, the maximum of (6.60) is reached at

$$\mathbf{P}_f^* = \frac{1}{2}\left(A + \frac{k}{\gamma}L'UL\right)^{-1}\mathbf{b},$$ (6.61)

$$A = \texttt{Diag}(a_s).$$

The inversion of the diagonal plus low rank matrix can be sped up by using the Woodbury formula (Sec. A2).

Constraints on the quadratic problem (6.60) can be introduced by the known relation (6.34) between current vs future optimum.[20] Similarly, slippage penalties can be added to the utility (6.60), but this will be an approximation because the results of Sec. 6.4.3 assumed no slippage.

6.5.4   Portfolio optimization using utility leak rate

Here we use the results of Sec. 6.4.4 to balance single-asset position value against multi-asset risk. Once the forecast path has been used to derive an optimal position path, utility loss due to the position away from the single-asset optimum P_s^* is given by the instantaneous rate (6.42). Adding multi-asset factor risk, we obtain an effectively single-period optimization problem for

$$\dot{F}(\mathbf{P}) = -\sum_s (k\sigma_s^2 + \lambda_s v)(P_s - P_s^*)^2$$

$$- k\sum_{ijss'} U_{ij}L_{is}L_{js'}P_s P_{s'},$$ (6.62)

with a structure similar to the future-position optimization of Sec. 6.5.3. Adding constraints to the QP problem (6.62) is straightforward.

6.5.5   Notes on portfolio optimization with slippage

Unlike linear impact, a singular structure of the slippage cost makes analytical optimization difficult. An exception is the closed-form solution of Sec. 6.4.5 obtained with a risk penalty but without impact costs. While providing an insight of the "comfort range" trading pattern, there is no obvious way to use it in the full multi-asset, multi-period optimization.

---

[20] One may wish to impose limits on both current $\mathbf{P}$ and future $\mathbf{P}_f$ leading to a narrower allowed box.

A pragmatic approach is to add to utilities like (6.60) or (6.62) terms $c_s|P_s - P_{0s}|$ penalizing for trading away from the current position $\mathbf{P}_0$ and tune heuristic scalings of c_s by simulation with proper costs. One should be aware though that positions for high-slippage assets can get stuck away from zero, which is suboptimal and should be handled outside the optimizer.

A wide class of portfolio optimization problems reduces to a modified QP with absolute value penalties such as[21]

$$\max \left[\sum_s (b_s P_s - c_s|P_s - P_{0s}|) - \sum_{ss'} C_{ss'} P_s P_{s'} \right] \tag{6.63}$$

with applicable box constraints. Problem (6.63) is convex and can be solved in well under a second for a universe of a few thousand assets.

Another option is to combine iterations of factor risk pressure in Eqs. (6.58)-(6.59) with an optimal control single-asset treatment, described in Sec. 6.7.

In general, it is difficult to "overfit the optimizer" (Sec. 7.2). Whatever tractable approximation of the full intractable optimization problem is adopted, the result is testable and tunable by simulation (Sec. 7).

6.6   Portfolio capacity

Estimate, with error bound, the number of molecules in the Earth's atmosphere.

From a quant interview

An important parameter of a quantitative strategy is its capacity, or maximum gross market value (GMV) it can handle.[22] Assuming a portfolio is performing at a certain size G, and the manager has calibrated the portfolio's transaction costs including slippage and impact, can we predict how the performance would scale at different portfolio sizes and determine its size limit?

---

[21] One could also add a second absolute value penalty $c_s'|P_s|$ to make closing positions easier than opening them: $|P| + |P - P_0|$ is constant for $P \in [0, P_0]$ and won't penalize trades toward zero.

[22] GMV is normally higher than assets under management (AUM) due to leverage (Sec. 6.9.)

A simple estimate can be done based on theory. Our trading cost model predicts the following structure of the mean daily pnl:

$$\text{pnl} = \text{Mean}(\mathbf{PR} - \mathbf{c}|\dot{\mathbf{P}}| - (1/2)\dot{\mathbf{P}}\Lambda\dot{\mathbf{P}}). \tag{6.64}$$

As a function of GMV G, the dependence is parabolic with some coefficients A, B, and C:

$$\text{pnl}(G) = BG - CG - AG^2, \tag{6.65}$$

where the gross pnl part is hopefully larger than the slippage part: $B > C$. Expression (6.65) is maximized at

$$G = \frac{B - C}{2A}, \tag{6.66}$$

although the rate of return

$$\text{ror}(G) = \frac{\text{pnl}(G)}{G} \tag{6.67}$$

is monotonously decreasing with the portfolio size G.

If capacity G^* is defined as the size at which the expected net pnl is maximized, it can be estimated from the current size G, gross pnl, and costs as follows:

$$G^* = G \, \frac{\texttt{gross\_pnl} - \texttt{slippage\_cost}}{2 \times \texttt{impact\_cost}}. \tag{6.68}$$

Note that this estimate assumes a uniform scaling of all positions with size. An optimal portfolio scaling would involve a decrease of the risk aversion k and corresponding changes in the effective forecast (6.29). The capacity then also depends on the spectrum of forecast horizons. Other things equal, longer horizons result in higher capacities.

The question of capacity for hedge funds as an industry was raised by Avellaneda and Besson,[23] whose analysis of hedge fund AUM and performance data indicates a statistically significant decrease of returns with increasing industry size.

---

[23] M. Avellaneda, P. Besson, *Hedge-funds: How big is big?*, CIMS-NYU Working paper, August 2005, available at http://www.math.nyu.edu/faculty/avellane/ HFCapacity.pdf.

6.7 Portfolio optimization with forecast revision

*Four dogs are standing at the corners of a square field and are allowed
to move only along the sides of the square. Their top speed is V.
A wolf is located at the center of the square and can move anywhere.
His top speed is 2V/3. The wolf can kill one dog, but two dogs
will kill the wolf. Prove that the dogs can coordinate to keep the wolf
inside the square.*

From a quant interview

In our portfolio optimization discussion so far, the forecast term
structure—expected return as a function of horizon—was taken at face
value, and the future position path $P(t)$ was chosen to optimize a utility
with multi-horizon impact costs. Using a terminology of control theory,
we shall call this approach *open-loop optimization*.

It is not immediately clear, however, how the open-loop portfolio optimization applies to the actual process of repeated, and therefore
revised, forecasting, as new data becomes available.[24] More generally, a
forecast $f(t, h)$ is a function of two variables: the time of forecasting t
and the horizon h measured from point t forward. The future position
path $P(t, h)$ optimal for $f(t, h)$ is used only for its initial part, and then the
whole process repeats. We shall call this portfolio construction workflow
a *semi-open-loop optimization*.

Instead of computing the position path, which will be soon revised
anyway, one could try a *closed-loop* approach. Closed-loop optimization
explicitly incorporates a continuous feedback of the forecast revision.
Instead of the future position path, one could seek an optimal trading
strategy

$$P^*(t) = S[f(t, h), \dot{R}(t)], \qquad (6.69)$$

a functional of past[25] and current forecasts and returns, to maximize, in
expectation, a utility such as

$$F[S] = E[P^*(t)\dot{R}(t) - k(P^*(t))^2]. \qquad (6.70)$$

---

[24] An exception would be a forecast-free problem such as basket unwinding (Sec. 6.4.4).
[25] Using earlier forecasts is needed for learning the rate of forecast revision.

A mathematical apparatus for maximizing in the space of functionals—strategies S in our case—doesn't seem to exist. A closest available approach is that of *optimal control*.[26]

An optimal control (OC) problem considers a system state space $\mathbf{x}(t)$ and a control variable $\mathbf{u}(t)$, possibly of a different dimension, which is used to minimize the cost function

$$J_{t_0} = \int_{t_0}^{T} g(\mathbf{x}(t), \mathbf{u}(t), t) \, dt + \Phi(\mathbf{x}(T), T). \tag{6.71}$$

The state is evolved according to the controlled dynamics,

$$\dot{\mathbf{x}}(t) = \mathbf{f}(\mathbf{x}(t), \mathbf{u}(t), t), \tag{6.72}$$

and is possibly subject to inequality constraints on both state and control variables. The state dynamics function $\mathbf{f}$ can be stochastic, in which case the task is to minimize the cost in expectation. The control $\mathbf{u}(t)$ can depend only on the state $\mathbf{x}$ observed during $[t_0, t]$ either directly or via a noisy measurement $\mathbf{y}(\mathbf{x})$.

An infinite-time, non-stochastic, unconstrained case with linear dynamics and quadratic cost g is called *linear quadratic regulator* (LQR):[27]

$$\min_{\mathbf{u}(t)} \int_{t_0}^{\infty} (\mathbf{x}Q\mathbf{x} + \mathbf{u}R\mathbf{u}) \, dt, \quad \dot{\mathbf{x}} = A\mathbf{x} + B\mathbf{u}. \tag{6.73}$$

The matrix R must be positive definite and Q positive semidefinite. The optimal solution for LQR is linear in the system state:

$$\mathbf{u}^*(t) = -R^{-1}B'L\mathbf{x}(t), \tag{6.74}$$

where the $n \times n$ optimal control matrix L satisfies the *algebraic Riccati equation*

$$A'L + LA - LBR^{-1}B'L + Q = 0. \tag{6.75}$$

Kalman filter,[28] a close relative of LQR, is used for minimizing deviations from a wanted path generated by noisy dynamics and subject to possibly noisy measurements.

---

[26] D.P. Bertsekas, *Dynamic Programming and Optimal Control*. Belmont, Athena, 1995.

[27] In a more general formulation, the integrand in (6.73) can also contain a cross term $\mathbf{x}S\mathbf{u}$. It can be eliminated by changing the control variable $\mathbf{u} = \mathbf{v} + C\mathbf{x}$ with $C = -(1/2)R^{-1}S'$.

[28] R. E. Kalman, *A New Approach to Linear Filtering and Prediction Problems*, Journal of Basic Engineering, 82(1), pp. 35–45, 1960.

Linear Quadratic Gaussian control (LQG) is a stochastic optimal control model with a Gaussian white noise. The LQG problem has a solution combining the features of LQR and the Kalman filter. An LQG approach to optimal portfolio control is possible for linear impact and no slippage costs.[29]

For nonlinear dynamics or non-quadratic loss, numerical solutions are used. A deterministic OC problem with T discrete time points can be solved in $O(T)$ steps using the *dynamic programming* (DP) algorithm based on Bellman's principle of optimality.[30] Consider a discrete deterministic version of Eq. (6.71),

$$J_0 = \sum_{t=0}^{T-1} g_t(\mathbf{x}_t, \mathbf{u}_t) + \Phi(\mathbf{x}_T), \quad \mathbf{x}_{t+1} = \mathbf{f}_t(\mathbf{x}_t, \mathbf{u}_t). \tag{6.76}$$

The principle of optimality says that a globally optimal solution has also optimal parts including *cost to go* from any intermediate time step t. Starting with the known terminal cost function,

$$J_T(\mathbf{x}) = \Phi(\mathbf{x}), \tag{6.77}$$

we can compute optimal controls $\mathbf{u}_t$ and cost to go functions backward in time:

$$J_t(\mathbf{x}_t) = \min_{\mathbf{u}_t} \left[g_t(\mathbf{x}_t, \mathbf{u}_t) + J_{t+1}(\mathbf{f}_t(\mathbf{x}_t, \mathbf{u}_t)) \right], \quad t = T - 1, \dots, 0, \tag{6.78}$$

and then compute the states $\mathbf{x}_{t+1} = \mathbf{f}_t(\mathbf{x}_t, \mathbf{u}_t)$ by forward iteration for $t = 0, \dots, T - 1$. Instead of (at best) a steep polynomial complexity of optimization in a T-dimensional space of controls $\mathbf{u}_t$, the DP algorithm of backward/forward propagation is linear in the number of time steps T.

Non-stochastic optimal control can be used to investigate optimal trading sequences for realizations of revised forecasts

$$v_t = \frac{\partial f(t, h)}{\partial h}. \tag{6.79}$$

The state variables are the forecast, the position, and the impact:

$$\mathbf{x}_t = (v_t, P_t, I_t), \tag{6.80}$$

---

[29] M. Abeille, E. Serie, A. Lazaric, X. Brokmann, *LQG for portfolio optimization*, arXiv: 1611.00997 [q-fin.PM], 2016.

[30] R. Bellman, *On the Theory of Dynamic Programming*, Proceedings of the National Academy of Sciences, 38(8), pp. 716–719, 1952.

with the dynamics

$$v_{t+1} = v_t + \varepsilon_t,$$

$$P_{t+1} = P_t + u_t, \tag{6.81}$$

$$I_{t+1} = I_t d + \lambda u_t.$$

Here ε_t are realizations of the forecast revision, the controls are the trades u_t, and $d < 1$ is the impact decay factor for the time step. The cost function is

$$g_t(v_t, P_t, I_t, u_t) = -(P_t + u_t)(v_t - (1 - d)I_t) + kP_t^2 + c|u_t|. \tag{6.82}$$

The costs to go J_t are convex piecewise parabolic functions of position. Such functions can be parameterized with a finite set of numbers, so the functional iteration (6.78) is computable. Solutions of this kind of OC problem can be generated for multiple Monte Carlo realizations of forecast revised at a known historical rate to compute the expected position comfort range (Sec. 6.4.5).

Qualitatively, forecast revision can be accounted for by suppressing the forecast amplitude to avoid slippage losses on revision-related roundtrips. The faster the revision rate relative to the forecast horizon, the more suppression is needed. If the utility function includes only linear and quadratic terms and no absolute-value terms (slippage), the difference between the semi-open- and closed-loop optimization appears less important.

6.8   Portfolio optimization with forecast uncertainty

The process of forecast revision discussed in Sec. 6.7 is due to the arrival of new information affecting the forecast—the PM's expectation of future returns. Now it is useful to recall that, even before any forecast revision, a future return is a random variable with an expectation and a variance. This variance has two components. The first part is an unpredictable noise due to single-asset and factor volatilities. The noise variance is much larger than the forecast and is accounted for by risk penalties in the portfolio mean-variance utility function. The second part is alpha risk (Sec. 4.9), which can be estimated in the course of forecast learning. This alpha variance part is smaller than the noise variance, but it can have more painful consequences: If noise risk is used to size the portfolio and to limit factor exposures, alpha risk, or *forecast uncertainty*, can lead to bad exposures.

Portfolio optimization under forecast uncertainty implies a utility function with uncertain parameters. Sampling uncertainty in return covariances requires shrinkage (Sec. 2.4.10) or a factor model (Sec. 4.2). Forecast uncertainty can be tackled in a few ways.

Robust optimization is an approach used in critical tasks requiring a high reliability of the outcome. The idea of robust optimization is to optimize the worst-case scenario. Financial alpha is typically weak with forecast uncertainty often of the order of the forecast itself making the worst case scenario overpessimistic and impractical.

A more reasonable approach is to optimize the uncertain utility in expectation. One can add a quadratic penalty term

$$-k_f \mathbf{P} \mathrm{cov}(\dot{\mathbf{f}}, \dot{\mathbf{f}}) \mathbf{P} \qquad (6.83)$$

term in the utility (6.9) due to the uncertainty in the forecast.[31] Unless the alpha risk aversion k_f is larger than the noise risk aversion k, such term would be small in comparison with the residual risk term in (6.11) and therefore inconsequential. Increasing k_f gives a heuristic, but tunable in simulation, way to account for forecast uncertainty. If the forecast is based on a linear regression of features (Sec. 2.4.3), the variance of regression coefficients (2.44) provides an explicit forecast variance by asset making it possible to penalize exposure to assets with outlier features.

Uncertain forecast contributes to the rate of forecast revision and can increase turnover and slippage losses. To estimate these effects, a Monte Carlo simulation can be used with forecast randomly sampled, with suitable autocorrelation, from the distribution predicted by the learning algorithm.

---

[31] D. Bauder, T. Bodnar, N. Parolya, W. Schmid, *Bayesian mean-variance analysis: Optimal portfolio selection under parameter uncertainty*, arXiv:1803.03573 [q-fin.ST], 2018.

6.9   Kelly criterion and optimal leverage

Sketch the graph of $x^y = y^x$ for $x, y > 0$. Hint: $2^4 = 4^2$.

From a quant interview

Variance is an important consideration for portfolio construction, but so is also drawdown. If it is impossible to prevent drawdowns, one should at least have some quantitative criteria on acceptable leverage and portfolio size consistent with staying in business. An obvious limit on the portfolio size is capacity due to nonlinear impact costs (Sec. 6.6). However, even for portfolio size well below its capacity, the question of the optimal risk appetite is meaningful and nontrivial.

Probabilistic models addressing optimal bet sizing for a gambler were considered by Kelly[32] in a context of information transmission via noisy communication channels and later by Thorp[33] in the investment context. In the simplest and widely popularized setting, a gambler receives a positive return $R > 0$ on the bet amount with probability p and otherwise (with probability $1 - p$) loses the whole bet. The question is what fraction ϕ of money at hand to bet repeatedly for a long-term gambling success. The Kelly criterion answers this question by maximizing the expectation of log wealth after one betting round. Starting with \$1 bankroll, the utility function

$$F(\phi) = p \log(1 + \phi R) + (1 - p) \log(1 - \phi) \qquad (6.84)$$

weighs the two outcomes,

$$\$(1 + \phi R) \quad \text{and} \quad \$(1 - \phi), \qquad (6.85)$$

with the respective probabilities. The maximum of (6.84) is reached at

$$\phi^* = p - \frac{1 - p}{R}. \qquad (6.86)$$

---

[32] J.L. Kelly, *A New Interpretation of Information Rate*, Bell System Technical Journal, 35(4), pp. 917–926, 1956.

[33] E.O. Thorp, *Portfolio Choice and the Kelly Criterion*. Proceedings of the Business and Economics Section of the American Statistical Association, 215-224, 1971.

For example, for a 50/50 chance to double or lose the bet ($p = 1/2$, $R = 1$), as well as for $R < (1 - p)/p$, it is best to bet nothing: $\phi^* = 0$, but for 60/40 odds, the gambler should bet $\phi^* = 0.6 - 0.4/1 = 20\%$ of the bankroll.

The Kelly criterion of probability-weighted logarithms (6.84) resembles the Shannon entropy (2.12) more than superficially. The two men have collaborated on the betting formula.[34]

More generally, the return R can be a random variable with a probability density $f(R)$[35] and the bet size ϕ can be any non-negative number including $\phi > 1$ when trading with leverage. The expected log wealth increase,

$$F(\phi) = \int_{-\infty}^{\infty} \log(1 + \phi R) f(R) dR, \qquad (6.87)$$

is maximized at

$$0 = F'(\phi) = \int_{-\infty}^{\infty} \frac{R f(R) dR}{1 + \phi R}$$
$$= \int_{-\infty}^{\infty} (R - \phi R^2 + \phi^2 R^3 - \ldots) f(R) dR. \qquad (6.88)$$

Assuming small returns, $\phi|R| \ll 1$, (6.88) gives the optimal leverage

$$\phi^* = \frac{E(R)}{E(R^2)} \approx \frac{\text{Sharpe}}{\sigma\sqrt{252}}, \qquad (6.89)$$

where σ^2 is the variance of daily portfolio returns.

Consider an example of a modest long-short book with mean daily return of 1 bps/GMV and annualized Sharpe of 2. Its root-variance is $\sigma = (1 \text{ bps})\sqrt{252}/2 \approx 8 \text{ bps/day}$, so Eq. (6.89) gives the optimal leverage $\phi^* = 159$. This high number suggest that something may be wrong with the Kelly criterion application to optimal portfolio leverage.

There are a few important assumptions made in the above procedure that are worth a closer examination.

---

[34] According to J. Case, *The Kelly Criterion: Fallacy or Kuhnian Paradigm Shift Waiting to Happen?*, SIAM News, 39(3), April 2006.

[35] The value of a long position cannot become negative, so $f(R) = 0$ for $R < -1$. For a long-short portfolio the loss can be unlimited and there is no such restriction.

1. First, applying logarithm before the expectation. Without the log, the utilities (6.84) and (6.87) would be linear in ϕ and inviting either zero or infinite leverage. It has been argued[36] that a concave utility is natural for the hardwiring of human brain.[37]

2. The definition of the mean return $E(R)$ and the variance σ^2 depends on the measurement horizon. Equivalently, this is a question of the definition of the bet round, which was assumed one day but could be one year or anything else. For portfolio returns modeled as a Wiener process with a drift, both mean and variance of return over n days are proportional to n. In the example above, changing the horizon from one day to one year results in the leverage $\phi^* = 32$.

3. Kelly's gambling problem assumes reinvestment of gains leading to an exponentially growing portfolio size whereas one would normally run at a fixed GMV book generating a linearly growing pnl.

4. Finally, a termination of a portfolio is usually caused by a certain drawdown from the previous peak rather than from inception. Largest drawdowns are due to serial correlations of daily returns, which are not captured by independent (i.i.d.) portfolio returns used in the Kelly model. Accounting for the prospects of a margin call and PM termination would significantly reduce the optimal leverage value.

To summarize, the Kelly criterion is an elegant way of bet or leverage sizing using a subjective choice of the betting horizon and the utility such as log return. Other concave utilities will result in different optima, so the reader's mileage may vary. Linear or convex utility choices generally result in reckless all-or-nothing bets not unlike the *Russian roulette*. For an optimal portfolio leverage level, no closed-form solution is recommended, but a PM can run simple simulations accounting for strategy-specific losing streaks and expressing risk preferences by a suitable utility function. An example of such simulation for varying leverage is presented in Fig. 6.3.

---

[36] D. Kahneman, A. Tversky, *Choices, values, and frames.* American Psychologist, 39(4), pp. 341–350, 1984.

[37] As an empirical evidence, a distinguished scientist consulting for this author would not renew his contract at some point citing that *money is perceived only logarithmically.*

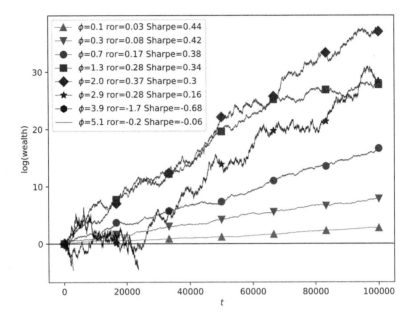

Figure 6.3   Log wealth simulations for the return distribution $f(R) = 0.49\ \delta(R + 0.01) + 0.51\ \delta(R - 0.01)$ expressing winning (losing) 1% with probability 51% (49%). Eight different leverage values are used. Kelly-optimal leverage $\phi = 2$ generates the largest mean rate of return (ror), a result generally dependent on the numpy.random.seed() setting. The Sharpe ratio of log returns is a decreasing function of leverage. Two most levered strategies terminated early after losing over 99% of the initial investment.

6.10   Intraday optimization and execution

Write a C++ class with methods translating (date,time) between a named time zone and UTC using a fixed number of arithmetic instructions. The class constructor should load the needed zoneinfo data available on Linux.

From a quant interview[38]

---

[38] This code was written by a successful quant developer candidate and extensively used in production systems well before a similar implementation by Google, https://github .com/google/cctz. An initial time zone handling appears in the <chrono> header of the C++20 standard library. A similar *Python enhancement proposal*, PEP 615, is currently active in the language development workflow. In the meantime, a contributed package is available: https://pypi.org/project/pytz.

Continuous time optimization makes math more manageable, but there is one special time scale of 1 day making it necessary to apply discrete treatment, especially in slippage-aware optimization. One of the mistakes learned by this author is not filling portfolio targets while chasing better execution opportunities (Sec. 7.1). Opportunistic execution involving both aggressive and passive (market making) orders requires a significant analytical and operational effort often outsourced to broker execution services or dedicated quant teams with high-frequency trading expertise (Sec. 6.10.3). Optimal execution of specified targets including algorithmic liquidation has long been a subject of active research[39] including aspects of execution risk.[40,41,42]

6.10.1 Trade curve

Compute the maximum deck area of a barge which could be pulled through an angular channel of width 1 with straight sides making a 90° turn. [$x/z + z/x : V$][43]

From a quant interview

One way to optimize intraday trading is to continuously run a forecasting and optimization loop generating periodic updates of the portfolio targets. Execution of the targets should be handled by a separate process working with each asset independently and looking for better ways of filling the targets based on real time market data. Strategy, a process responsible for forecasting and portfolio construction, cannot keep up with every single tick update, but it can generate position targets

---

[39] D. Bertsimas, A. Lo, *Optimal Control of Execution Costs*, Journal of Financial Markets, 1, pp. 1–50, 1998.

[40] R. Almgren, N. Chriss. *Optimal Execution of Portfolio Transactions*, Journal of Risk, 3, pp. 5–39, 2000.

[41] O. Gueant, *The Financial Mathematics of Market Liquidity: From Optimal Execution to Market Making*, CRC Press, 2016.

[42] A. Barzykin, F. Lillo, *Optimal VWAP Execution Under Transient Price Impact*, Available at SSRN: https://ssrn.com/abstract=3380177, 2019.

[43] Answering this difficult question can take forever. The shortest solving time of 15 minutes was recorded by a bright theoretician, one of the discoverers of quasicrystals and a scientific founder of Numerix, a global fintech company. Early on, the author had applied for a job at Numerix but did not get one due to insufficient coding skills.

P^* with their sensitivity to the trade price p, e.g., due to a known dependence of a short-horizon mean reversion forecast on price. Depending on how bid and ask prices fit on the *trade curve* $P^*(p)$, the trader process can generate orders of different aggression level.[44] The trade curve would normally have a plateau at the current position P_0 with the width proportional to slippage expressing the comfort range of Sec. 6.4.5.

Getting into execution level detail may be a good thing, but one should keep a bigger picture in mind: portfolio targets based on longer-horizon forecasts should be filled so production trading is matched by historical simulation (Sec. 7.1). If filling a target is deemed too expensive by the execution process, this should be part of TCA and known to the strategy process, so unrealistic targets are not generated in the first place.

6.10.2 Forecast-timed execution

Write Python code to implement the Nasdaq closing cross for a given list of on-close orders.

From a quant interview

Forecast combining methods discussed in Chapter 3 work best for the same horizon. This is normally not a limitation because a slower forecast has a measurable realization curve whose initial part can be used for combining with faster forecasts. However, given the approximate nature of optimizing fast forecasts with slippage (Sec. 6.5.5), it can be beneficial to move the fastest forecasts from portfolio optimization to execution algos. Optimization using only slow forecasts can be more accurate in setting daily position targets $\mathbf{P}^*$. A fast forecast with an intraday horizon can be used for timing execution toward the target by solving an auxiliary single-asset intraday optimization problem.

Let $f(t)$ be the intraday forecast profile known at the current time t_0, starting with $f(t_0) = 0$. We optimize the intraday trading pnl with a quadratic regularization term,

$$F[P(t)] = \int_{t_0}^{t^*} [\dot{f}(t)P(t) - c|\dot{P}(t)| - \mu\dot{P}^2(t)]dt, \qquad (6.90)$$

----

[44] A talented quant analyst proved a theorem stating that trading by such a curve can never lose money—under certain assumptions.

subject to the boundary conditions $P(t_0) = P_0$ and $P(t^*) = P^*$. Varying this utility gives the optimality condition

$$2\mu\dot{P} + c \; \text{Sign}(\dot{P}) + f(t) = A, \tag{6.91}$$

or the *soft thresholding* trading rate

$$\dot{P} = \frac{1}{2\mu}\begin{cases} A - c - f(t), & f(t) < A - c, \\ 0, & A - c < f(t) < A + c, \\ A + c - f(t), & A + c < f(t). \end{cases} \tag{6.92}$$

The integration constant A is determined from the boundary conditions by the nonlinear equation

$$\int_{t_0}^{t^*} [A - c - f(t)]^+ dt = 2\mu(P^* - P_0), \quad x^+ \equiv \max(x, 0). \tag{6.93}$$

If the intraday forecast f is smaller than slippage, $|f(t)| < c$, the optimal solution does not allow roundtrips. Then, for a buy target $P^* > P_0$, we have the initial trading rate

$$\dot{P}(t_0) = \left[\frac{P^* - P_0}{t^* - t_0} + \frac{\text{Mean}(f)}{2\mu}\right]^+,$$

$$\text{Mean}(f) = \frac{1}{t^* - t_0} \int_{t_0}^{t^*} f(t)dt. \tag{6.94}$$

Eq. (6.94) describes the execution timing policy: trade faster when the intraday forecast is in the direction of the daily target, and slow down or stop when it is not. The policy works best when the intraday forecast is revised and changes sign multiple times during execution, so multiple intraday trading opportunities are utilized. If the intraday forecast has the same sign all day, Eq. (6.94) indicates whether the execution should be front- or back-loaded. The regularization parameter μ could be measured in TCA as instantaneous impact (5.9) or selected based on desired volume participation rate subject to guaranteed filling of the daily target.

6.10.3 Algorithmic trading and HFT

What is the minimum cruising altitude for an aircraft to have line-of-sight views of both Chicago and New York City?

From a business meeting

The times when an investor wishing to make a trade had to pick up a phone and call her broker, who would then place the trade at the exchange via an *open outcry*, are long gone. Now even retail investors must use a web browser or a trading app to buy or sell securities. Computer-driven order management is even more important for larger institutional trades, which need to be sliced and diced to limit their market impact (Chapter 5).

Unlike goods sold at Amazon's Whole Food Markets, financial markets trade standardized and reusable securities, which are ultimately just bytes of computer records. This process is easily automated. There are at least three types of computer programs involved in equity and other continuous auction markets:

1. Liquidity providers, or market makers, are processes maintaining passive limit orders on the limit order book. Market makers attempt to benefit from the spread cost paid by active traders while limiting their own inventory and risk exposure.
2. Liquidity takers are processes responsible for building a target position for desired portfolio exposure while trying to minimize transaction costs. This can be accomplished with either more aggressive limit orders or market orders.
3. The exchange (auctioneer) matching engine provides a common framework for the market, maintains limit order books, crosses matching orders, and disseminates quote and trade data. Public exchanges differ by rules, matching algorithms, fee structure, and their APIs. There are also private dark pool markets not quoting standing orders. The largest dark pools are run by major brokers who internalize client flow, ostensibly to limit the market impact of large orders.

Market makers and market takers operate for trading profits under significant risks and can be combined into hybrid "passive-aggressive" strategies. An exchange is a service to market participants earning a fee from crossed trades.

Market participants compete with each other on the same (buy or sell) side and play a tactical game with the other side: the buyers want to buy cheaper and the sellers want to sell at a higher price, but the two sides ultimately need each other to make their trades. Liquidity takers have to build a target position within a certain time frame and often cross the spread to meet their targets. Liquidity providers prefer better price to expedience but must limit their positions and related risk. The double auction market is designed to establish an orderly middle ground, aka competitive fair price. A well automated auction is needed to avoid the time-consuming manual negotiation of the sort you engage in when buying a used car or a house, often an unpleasant price discovery process.

Academic and professional literature on the market microstructure is ample.[45] An early view of the market as a mathematical game was proposed by von Neumann.[46] The Nash equilibrium[47] and further developments of game theory feature a number of elegant results about the optimal behavior of rational players interacting in zero-sum and other strategic games. Unfortunately, the theory is still too simple to describe dynamics of a two-sided auction in any realistic detail.[48] There are also negative game-theoretic results, including a theorem stating that no double-sided auction mechanism can be efficient, budget-balanced, and individually rational at the same time.[49]

Algorithmic execution of active and passive strategies can range from basic flow scheduling aiming to track time-weighted average price

[45] J.-P. Bouchaud, J. Bonart, J. Donier, M. Gould, *Trades, Quotes and Prices. Financial Markets Under the Microscope*, Cambridge University Press, 2018, and references therein.
[46] O. Morgenstern, J. von Neumann, *Theory of games and economic behavior*, Princeton University Press, 1953.
[47] J. Nash, *Non-Cooperative Games*, Annals of Mathematics, 54(2), pp. 286–295, 1951.
[48] S. Phelps, S. Parsons, P. McBurney, *An Evolutionary Game-Theoretic Comparison of Two Double-Auction Market Designs*, In: P. Faratin, J.A. Rodriguez-Aguilar (eds.) Agent-Mediated Electronic Commerce VI. Theories for and Engineering of Distributed Mechanisms and Systems. AMEC 2004. Lecture Notes in Computer Science, vol. 3435. Springer, Berlin.
[49] R. B. Myerson and M. A. Satterthwaite. *Efficient mechanisms for bilateral trading*, Journal of Economic Theory, 28:265-281, 1983.

(TWAP) or volume-weighted average price (VWAP) to advanced order management using microstructure alpha extracted from limit order books on multiple exchanges.

Micro alpha differs from a regular financial forecast (Chapter 2) in a few ways. First, at the micro level one has to distinguish between bid and ask prices at multiple book depth levels instead of just one price. Second, order book changes are discrete events occurring at irregular time intervals and at price levels quantized by the book's *tick size*. The events include orders placed, canceled, or executed rather than simple or log return. If it was acceptable—and even advantageous (Sec. 2.12)—to separate portfolio-level forecasting from trading costs (Chapter 5), micro forecasting needs to be run on an impact-aware basis. Explicitly or implicitly, micro alpha involves probabilities of future book events conditional on an order being added or removed. The task is further complicated by the presence of dark-pool-style hidden orders allowed on most exchanges. It is also understood that a thin market (small bid or ask quote size) reflects a potentially larger liquidity not revealed by traders for fear of market impact. This undisplayed liquidity is an important latent structure (Sec. 2.4.17).

Given sub-millisecond time scales of the order book events to keep up with, micro alpha is usually learned in terms of features whose updates require only a handful of FLOPs. The micro alpha can be as simple as recommending aggressively taking a newly improved bid order or canceling an existing passive order based on more complex order book patterns. The finite speed of information propagation and handling adds a new level of complexity to the market microstructure.

In addition to deriving micro alpha from a single venue order book, *cross-market arbitrage* presents a much simpler and more important trading opportunity. Due to the fragmentation of financial markets into multiple competing exchanges and dark pools in both the US and Europe, it is possible to profitably trade identical or closely related instruments, such as equities and futures, when having an edge in the speed of order book data access. Creation of multiple trading venues was triggered by the US Regulation National Market System, or Reg NMS, established in 2005. Reg NMS Rule 611 requires the exchanges to communicate and route orders among each other to get the best execution price across US markets—the national best bid and offer (NBBO) defined by Reg NMS rule 600.

Given the extreme time sensitivity of micro alpha and cross-market arbitrage, a competitive advantage is gained by using low-latency, or high-frequency, strategies and co-located access infrastructure. High frequency trading (HFT) has been a prominent part of the financial landscape starting around 2005. The race for faster communication lines famously included a Spread Network fiber line between Chicago and New York whose construction was depicted in an influential book by Michael Lewis[50] and in the movie *The Hummingbird Project*.[51] Underground fiber optic cables provide high bandwidth and reliability, but the Spread Network story reveals a crucial design flaw due to missing the basic physics fact that light travels about 30% slower in glass than in the air. As a result, the expensive fiber line lost the latency battle to old-fashioned line-of-sight microwave networks using transceivers mounted on cell towers.[52] A microwave network may be unsuitable to carry the full stream of market data, but it can transmit a subset of critical information needed for an HFT strategy. Periods of inclement weather conditions between New York and Chicago have been linked to drops in overall trading volume and milder adverse selection for non-HFT traders.[53] Space could be the next HFT frontier.[54] It appears that the profitability of pure HFT portfolios,[55] a crowded and low-capacity arena, has significantly reduced since its heyday around 2009, and the focus of the HFT algorithms has shifted toward more efficient execution of other portfolios.

To keep up with increased volume of incoming trading orders, and almost the same number of cancellations,[56] exchanges have been

---

[50] M. Lewis, *Flash Boys*, Norton & Co, 2014.

[51] The only hilarious detail in the otherwise gloomy film is the idea of Anton Zaleski, a nerdy Russian coder, to use neutrinos, which pass freely through the Earth's crust at the speed of light, for transmission of financial data.

[52] S. Antony, *The secret world of microwave networks*, Ars Technica, November 3, 2016.

[53] A. Shkilko, K. Sokolov, *Every Cloud Has a Silver Lining: Fast Trading, Microwave Connectivity and Trading Costs*, The Journal of Finance, 75(6), pp. 2899–2927, 2020. Available at SSRN: https://ssrn.com/abstract=2848562.

[54] S. Rosov, *SpaceX Is Opening Up the Next Frontier for HFT*, Market Integrity Insights, CFA Institute, June 25, 2019.

[55] M. Kearns, A. Kulesza, Y. Nevmyvaka, *Empirical Limitations on High Frequency Trading Profitability*, Available at SSRN: https://ssrn.com/abstract=1678758, 2010.

[56] This author has run a book with HFT execution following a trade curve (Sec. 6.10.1). About 1% of orders were executed and 99% canceled. The strategy was soon shut down

aggressively upgrading their compute infrastructure, including acquiring HFT shops with low-latency expertise.[57] In an opposite move, the SEC approved IEX as the nation's 13th stock exchange.[58] IEX's distinctive feature is a "speed bump" made of a 38-mile fiber cable coil delaying all incoming and outgoing messages by 350 microseconds. The additional latency does not affect throughput and is specifically designed to diffuse the latency advantage of HFT over other traders. The market share of the IEX has been in the range of 2-3%.[59]

6.10.4   HFT controversy

Two bored cowboys, Bill and Joe, are riding on horseback. They see a pile of horse shit. "Hey Bill, I bet you $50 you can't eat this shit," says Joe. "Sure I can," says Bill. He proceeds to eat it, and Joe hands over $50. Soon they come upon a pile of bull shit. "Hey Joe, I bet you $50 you can't eat this one." "Oh yeah?" says Joe, and immediately does it. Soon they are bored again. "Looks like we just ate a lot of shit for free, didn't we?" "Well, at least we increased the US GDP by $100."

Old Soviet folklore

While being credited for improving market liquidity and reducing bid-ask spread, HFT has been also subject of criticism and regulatory scrutiny, notably after the publication of the 2014 book *Flash Boys* by Michael Lewis. There are three main lines of critique: information asymmetry, conflict of interest, and arms race.

Information asymmetry means that some market participants have better or faster access to material information than others. While this is definitely a concern, such asymmetry has always existed in the financial markets. The asymmetry depends on the resources a trader is willing to invest in data acquisition and delivery. A retail investor would

---

on compliance concerns about the high cancellation rate: the non-HFT fund was not used to such numbers.

[57] A. Osipovich, *NYSE Aims to Speed Up Trading With Core Tech Upgrade*, Wall Street Journal, Aug 5, 2019.

[58] N. Popper, *IEX Group, Critical of Wall St., Gains Approval for Stock Exchange*, The New York Times, June 17, 2016.

[59] Assuming HFT market makers stand on one side of each trade at other exchanges, the non-HFT market share of IEX should be larger than this.

likely trade on a delayed quote. A mid-frequency portfolio manager could settle for Level I NBBO feed (but would probably pay a lot more for other data, see Sec. 2.1). An HFT prop shop wouldn't care much about analyst estimates (Sec. 2.1.4) but would subscribe to direct exchange feeds over the fastest available lines.

HFT market making competition does reduce the bid-ask spread but not necessarily trading costs to the party on the other side of the trade. By conservation of money in a trading transaction, the aggregate HFT pnl, which has peaked at about \$5B in 2009,[60] is a cost to HFT's counterparties. Incidentally, one can also argue that the profits of market-neutral hedge funds are costs to pension funds and other traditional investors. These costs could be seen as the price of the needed market liquidity and efficiency, but then there are concerns that *this* kind of liquidity could be overpriced (more thoughts on this in the Afterword).

HFT quotes on multiple venues create a *liquidity mirage*,[61] an apparent increase of the composite market depth that can quickly disappear upon an execution at any one venue. Whether treated as slippage or impact, the cost is primarily in the reaction of the market to a trade order. The other side of the quote often quickly moves away inviting the trader to post a higher buy or lower sell quote—the market maker's micro alpha at work. This requires more aggressive (worse priced) orders to get portfolio fills and translates into higher trading costs for a portfolio manager.[62] Execution latency was found to be adversely affecting slow liquidity providers even more than liquidity takers.[63] The larger the portfolio and the faster its turnover, the more adverse selection is expected from trading on markets exposed to advanced HFT algorithms. Possible remedies for a large portfolio include using dark liquidity or instructing your broker to execute trades on IEX.

Conflict of interest is more troubling. Both anecdotal and other evidence exists that some brokers have sold their clients' order flow to

---

[60] J. Parsons, *HFT: Not so flashy anymore*, The TRADE News, June 14, 2017, https://www.thetradenews.com/hft-not-so-flashy-anymore.

[61] D. Dobrev, E. Schaumburg, *The Liquidity Mirage*, Liberty Street Economics (Federal Reserve Bank of New York blog), October 2019.

[62] By the author's observation, by 2011 it became difficult to execute a mid-frequency portfolio by mostly passive orders.

[63] R.P. Bartlett, J. McCrary, *How rigged are stock markets? Evidence from microsecond timestamps*, Journal of Financial Markets, 45, pp. 37–60, 2019.

HFT firms for selective execution, or have granted such firms privi-
leged access to their dark pools, without disclosing these arrangements
to their clients. Unlike investment advisors such as hedge funds or pension plans, which are subject to a *fiduciary duty* standard, broker-dealers
are bound only by a lesser *suitability standard* when trading on the clients'
behalf. Depending on the broker and the time period, portfolio managers' mileage has varied.[64]

Arms race is perhaps the easiest aspect to explain about the otherwise complex high frequency trading phenomenon. If makes perfect
sense to pay for being on the right side of information asymmetry. But
other players will soon be forced to build faster lines, arrange for a better
colocation, or develop smarter inter-market arbitrage. Non-HFT traders
will also upgrade their connectivity and execution algos to incorporate micro alphas and multi-venue execution. To stay competitive, both
HFT and non-HFT traders alike will have to spend more on execution
complexity and speed, gradually approaching its physical limit. Once
everybody has reached that limit, there is no more upside, just as when
everyone was slow, but the costs are higher.

People and businesses respond to opportunities and stimuli, even
when the response is expensive and leads to a wasteful equilibrium.
Situations like this should be resolved by better rules imposed by regulators. Reg NMS and market fragmentation in the name of competition
have led to one of those *cobra effects*.[65] Just like choosing between a
single-payer medical insurance vs multiple competing insurers, the
optimal solution is not immediately obvious on quantitative grounds,
bears elements of ideology, and depends on whom you ask.

---

[64] This author ran statistical comparison of contemporaneous execution quality in the
same stocks by different brokers in 2008-2011. For example, slippage measured consistently worse at Credit Suisse than at Morgan Stanley. It was difficult to retrieve from
the brokers a detailed information of how much of the flow went to their dark pools vs
public exchanges. Around the same period, interviewing quants working for a major
brokerage revealed apparent holes in the Chinese wall which is supposed to separate
the broker's client and prop trading businesses. Statistical and anecdotal data on possible front-running was used for dynamic weighting of order flow split among multiple
executing brokers.

[65] S.D. Levitt, S.J. Dubner, *Freakonomics: A Rogue Economist Explores the Hidden Side of
Everything*, William Morrow, New York, 2005.

Chapter 7

Simulation

What happens if a big asteroid hits Earth? Judging from realistic simulations involving a sledge hammer and a common laboratory frog, we can assume it will be pretty bad.

Dave Barry

Computer simulation is a digital modeling of a deterministic or random process, which would be expensive or impossible to set up in reality. Simulations have been used in many fields, most famously starting with physicists simulating nuclear detonation for the Manhattan project. The design of the early nuclear weapons was helped by ENIAC, the *Electronic Numerical Integrator and Computer*, a 60,000 lbs machine consuming 150 KW of power and performing 50,000 instructions per second.[1] During the same time, the Soviet nuclear effort did not

---

[1] https://www.atomicheritage.org/history/computing-and-manhattan-project.

have access to comparable computing power, and the weapon research was aided by analytical calculations, spying, and testing.[2]

A simulation is based on a set of rules such as discretized partial differential equations in physics or trading rules in finance. A historical trading simulation, or *backtest*, seeks to model the impossible—trading using current ideas on the past market data—in the hope a quant strategy performing in such a *Gedankenexperiment* would be successful in the future. The purpose of a trading simulation is to put all the complex components of the quant process together to see what the result might look like in terms of summary characteristics such as position turnover, rate of return, Sharpe ratio, and drawdown, under applicable costs and constraints. Of special interest is the question of strategy performance during riskier periods such as the quant dislocations of 2007 and 2020 (Sec. 4.7) or the global financial crisis of 2007-2008.

The other purpose of a simulator software is production trading: daily production is the last day of historical simulation in most respects except for execution that is real rather than simulated. The production trading process has its specifics and could be driven by a code independent of the historical simulator; however, such design would be more prone to unwanted deviation of production from simulation and run against the programmer's doctrine of code reuse. Other things equal, less code is better than more code (Sec. 7.5).

In addition to alpha and portfolio construction ideas, a bug-free, efficient, and reusable code implementing those ideas is a major and carefully guarded asset of a quantitative trading business. A realistic trading simulator is a critical part of quantitative portfolio management, but it is best used sparingly as explained in Sec. 2.12.

---

[2] The first Soviet plutonium bomb RDS-1 was detonated 4 years after the first test of a similar device in Alamogordo, NM in 1945. The author's grandfather was a Soviet military engineer overseeing the first nuclear tests at the Semipalatinsk site in Kazakhstan in 1949: https://ru.wikipedia.org/wiki/Малютов,_Борис_Михайлович. General Malyutov's first paid job, as an elementary school student from a poor peasant family in rural Central Russia, was tutoring his more fortunate classmates in math for food.

7.1   Simulation vs production

Beware of bugs in the above code; I have only proved it correct, not tried it.

> Donald Knuth

To model the impossible, the simulator should first be good at modeling things actual and possible. It is important to test the simulator in the reality-check mode. Historical trading simulated on actually used point-in-time raw data, alpha signals, portfolio construction, portfolio size, and constraints must match real production data sufficiently well. If the reality check fails, the quant research process is likely broken and the business may be driving in the dark without headlights. Indeed, gross alpha returns in an efficient market are just slightly above trading costs, and even a small systematic error in either alpha performance or costs can change the sign of their difference. There are several possible reasons for a simulation to fail matching actual trading:

1. Incorrect slippage and/or impact model. Markets are responsive to intervention by any new participant, especially trading at a size, and any impact model is just an approximation (Sec. 5.2). Trading costs change over time and need to be periodically recalibrated and recorded point-in-time (PIT) like any other data.

2. Self-fulfilling prophecy due to historical prices already affected by the portfolio (Sec. 2.6).

3. Inadequate modeling of probabilistic execution, especially when using elements of market making in the execution engine (Sec. 6.10). Limit order book queue is subject to complicated dynamics[3,4] and is affected by evolving algorithms of HFT market makers (Sec. 6.10.3). Unless probabilistic execution can be modeled reliably, production should use a guaranteed execution of portfolio targets (Sec. 6.10.2).

4. Using data not available in the past or not PIT (Sec. 2.1.1).

---

[3] R. Cont, S. Stoikov, R. Talreja, *A Stochastic Model for Order Book Dynamics*, Available at SSRN: https://ssrn.com/abstract=1273160, 2009.

[4] W. Huang, C.-A. Lehalle, M. Rosenbaum, *Simulating and analyzing order book data: The queue-reactive mode*, arXiv:1312.0563 [q-fin.TR], 2014.

5. Survival bias (Sec. 2.1.2), another violation of the PIT principle.

6. Various bugs, notably involving lookahead (Sec. 2.1.1).

Poor alpha performance, including due to overfitting, or bad portfolio optimization do not contribute to the deviation of simulation from production.

There are of course important uses of the simulator not meant to be compared with production. These include testing new ideas and datasets on past market data, before the ideas or data even existed.

7.2   Simulation and overfitting

A computer program does what you tell it to do, not what you want it to do.

A well-known truth

A lot of our discussion so far concerned a careful distinction between the past and the future, with the grand purpose to realistically predict, and optimize for, the future portfolio performance. Due to the competition-based market efficiency, future returns depend on past data very weakly (Sec. 2.3.3). A buggy lookahead (Sec. 2.1.1) introduces a spurious predictability enthusiastically grabbed by ML forecasts hungry for any x vs y mutual information. Assuming that such deadly bugs are fixed, we are not out of the woods just yet.

A simulator, as any other piece of software, is meant to be run more than once. If the simulator is repeatedly used to "improve" a strategy by tuning forecast parameters for a better pnl, chances are the forecasts will be overfit (Sec. 2.12). Forecasts, the most important part of the quant process, should be fitted and hypertuned in as few passes over historical data as possible, ideally just once using a version of AutoML (Sec. 2.4.18) or an online hyperparameter optimization (Sec. 2.4.7). Once forecasts are fixed and recorded PIT, the simulator can be used, finger-crossed, for tuning risk factors and portfolio construction, playing with scenarios of portfolio sizing (Sec. 6.9), and so forth. This activity is not totally immune to overfitting, but its danger is now lower.

In general, one can rank the sins of overfitting from mortal to venial as (1) forecasts and their combining, (2) risk management, (3) portfolio construction—in that order.

7.3   Research and simulation efficiency

Write C++ code for managing, in multiple threads, a large number of tasks with given dependencies (via a direct acyclic graph) and expected complexity levels. The thread manager should load a specified number of cores to execute all tasks in the shortest possible time.

From a quant interview[5]

An efficiently designed ML framework and trading simulator claim modest computing resources and speed up the quant research cycle. Computational efficiency is more important for historical ML and simulations, which are long and many, than for production. Most of computational costs are incurred by alpha generation (Sec. 2.4.19), perhaps less so if online learning (Sec. 2.4.13) is implemented. Once the forecasts are produced and combined, the remaining nontrivial task is portfolio construction, which needs only current data for forecasts, prices, risk loadings, costs, and so forth. This implies that the simulator can run in a date/time loop accessing all data *cross-sectionally* without loading the whole history in RAM.

Among other considerations, this suggests that cross-sectional, or row-oriented data storage formats with contiguous data blocks for same time, all assets are preferable over serial (same asset, all times), or column-oriented formats. A cross-sectional simulation workflow implies multiple reader processes potentially running over extended periods of time while the data storage is updated with new data. A number of optimized binary data storage formats provide efficient row-, column-based, or hybrid access, but few support read/write concurrency. A well-designed custom concurrent data format optimized for the heaviest use cases can speed up big-data ML research and simulation.

An alternative to pure cross-sectional storage is striped column-wise storage with sufficiently large row groups corresponding to blocks of consecutive times. This hybrid design seeks a balance between better

---

[5] A quant developer candidate posted his answer to this at https://github.com/ Chivelazur/task_manager and included it in his resume. Modern programming languages such as Julia, Python, or C++20 support asynchronous multitasking either as a built-in feature or via standard library modules. A Python module for multi-core management of parallel processes is available at https://github.com/michael-isichenko/ multicmd.

column-wise compression and queries with cross-sectional access logic. Google Dremel is a storage architecture designed for web-scale (petabyte) datasets representing both flat and hierarchical data with efficient *in situ* retrieval capabilities.[6] Apache Parquet[7] is an open-source storage based on the Dremel's *Record shredding and assembly* algorithm and usable for data storage either locally or in a distributed Hadoop system.

With cross-sectional online ML and simulator infrastructure, memory and processor resources can be used for running multiple learners and/or portfolios in parallel in one process instead of multiple simulations. The portfolios can use different sets of alphas, risk models, optimizer parameters, costs models, and constraints, while sharing common read-only resources such as current forecasts, market data, and risk loadings, thereby further reducing computational resources requirements (Sec. 2.4.19).

7.4 Paper trading

In addition to historical simulation, it is useful to continuously simulate real-time production trading. This process is called *paper trading*.[8] Paper trading is a process identical to the production trading process except for execution: its orders are sent to a software agent emulating an exchange or broker algo execution rather than to a real exchange via a broker. The benefits of paper trading include:

1. A quality assurance (QA) environment for testing production system updates before an actual production deployment.
2. Monitoring for a deviation of production data from paper trading. A significant difference would indicate a bug or a need for recalibration of the execution model or trading costs.
3. Monitoring real-time performance of a portfolio proxy when the actual portfolio is downsized due to a dislocation (Sec. 4.7) or some other reason.

---

[6] S. Melnik, A. Gubarev, J.J. Long, G. Romer, S. Shivakumar, M. Tolton, T. Vassilakis, *Dremel: Interactive Analysis of Web-Scale Datasets*, Proceedings of the VLDB Endowment, 3(1), 2010.

[7] https://parquet.apache.org/documentation/latest.

[8] The nomenclature varies across the industry. Some teams use the term *simulation* for real-time paper trading, and *backtest* for historical simulation.

Just like for a historical simulator, things should look as good (or bad) on paper as in reality.

7.5   Bugs

The unwritten motto of United States Robot and Mechanical Men Corp. was well known: "No employee makes the same mistake twice. He is fired the first time."

Isaac Asimov, *Catch That Rabbit*[9]

Quantitative trading is based on software written in various programming languages such as Matlab, R, Java, C#, C, C++, or Python, the last two being used more frequently than others. The software includes scripts and programs for data acquisition, processing, cleaning and storage, machine learning and forecasting, portfolio construction, historical simulations and tuning of parameters, placement of trades, maintenance of positions and other back-office bookkeeping, monitoring the health of production processes, paper trading, maintenance of code repositories, data backups, and so forth. A source code implementing all these functions for a mature quant team would normally include $10^5 - 10^6$ lines and grow over time.

Whatever the programming language(s), there is a finite probability $p \ll 1$ of planting a bug, i.e., a coding error, on each new line of the source code. Assuming an independent error rate for each of the N lines of the source, the probability of being completely bug-free is exponentially small,

$$q(N) = (1 - p)^N, \tag{7.1}$$

under a safe assumption of $p > 10^{-6}$.

There are several approaches to reducing the chance of bugs, but it is virtually impossible to get rid of them all in a large software system, so debugging is a a major part of programming.[10] With Eq. (7.1) in mind, we want a cleaner and smaller code. A compiler or an interpreter helps detecting typos and syntax errors. A strongly typed language, such

---

[9] This short story published in 1944 was one of the first to use the term *bug* in the modern computer context, as well as to describe a way of debugging.
[10] A developer who worked for this author liked to use the word *bugging* as a synonym for programming.

as C++, is likely to spot more of unintended assignments or passing wrong arguments to functions (perhaps at the expense of more lines of code) than a *duck-typed* language, such as Python. Unlike Perl, an older scripting language, the Python interpreter won't check syntax of parts of code not being executed. The full source syntax and compliance with the recommended PEP8 coding style can be checked with external tools, such as `py_compile`, `pylint`, or various integrated development environments (IDE). Those tools can also check optional static typing of variables, function arguments, and return values supported by type hints added to Python3 following PEP3107, PEP484, and other proposals. Upon an easy automatic cleanup, there will likely be bugs not detectable by the machine and requiring human vigilance.

A major goal of better coding is resisting the exponential (7.1). There are several well-known general approaches such as modular code design with clear separation of functionality and extensive test suites for each component, but no bullet points can capture all aspects of good coding, just like it is hard to explain, other than by example, how to write good poetry. In the author's experience, nothing works better than looking at the code of good programmers and asking questions as to why something is written the way it is and not like *that*. Collaborating with experts on the same project is the best way to improve one's coding (as any other, for that matter) skills.

It pays to stick to a set of conventions and follow the *principle of least astonishment*.[11] Given that a programmer spends more time reading code than writing it, write laconic and readable code with descriptive names for classes, variables, and functions. Using meaningful nouns for objects and verbs for functions makes a plain English coding style much preferable over any explanatory comments. C++ macros can be used to avoid some error-prone repetitions and to reduce visual noise in the code by wrapping function calls with error/exception handling in a single line. A few such macros are shown in Listing 7.1. Macros should carry clear semantics and be used only when they help readability.[12]

---

[11] However, if a code implements a non-obvious mathematical algorithm, it may be better to start with LaTeX before writing it in C++ or Python.

[12] This author's obsession with C++ readability once lead to the curious macro '`#define but &&`' allowing conditionals like '`if(a > b but a < c)`'. No wonder the Python architect preferred the keywords and and or to the symbols `&&` and `||`.

Listing 7.1 Examples of helpful C++ macros.

```
//before: iterate over a symmetric matrix
for(int i=0; i<n; ++i) {
    for(int j=i; j<n; ++i) { //buggy increment
        if(!Manipulate(a(i,j))) { //4 lines per call with err handling
            fprintf(stderr, "failed at (%d,%d)", i, j);
            return false;
        }
    }
}

//loop macros:
#define FOR(i, end)         for(int i=0, end__=(end); i<end__; ++i)
#define FOR2(i, beg, end) for(int i=(beg), end__=(end); i<end__; ++i)
#define RFOR(i, end)        for(int i=(end); i-- > 0;) //reverse for loop

//error handling variadic macro printing error location:
#define TEST(ret, msg_format, ...) {if(!(ret)) {\
    fprintf(stderr, "ERR(%s:%d) " msg_format "\n",\
    __FILE__, __LINE__, ## __VA_ARGS__); return false;}}

//and after: corrected compact loop
FOR(i, n) {
    FOR2(j, i, n) {
        TEST(Manipulate(a(i,j), "failed at (%d,%d)", i, j));
    }
}
```

Another guideline is to name related things related names using common substrings. For example, subclasses of a Learner class can be called OLSLearner, GPLearner, KernelLearner, and so forth. This is a useful convention making it much easier to search related pieces of code.

A quantitative codebase would inevitably include a number a mathematical algorithms that are hard to write and even harder to read. These must be entirely trusted both in terms of correctness and performance guarantees. Examples include linear algebra (linear equation solvers, matrix inversion, eigendecomposition, SVD), root solvers, clustering, learners (OLS, Lasso, GP, TVD, KNN, DNN, etc.), convex optimization (LP, QP, specialized), and so forth. Many of these algorithms are available in open-source or commercial libraries that keep improving but some need to be implemented in-house. Extensive *unit testing* is a must for such black-box algorithms. In the *extreme programming* view of software development,[13] tests are written before the program and are integral part of the codebase. A bug is not a problem; a missing unit test is. LAPACK (Linear Algebra PACKage) is one of the

---

[13] http://www.extremeprogramming.org.

most trusted, although not bug-free,[14] mathematical libraries that has been in academic and open-source development since 1970's. LAPACK is used in the Python numpy library and in many other open-source and commercial software tools.

Although programming languages keep improving, it is still useful to generate certain repetitive code programmatically. To keep related things near each other, one can write bilingual code exemplified in Listing 7.2. Mixed-language code generators like this have been used by the author for the compact maintenance of multiple ML and forecast objects. Autogenerated C++ code is also useful for data loaders, serializers, stringification of enum types, and other low-level tasks.

Listing 7.2 Bilingual C++/Python file generating repetitive C++ code.

```
#include "MyHeader.h"
#if 0
""" C++ below ignored by Python as a docstring
#endif
#define xcode(code) #code

typedef const char* CC; //a handy shortcut
struct ForecastConfig {CC key, spec, features;};
static const ForecastConfig _forecastConfigs[] = {
  {"LearnerA:Data1", "1000|20 ...", xcode(x[0] = Max(field1, field2);)},
  {"LearnerB:Data2", "1000|5 ...", xcode(x[0] = Cap(field3, 0.02);)},
  //...
};
#include "generated_ForecastConfig.cpp" //generated by Python below
#//"""
#if 0 //end C++, begin Python
import os, sys, re

objects, specs = ParseForecastConfig(__file__) # from _forecastConfigs
Write_generated_ForecastConfig(objects, specs)
#endif
```

Quantitative code handles a lot of numeric data and arithmetic operations (Sec. 2.4.19). Once a wrong number goes down the graph of dependencies, it is very hard to find where the problem first occurred. It is important to check early for any abnormal conditions including inconsistent or missing data. Handling missing data needs to be thought through at the system design stage. It is common to use numpy.nan, a special floating-point value not representing any valid number, in Python

---

[14] https://github.com/Reference-LAPACK/lapack/issues.

where pretty much all of the arithmetic must be vectorized for performance reasons. One must then be prepared for the consequences of "seamless" propagation of nans through arithmetic and to distinguish legitimately missing values from those coming from $\log(negative)$ or other bugs. In C++, there is no vectorization constraint, and it is possible to designate a special non-nan, such as FLT_MAX or another unusual number, as a missing value and use lots of IsMissing() checks around the code.[15] It is then possible to configure the code to raise an arithmetic exception on the first invalid operation or nan. To flag missing data, it is also possible to use numpy masked arrays or ML weights (Sec. 2.4.3), but note that nan*0 equals nan rather than zero.

A quant programmer should be reasonably paranoid about checking all inputs and function calls that can potentially fail. In addition to bad external data, any new algorithm or piece of logic can be buggy and should be tested under multiple conditions. A useful practice for C++ or Python classes is defining an Invariant() method verifying that things that must hold do so. For example, any constraint-compatible deviation from the solution of a QP optimizer (Sec. 3.3) must result in a smaller value of the utility function than at the optimum, the eigenvectors of a symmetric matrix must be orthogonal, and so forth. Assertion-style checks for the invariants can be enabled in a debug mode and disabled in the optimized build. Likewise, fairly frequent index-out-of-range bugs can be caught by redefining, via inheritance, library functions such as std::vector<T>::operator[]() to perform a range check in the debug mode.[16]

In addition to low-level bugs usually due to typos, there can be higher-lever logical bugs appearing at the system design level. Lookahead (Sec. 2.1.1) is one of them. At one point, being frustrated with

---

[15] This author has used the Avogadro number for a recognizable missing value. Most other physical constants are smaller and wouldn't cause a floating point exception, which is a good thing to have in a buggy arithmetic. One quant shop used, following a vendor convention, -999.0 for a missing price. A later adoption of an advanced C++ matrix library with expression evaluation and vectorized loops lead to nonintuitive results. Cleaning up the mess was difficult due to hard to grep conditionals spread over the codebase. Some tests looked like x==-999.0 and others more like x < 0. A *function* is perhaps the single most useful invention of computer programming.

[16] The C++ standard library has a range-checked version of vector element access via std::vector<T>::at(), but replacing all instances of x[i] with x.at(i) is harder than setting DEBUG=1 at compile time.

a hard-to-find suspected lookahead, the author went to the extreme of deriving all C++ ML data structures from a time-tracking `Timestamped` base class and updating the timestamp of any combination of data to the maximum timestamp of the dependencies. Asserting that any used data is not past the current simulation time helped to find the bug.

A design bug with severe production consequences was once made in the author's early version of the order management system (OMS). The OMS was sending DMA trade orders via a broker gateway without waiting for receipt acknowledgments ("acks") for earlier orders. Orders sent but not followed by executions were deemed never executed and sent again in a portfolio rebalancing loop. A peculiar breakdown in the broker (which was Lehman Brothers at the time) system led to an accumulation of client orders, failure to respond with acks, and subsequent batch execution of the large order backlog. This incident resulted in a shock price impact used for the expensive TCA study mentioned in Sec. 5.2.

In a quant research environment, there is a certain amount of temporary, often low-quality code written for testing new ideas or addressing urgent issues. Some of it ends up in the system core building up layers of legacy code. Many quants are not strong programmers and learn better coding practices as it goes. Older, poorly written legacy code is hard to understand, too fragile to maintain, and scary to touch when you must. It is not uncommon for established quant teams to periodically undertake a laborious code redesign or refactoring, including using newer language features, new libraries, or new programming languages.

Software bugs are easier to detect in a collaborative coding environment with peer code review. Open source software development, while not exactly an option for quant traders, has long preached the Linus' law: *given enough eyeballs, all bugs are shallow.* This, and other collaborative ideas have been popularized by Eric Raymond.[17] Echoing the principle of least astonishment, Raymond remarks that *smart data structures and dumb code works a lot better than the other way around.* GNU/ Linux, an open-source Unix operating system started by Linus Torvalds and helped by over 15,000 developers worldwide,[18] is now the main OS

---

[17] E.S. Raymond, *The Cathedral and the Bazaar*, O'Reilly Media, 2000.

[18] J. Corbet, G. Kroah-Hartman, https://www.linuxfoundation.org/blog/2017/10/ 2017-linux-kernel-report-highlights-developers-roles-accelerating-pace-change.

used by quantitative hedge funds and top machine learning and internet companies. Linux has also landed on Mars.[19]

Discovery of bugs and security vulnerabilities is a critically important task in software and internet service industry. There, an industrial-strength approach of *fuzzing* has been used for testing software with multiple adversarial random inputs searching for a regression, not to be confused with ML regression (Sec. 2.4.1). ClusterFuzz,[20] a fuzzer developed by Google, has been used to fix over 25,000 bugs in Google software including Chrome. In line with Eq. (7.1), it can take exponentially many fuzzing runs to find all bugs in a program.[21]

Automated debugging is more suitable for programs with well-defined functionality, such as a web browser. Bugs in quant trading systems are much harder to detect. It is quite possible that a system performance is degraded due to subtle coding errors, but whether it is bugs or just the market efficiency is anyone's guess. Gregory Zuckerman[22] describes a plausible story of David Magerman's discovery of a few bugs in RenTec's early statistical arbitrage code leading to a major success of the Renaissance Technologies' equity trading model, the most profitable—or perhaps the least buggy—statarb system ever built.

---

[19] E. Ackerman, *How NASA Designed a Helicopter That Could Fly Autonomously on Mars*, IEEE Spectrum, February 17, 2021.

[20] https://github.com/google/clusterfuzz.

[21] M. Böhme, B. Falk, *Fuzzing: On the Exponential Cost of Vulnerability Discovery*, ESEC/FSE Virtual Events, November 2020.

[22] G. Zuckerman, *The Man Who Solved the Market. How Jim Simons launched the quant revolution*, Portfolio/Penguin, 2019.

Afterword: Economic and Social Aspects of Quant Trading

Describe all methods of making noise. Which one is the most efficient?
Peter Kapitza[1]

---

[1] From Kapitza's collection of physics problems for the first (1948) class of Moscow Institute of Physics and Technology (MIPT), the author's *alma mater*. It was estimated that over 40% of science publications produced by PhysTech alumni come from affiliations in the US alone, reflecting a brain drain from Russia to the West—or perhaps the *publish or perish* environment in the US academia. The Unites States has traditionally benefited intellectually from upheaval in Europe and other regions and became home for highly productive scientists like Enrico Fermi from Italy, Albert Einstein from Germany, George Gamow from Russia, or the Hungarian "Martians" including John von Neumann, Eugene Wigner, Edward Teller, and others. What is seen more recently, and the author is part of it, is the new, *occupational brain drain* from science and engineering to finance.

After answering, more or less, the question of *how*, one may want to ask *why*? Why do quant analysts and portfolio managers do what they do? Serving hedge fund investors and paying their own bills, mortgages and alimonies aside, what is the purpose of quantitative trading of securities in a bigger social picture?

The main purpose of stock markets in a capitalist economy is to provide an information framework and liquidity (primary and secondary) to investors. The idea is putting passive savings money to work, with the help of entrepreneurs, to create things like railroads, internet search engines, or electric cars. The primary market includes initial public offerings (IPO), an investment banking function not normally involving quants. But without the secondary market for existing outstanding shares the primary equity market wouldn't exist in the first place: an investor needs to be sure that his IPO stake can be sold later when he sees fit and that his holdings can be diversified with other investments to control risks. Market makers and quant traders, among others, generate such liquidity. It is fair to assume that most of quant equity volume is generated by technical alphas such as short term mean reversion and momentum.

The other purpose of the secondary stock market is price discovery for shareholder feedback. Investors in publicly traded companies are not normally privy to day-to-day company business, but they can easily follow the stock price and have their say by dumping depreciating stock or changing company management or officer compensation policy by voting their shares. Price or mispricing discovery involves research and trading on company financials, analysis of competition, and other fundamental data.

Efficient and transparent, as opposed to insider-driven or manipulative, financial markets encourage broader investor participation. Efficient markets also facilitate capital formation via IPOs or bonds if the issuers know the cost of raising capital is reasonable[2] and their securities will be fairly priced.

It is then natural to ask how many quants are needed to serve the good purpose of liquidity and price discovery. More broadly, this is a

---

[2] A.W. Butler, G. Grullon, J.P. Weston, *Does Stock Market Liquidity Matter? Evidence from Seasoned Equity Offerings*, 2003. Available at SSRN: https://ssrn.com/abstract=471721.

question asked about the financial industry in general, primarily in the academic literature.[3,4,5] By some estimates,[6] which are likely missing much of the proprietary trading and HFT activity, the cost of financial intermediation in the US, defined as profits and wages in the financial industry, is 9% of the GDP, and it is largely attributable to trading in the secondary markets.

What are more efficient ways to maintain liquid and transparent financial markets? How much secondary liquidity is enough to get the markets' job done? How many people need to be employed in finance and trading? How do we like that thousands of talented scientists, engineers, or computer programmers develop and support trading models instead of conducting science research, teaching, putting green sources of energy to work, or creating robots for performing tedious jobs? Should innovations of machine learning and cloud computing be used for running more efficient and less costly financial markets or for a negative-sum market-neutral game or the HFT arms race? Is it normal to routinely pay successful quant traders end-of-year bonuses well in excess of the Nobel Prize?

Many quants tend to appreciate such questions and get involved in educational and scientific philanthropy and volunteering. Good examples include Math for America and Simons Foundation funded by Jim Simons, mathematician and the founder of Renaissance Technologies, the most successful quantitative hedge fund.[7] Simons Foundation supports research and education in math, physics, and life sciences as well as the arXiv, a major source of references cited in this book. Capital Fund Management (CFM), a Paris-based quant fund founded and run by prominent French scientists invests, via CFM-Foundation, in data science research in France, UK, and the US. The donors of the National

---

[3] R.J. Shiller, *Finance and the Good Society*, Princeton University Press, 2012.
[4] S.G. Cecchetti, E. Kharroubi, *Why does financial sector growth crowd out real economic growth?* BIS Working Papers, No 490, 2015.
[5] G. Mukunda, *The Price of Wall Street's Power*, Harvard Business Review, 92(6), pp. 70–78, 2014.
[6] T. Philippon, *Has the US Finance Industry Become Less Efficient? On the Theory and Measurement of Financial Intermediation*, The American Economic Review, 105(4), pp. 1408–1438, 2015.
[7] G. Zuckerman, *The Man Who Solved the Market. How Jim Simons launched the quant revolution*, Portfolio/Penguin, 2019.

Museum of Mathematics include many successful quant traders. A group of quants from D.E. Shaw & Co., including prize winners of national and international math competitions, started Math-M-Addicts, a highly regarded New York City math enrichment program, at which this author had an honor to teach—and to polish some of his interview questions.

The financial industry is heavily, if inefficiently, regulated. Quoting a senior quant and a math educator, it would be *conceptually nice* if quants also volunteered developing rational models for regulators to benefit the industry and the society at large, while avoiding more "cobra effects," which have propensity to happen when conflicts of interest or bad regulations meet sharp minds.

One idea is to replace the continuous double auction exchange mechanism with batch auctions once a second,[8] once every 10 minutes,[9] or perhaps just once a day. A daily opportunity of portfolio rebalancing appears sufficient for market liquidity, especially for investors operating on the time scale of economic and human reasoning. Access to nanosecond-level real-time order book structure, while creating business and profit opportunities, also poses a prisoner's dilemma not unlike the cold-war-era arms race. No doubt this model works and keeps many folks busy, but from an economist's perspective, this way of providing market liquidity may look like a *Rube Goldberg machine*. Doing without intraday market data, HFT, algorithmic execution, flash crashes, and such would probably send some quants to fundamental microeconomic analysis or back to their headhunters or perhaps to the real sector. Higher financial transaction taxes (FTT) on some European exchanges are designed to limit HFT, but they also decrease liquidity.[10]

Any financial regulation, such as exchange rules, needs a solid and transparent quantitative cost-benefit analysis rather than lobbying or political activism. Design of transparent, liquid, and elastic financial

---

[8] E.B. Budish, P. Cramton, J.J. Shim, *The High-Frequency Trading Arms Race: Frequent Batch Auctions as a Market Design Response*, SSRN Electronic Journal 130(4), 2013.

[9] P. Jusselin, T. Mastrolia, M. Rosenbaum. *Optimal auction duration: A price formation viewpoint*, arXiv:1906.01713 [q-fin.TR], June 2020.

[10] J.-E. Colliard, P. Hoffmann, *Financial transaction taxes, market composition, and liquidity*, European Central Bank Working Paper Series, No 2030, February 2017.

markets free of gaming or negative externalities is an interesting and important interdisciplinary problem involving psychology, economics, mathematics, computer science, game theory, and other fields.

Finally, why was this book written, and what message is it trying to convey? Quoting Vonnegut once again, *There isn't any particular relationship between the messages, except that the author has chosen them carefully, so that, when seen all at once, they produce an image of life that is beautiful and surprising and deep.*

Appendix

A1   Secmaster mappings

When multiple vendor data are provided historically in different symbologies, the data needs to be mapped to a common "house" symbology. The house symbology can be either one of the vendors' or house-specific. Data management can be implemented in one of two ways: (a) remap and store data in house symbology on each vendor data update, or (b) store data in vendor-native symbology. Both approaches have advantages and disadvantages. If all external data is remapped on entry, reader processes do not have to load the secmaster, but all potentially big data storage has to be rerun on any change of (small) secmaster mappings. Storing data in vendor symbology is simpler and more in line with PIT data management (Sec. 2.1.1) but requires remapping to house symbology in reader processes. With suitable implementation, the remapping can be efficient and impose low overhead. Here we describe a possible historical remapping algorithm.

Vendors using their own symbologies, including MSCI Barra, Bloomberg, Thompson Reuters, Refinitive, Compustat, Factset, and many others, provide historical mappings from their security IDs to a few common identifiers such as ticker, CUSIP, SEDOL, ISIN, FIGI, RIC, among others. A vendor secmaster is a data structure implementing a dictionary of *histories* for each (`vendorID, field`) tuple as a key. A history is a list of (date, value) tuples. Using common identifier fields, the mapping

$$\texttt{commonID\_value} = V_A(\texttt{date, A\_vendorID}) \qquad \text{(A1.2)}$$

can be inverted to get the inverse history

$$\texttt{A\_vendorID} = V_A^{-1}(\texttt{date, commonID\_value}). \qquad \text{(A1.3)}$$

Each history normally includes just a few entries. Chaining this with mappings of vendor B gives a B → A remapping:

$$\texttt{A\_vendorID} = V_A^{-1}(\texttt{date}, V_B(\texttt{date, B\_vendorID})). \qquad \text{(A1.4)}$$

Complications appear when vendors' secmasters disagree on the forks in the genealogical tree of securities and due to data errors. As a result, the same A_vendorID can be claimed by multiple B_vendorIDs on the same date when remapped via different common identifiers. These situations need to be resolved algorithmically, for example, by maintaining a stack of such claims and assuming that any new claim shall be granted by temporarily suspending earlier claims for A_vendorID. Priority of recent claims over older claims is motivated by the observation that vendors err on security delistings more often than on listings or ticker changes.

A2 Woodbury matrix identities

Let 1 be an $N \times N$ identity matrix, and X an arbitrary $K \times N$ matrix. Then, for any power n, we have

$$(1 + X'X)^n = 1 + C_n^1 X'X + C_n^2 X'XX'X + \dots$$
$$= 1 + X'(C_n^1 + C_n^2 XX' + C_n^3 (XX')^2 + \dots)X$$
$$= 1 + X' h_n(XX')X, \qquad \text{(A2.5)}$$

where C_n^k are "n choose k" binomial coefficients and the h_n operator is used:

$$h_n(Y) \equiv Y^{-1}((1 + Y)^n - 1). \qquad \text{(A2.6)}$$

Note the following special cases:

$$h_{1/2}(Y) = (1 + \sqrt{1 + Y})^{-1}, \tag{A2.7}$$

$$h_{-1/2}(Y) = -(1 + Y + \sqrt{1 + Y})^{-1}, \tag{A2.8}$$

$$h_{-1}(Y) = -(1 + Y)^{-1}. \tag{A2.9}$$

If $K < N$, raising an identity plus rank K matrix to a power only requires computing the same power of a smaller $K \times K$ matrix. For $n = -1$, (A2.5) becomes the Woodbury formula

$$(1 + X'X)^{-1} = 1 - X'(1 + XX')^{-1}X. \tag{A2.10}$$

It can be generalized for the identity replaced by a diagonal matrix D:

$$(D + X'X)^{-1} = D^{-1} - D^{-1}X'(1 + XD^{-1}X')^{-1}XD^{-1}. \tag{A2.11}$$

Other versions of the Woodbury formula with a symmetric U include:

$$(1 + DX'UX)^{-1} = 1 - DX'(U^{-1} + XDX')^{-1}X \tag{A2.12}$$

$$= 1 - DX'(1 + UXDX')^{-1}UXD. \tag{A2.13}$$

Unlike (A2.12), Eq. (A2.13) can be used for rank-deficient U. Formula (A2.12) tends to generate a higher numerical error for large matrices.

Various version of the Woodbury formula can be used to speed up matrix inversion or linear system solution, normally an $O(N^3)$ problem, down to $O(NK^2)$ for diagonal plus rank K matrix. A few more related matrix identities are based on Schur complement in block matrices.[1]

A more general matrix inversion formula is[2]

$$(A + BCD)^{-1} = A^{-1} - A^{-1}B(DA^{-1}B + C^{-1})^{-1}DA^{-1}. \tag{A2.14}$$

Here A and C are square, and the rest of the matrices have sizes compatible with multiplication. This formula can be used for an incremental update of the inverse of a $K \times K$ covariance matrix

$$C_{kk'} = \sum_i w_i x_{ik} x_{ik'}, \quad \text{or} \quad \delta C = \mathbf{x}' w \mathbf{x}. \tag{A2.15}$$

---

[1] J. Gallier, *Notes on the Schur Complement*. University of Pennsylvania, 2010.
[2] H.J. Kushner, G.G. Yin, *Stochastic approximation and recursive algorithms and applications*, Springer, 2003.

The change of C by a new $1 \times K$ observation of $\mathbf{x} = \mathbf{x}_i 1$ is a rank-one update. Then, instead of the full $O(K^3)$ inversion, Eq. (A2.14) gives an $O(K^2)$ update of C^{-1} upon a new observation:

$$\delta C_{kk'}^{-1} = -\frac{\xi_k \xi_{k'}}{w + \boldsymbol{\xi} \cdot \mathbf{x}}, \quad \text{where} \quad \xi_k = \sum_{k'} C_{kk'}^{-1} x_{k'}. \tag{A2.16}$$

A3   Toeplitz matrix

Toeplitz matrices are diagonal-constant matrices whose (i,j) elements depend only on $i - j$. A special case of a symmetric Toeplitz matrix

$$A_{ij} = a^{|i-j|}, \tag{A3.17}$$

or its continuous analog

$$A(t, t') = e^{-v|t-t'|}, \tag{A3.18}$$

is applicable to the impact model with exponential decay (Sec. 5.2). The determinant of a finite $n \times n$ matrix A is

$$\det(A) = (1 - a^2)^{n-1}, \tag{A3.19}$$

and its inverse is tridiagonal:

$$(A^{-1})_{ij} = \frac{1}{1 - a^2} \begin{cases} 1, & i = j \in \{1, n\}, \\ 1 + a^2, & i = j \notin \{1, n\}, \\ -a, & |i - j| = 1, \\ 0, & |i - j| > 1. \end{cases} \tag{A3.20}$$

This result was found using Wolfram `Mathematica`, motivated by the surprisingly local solution of an infinite-dimensional analog. The linear integral equation

$$\int e^{-v|t-t'|} f(t') dt' = u(t) \tag{A3.21}$$

is solved by repeated differentiaton:

$$f(t) = \frac{v}{2} u(t) - \frac{2}{v} \ddot{u}(t). \tag{A3.22}$$

In the limit $n \to \infty$, $a \to 1$, A^{-1} is asymptotically Toeplitz with the eigenvalues[3]

$$\lambda_k = a^2 - 2a \cos \frac{k\pi}{n+1} + 1, \quad k = 1, ..., n, \qquad \text{(A3.23)}$$

meaning that A is positive definite for $0 < a < 1$.

---

[3] S. Noschese, L. Pasquini, L. Reichel, *Tridiagonal Toeplitz Matrices: Properties and Novel Applications*, Numerical Linear Algebra with Applications, 20(2), pp. 302–326, 2013.

Index

Question Index

Quotes Index

Stories Index